D0394825

EAGLE VALLEY LIBRARY DISTRICT
P.O. BOX 240 600 BROADWAY
EAGLE, CO 81631 / 328-8800

DEMOCRACY
Betrayed

THE RISE OF THE SURVEILLANCE SECURITY STATE

William W. Keller

COUNTERPOINT

BERKELEY

Copyright © 2017 by William W. Keller

All rights reserved under International and Pan-American Copyright
Conventions. No part of this book may be used or reproduced in any manner
whatsoever without written permission from the publisher, except in the case
of brief quotations embodied in critical articles and reviews.

Library of Congress Cataloging-in-Publication Data is Available

Cover design by Faceout, Charles Brock
Interior design by Domini Dragoone

ISBN 978-1-61902-912-5

COUNTERPOINT
2560 Ninth Street, Suite 318
Berkeley, CA 94710
www.counterpointpress.com

Printed in the United States of America
Distributed by Publishers Group West

10 9 8 7 6 5 4 3 2 1

For Lonna

ACKNOWLEDGMENTS

Various teachers and friends have informed this book. I think first about Frances Richardson Keller, who taught me history and writing. I have had the great fortune of knowing extraordinary thinkers. Theodore J. Lowi is a lifelong mentor and friend. I had the privilege of studying with him at Cornell University, where I was also influenced by the intellectual honesty and deep scholarship of Sidney G. Tarrow. At Princeton University, I was profoundly lucky to take courses from Thomas Kuhn and Carl Hempel, both of whom taught me to look beyond the received wisdom, especially in the progress of science. John Hope Franklin and William H. McNeill both took an interest in me when I was quite a young man at the University of Chicago. To all of them, my heartfelt thanks.

Several friends and colleagues commented on drafts of the manuscript. Margaret Crosby, Jacques Hymans, Bruce Jentleson, Loch Johnson, Ren Keller, Louis Pauly, Thomas Rawski, Simon Reich, David Robertson, and Charlie Savage all made helpful comments, saving me from various errors and omissions. I am not sure we are all in complete agreement, but as far as that goes, none of them is a stranger to political or intellectual controversy.

My agent, Claire Gerus, helped me to focus the scope and expand the range of the manuscript. The book most certainly benefited from close review by two extraordinary editors, Roger Hayden of Cornell University Press and Dan Smetanka of Counterpoint Press. Both read the full manuscript and helped to improve it in many ways.

—W.K.
The Sea Ranch,
California

Table of Contents

///

STATE OF PLAY

History tells us that great leaders arise when the Republic is in peril. George Washington united a fractious people throughout the Founding. Abraham Lincoln presided over the Civil War and the abolition of slavery. And Franklin Roosevelt confronted the Great Depression and then fascism during World War II. In the 21st century, democracy again faces a sustained challenge, an onslaught to the core values of Western democratic peoples. The threat comes not so much from violent extremism, as is commonly supposed, but from our responses to it that diminish our civil liberties and our freedom.

Western leaders appear to have lost their compass. They have delegated the safety of the nation to a newly empowered class of internal security and intelligence professionals. These unelected officials privilege security over liberty, secrecy over transparency, surveillance over privacy, detention over rule of law, and power over democratic accountability. While they proclaim democratic values, their handiwork is evident in a hardened society in which local police deploy SWAT units with military weapons, public buildings are closed to the public, and daily communications among ordinary persons are monitored and recorded. No great leader has yet arisen to confront this challenge. Indeed, most seem captured by or complicit with the pervasive security and intelligence apparatus.

For 200 years, the U.S. Capitol Building was a beacon to free peoples, its beautiful tiled floors, ornate columns, vaulted ceilings, storied chambers, and cultural treasures open to the public. But that was before 9/11. Today it is a fortress, its empty halls defended by police toting automatic weapons. Visitors are shunted to a new Visitor Center, which cost $621 million to build. It is a secure dugout located beneath the parking lot on the eastern front of the Capitol Building. It is a place where members do not go and business is not transacted. It is, instead, a cavern filled with historical tributes and propaganda. There was a time, not long ago, when the U.S. Capitol Building provided inspiration to millions of visitors; today it is the refuge of some 535 members of Congress, their staffs, and major donors.

Secrecy has always been a central feature of statecraft. As Cardinal Richelieu—who used authoritarian methods to consolidate the French state under King Louis XIII—famously put it, "Secrecy is the first essential in affairs of state." And so it is today, especially in the conduct of foreign affairs. But Richelieu's aphorism applies as well to *internal security*, which is increasingly equated with national security, and typically opaque—even to most elected officials. Moreover, the relationship between foreign policy and internal security is often blurred. It is a reversal in which internal security considerations drive foreign military commitments and Counterterror Wars. Intelligence agents and elite military units conduct combat operations side by side.

A country that places all of this security over the rights of its populace is in a condition that I call Secure Democracy. In Secure Democracy, the secrecy that shrouds our internal security is a clear and present danger to liberalism. An apparatus we will come to know as the Security Industrial Complex hides hundreds of thousands of security personnel and their activities from public scrutiny, and often from the investigatory powers of prosecutors in the courts. As a consequence, many activities take place that are contrary to rule of law. They are seldom discovered. And even when they are, agents and other perpetrators are rarely held accountable. The cases against them are dropped or sealed because pursuing them might reveal intelligence sources and methods or other classified information. It is ironic indeed that many of the prisoners illegally detained at the U.S. Naval Station at Guantánamo Bay could not be prosecuted for the same reasons.

The great documents that establish modern liberal states have little use for internal security and do not even refer to it—the U.S. Constitution (1787), the French Declaration of the Rights of Man (1789), and, most recently, the Charter of Fundamental Rights of the European Union (2009). Indeed, these documents can broadly be construed as efforts to establish and maintain an open society. They pierce the secrecy and limit the powers of the executive state, making it more transparent, flexible, responsive to rule of law, and tolerant—so that the rights of individuals can be protected against the powers of government.

State secrecy and internal security are pervasive elements of Secure Democracy. This can be seen in the precipitous rise in security budgets, the construction of extensive new counterterrorism facilities, and dramatic increases in the numbers of police and intelligence agents in the post-9/11 period. When extraordinary powers of internal security are fully established and accepted as a legitimate state function, it is extremely difficult for an individual, civil-society groups, or even other parts of the government to challenge them. Excessive internal security is, accordingly, a structural element of Secure Democracy. It poses a threat to the open society and generally to the rights and liberties of everyone.

The advent of ubiquitous government surveillance in the United States, Western Europe, and the democracies of Asia is another indication of Secure Democracy. The interests of the state and the private sector certainly diverge at points, as the confrontation between the Federal Bureau of Investigation and Apple over unlocking iPhones has shown. Nevertheless, companies in the digital sector make all manner of surveillance software and equipment, as well as personal information, available to governments. And governments privilege companies that cooperate in security matters. Both engage in pervasive surveillance, so much so that privacy—once a cornerstone of liberal democracy—is now a contested right. It is impossible to keep personal information private in Secure Democracy. It is stolen, misappropriated, hacked, compiled, aggregated, analyzed, manipulated, traded, and sold as a commodity in the digital marketplace.

Personal information also resides in the data centers of thousands of intelligence and police units, both foreign and domestic. The laws relating to privacy that attempt to regulate surveillance and data mining by intelligence agencies are outdated, obtuse, and ineffective in the extreme. Secure Democracy places secret state interests above the privacy concerns of citizens, using ever-evolving, state-of-the-art surveillance software and equipment to gather personal information on everyone. Presidents and prime ministers can order large-scale, indiscriminate data collection on their own authority. The technologies of the digital age are the coin of the realm, integrating many aspects of the public and private spheres. Not even German Chancellor Angela Merkel could operate her cell phone without being hacked by the U.S. National Security Agency.

Another key element of Secure Democracy is the emergence of a threat, an apparently permanent one. It is analogous to the Cold War era, when Communism became the common enemy against which to organize the coercive powers of the state, most prominently the military. There were some now-discredited internal manifestations such as McCarthyism and the loyalty-security boards of the 1950s. With the collapse of world Communism, however, after a post–Cold War period of drifting and confusion, terrorism became the new *bête noire*. Politicians, intelligence officials, and, most promiscuously, the media hype the threat of terrorism. They do it even when the incidence of such events in the United States and Western Europe is minuscule compared to other causes of death and dismemberment. It is fear mongering, plain and simple. Since 9/11, the United States has engaged in a permanent war on terrorism, even if we do not always call it that, now with lethal attack drones. Special Forces and the Cyber Command are deployed globally. Under Secure Democracy, governments embrace a state of permanent emergency, killing fighters in foreign lands by remote control, sometimes even their own citizens—as the U.S. and U.K. governments have demonstrated. In an emergency, the executive can preempt the roles of judge, jury, and executioner.

Secure Democracy also promotes and enables law enforcement at all levels of government—and to an increasing extent, local police—who take the gloves off, especially when dealing with minorities, poor people, and other vulnerable populations. Although official statistics are not kept on the numbers of persons shot or killed by the police, high-profile police violence took center stage in 2014 through 2016 in the United States, focusing attention on volatile race relations and federal government programs that have armed the police with military-grade weapons, as well as providing them with funding and training in counterterrorism. Big-city police forces now operate sophisticated intelligence units that maintain close relations with national intelligence agencies and many counterparts in foreign countries. Secure Democracy incorporates the local police as the front line against terrorism and other threats to internal security.

It also penetrates local and civil society. Government intelligence agencies employ many thousands of agents and informants who infiltrate groups suspected of terrorism or other criminal activities They are given wide latitude in their operations and are permitted to engage in "otherwise illegal activity." These government employees can act as *agents provocateurs*—providing money, motivation, planning, logistics, weapons, and munitions to individuals and groups who would otherwise not have undertaken these activities and would not have been able to execute them if they had. Here the Federal Bureau of Investigation has blurred the line between national security and criminal investigations, creating cases in which the accused is not permitted to see the classified evidence against him, even when sentenced to jail.

Unelected intelligence officials seize significant power under Secure Democracy, vastly expanding their budgets and operations. They conduct disinformation campaigns with relative impunity, and supply elected officials, including heads of state, with misleading and incorrect information. It may be relatively harmless and self-serving, such as the discredited claim made in 2013 by the then-director of the National Security Agency, General Keith Alexander, that his agency had helped to foil 54 terrorist plots against the West. Or it may have grave consequences, as in the 2002 allegations that Iraq possessed weapons of mass destruction and harbored or supported al Qaeda. Political elites cherry-picked faulty and manufactured intelligence to justify invading Iraq with the consequent devastation of Iraqi society.

Secure Democracy also enables the executive to undertake activity that is universally recognized as abhorrent and illegal in all liberal democracies. Acting on trumped-up and misguided authority, the Central Intelligence Agency rounded up and tortured hundreds of suspected terrorists in secret and without reference to rule of law or any form of due process. In cases of mistaken identity, the agency even tortured innocent persons. When political authorities called the agency to task, its leadership became recalcitrant and pushed back against criticism. They even hacked the classified computers of their oversight committee of Congress, the Senate Select Committee on Intelligence, attempting to intimidate committee staff investigating CIA malfeasance. Committee chair Dianne Feinstein took to the Senate floor to denounce the defiance of John Brennan, the director of the Central Intelligence Agency. But he remained obstinate to the end, refusing to cooperate fully with the Senate, and he lost no opportunity to contradict and oppose the release of the committee's report on CIA torture programs. Over 90 percent of the Senate report remains classified and unavailable to the public.

Infiltration of civil society, universal surveillance, and secret torture programs are not the only miscarriages of justice under Secure Democracy. Secret *ex parte* courts authorize shady and antidemocratic activities conducted by intelligence and law-enforcement agencies, which would not be considered in open courts. While there were some positive modifications to the Foreign Intelligence Surveillance Court under the USA Freedom Act of 2015, the court still operates in secret and conducts non-adversarial proceedings. In liberal democracy, there is no such thing as secret justice. Anyone should be able to enter the courtroom and review the record of the court. Secret courts are everywhere the harbingers of tyranny.

The most often stated objective of Secure Democracy is to protect society from "terrorism," even though that term has no precise meaning or agreed definition. This mission is to a large extent self-reinforcing. I call it the "terror-counterterror-terror dynamic." When terrorist incidents occur, intelligence agencies, military units, the media, and political authorities overreact. This can occur on a grand scale, such as the invasions of Iraq and Afghanistan, or on a smaller scale, such as the Boston Marathon bombing, when a thousand intelligence and law-enforcement officials converged on Boston. They locked the city down, took over private homes, and discharged automatic weapons, strafing a suburban neighborhood where a single suspect was wounded and hiding in someone's backyard.

The frequency of international terrorism increased in the 1990s, including bombings of the World Trade Center in 1993 and the U.S. embassies in Nairobi and Dar es Salaam in 1998—culminating in the attacks of 9/11 and a spate of assaults thereafter in Baghdad, Bali, Brussels, Karachi, London, Madrid, Mumbai, Paris, Sadr City, and elsewhere. The reaction in the West was to build up counterterrorism and intelligence assets. These new powers are directed both internally and against suspected terrorists in the Middle East, Northern Africa, and South Asia. But rather than stemming global terrorism, they stimulate it, mostly in the form of suicide bombings in countries under occupation or suicide attacks in Western cities. In Secure Democracy, terror elicits indiscriminate counterterrorism (such as ubiquitous surveillance and foreign wars), which in turn stimulates more terrorism, often motivated by revenge. It is a self-reinforcing mechanism, an extended cycle of terror, counterterror, and more terror that is clearly detrimental to modern liberal democracy.

The first chapter of this book argues that Secure Democracy is supplanting liberal democracy in the aftermath of 9/11, and in response to an irrational fear of terrorism. It is occurring in the heyday of the digital revolution, a period of singularity, when it is impossible for most people to comprehend fully the technological change all around us. As a society, we have yet to grasp the meaning of universal digital interconnection, its impact on developmental psychology, or its transformation of government and society.

Most intelligence and internal security activity is classified. Even core budgetary, planning, legal, operational, and historical documents are secret. Accordingly, Chapter II assesses the scale and scope of the Security Industrial Complex, mainly in the United States, but also with reference to the modern liberal democracies of Europe. The massive blueprint of this complex demonstrates a growing interdependence between internal and military security units and operations, both within and among nation-states. One thing is clear: The buildup of the surveillance security state is a response to psychological shock, the fear of terrorism made manifest in the 9/11 attacks on New York and Washington, and other major terrorist events around the world.

Chapter III turns to the history and magnitude of terrorism. It demonstrates an irrational disconnect in which extreme internal security powers of government have been amassed in response to the *fear of terrorism*, when terrorism in the West is minimal at best. The chapter compares internal and military security, suggesting that the two are closely aligned, and that both embody dangerous elements that are psychologically driven, yet pathological and highly irrational. The race to modernize the nuclear arsenal, initiated by the Obama administration, is a telling example.

All terrorism is not the same. The fourth chapter distinguishes between so-called catastrophic terror and several categories of small-scale episodic terrorism. Catastrophic terrorism is mainly, perhaps exclusively, the province of states and typically occurs in the context of war. The United States killed 30,000 in the fire-bombing of Dresden and 100,000 in Tokyo. One hundred and fifty thousand perished in Hiroshima and 75,000 in Nagasaki. Germany killed 6 million in the Holocaust, and Turkey executed between 800,000 and 1.2 million in the Armenian Genocide. Terrorists are unlikely to match this scale of destruction. The number in 9/11, some 3,000 fatalities, pales in comparison but still constitutes the largest non-state act of terrorism to date. The chapter argues that internal security should focus on keeping weapons of mass destruction out of the hands of people who would use them, not on millions of ordinary people. It turns out that the global nonproliferation regime is well suited to this task.

Chapter V presents case studies of the several different kinds of episodic terror, such as *"lone wolf" single-point security failures, attacks perpetrated by organized groups,* and *conspiracies inspired by the government.* It presents a typology of terror with illustrative stories. These draw out the motivations and political machinations of the intelligence and law-enforcement agencies as they pursue opportunities to justify their outsize budgets and political ambitions. Indeed, the Federal Bureau of Investigation infiltrates mosques and other organizations in an attempt to organize and empower terrorist cells, only to arrest their hapless recruits at a later date. Chapters VI and VII engage the operations of Secure Democracy, specifically detention and torture in the former, and surveillance and control in the latter.

The concluding chapter strives to present an optimistic picture. It asks if authoritarian forms of governance will overwhelm liberalism in the end. Is liberal democracy an ephemeral construction, a highly evolved system of governance beginning sometime between the Peace of Westphalia and the Declaration of the Rights of Man, and lasting only about 250 years? The rise of the surveillance security state forces us to contemplate the possibility that modern liberal democracy has now become obsolete as a governing force. The chapter analyzes possible legal remedies, challenges to Secure Democracy from civil society, and a divergence of interests among intelligence agencies and corporate giants in the digital economy. It holds out some hope that a confluence of these elements might possibly confront Secure Democracy—but only if ordinary citizens are roused en masse and comprehend the decline of freedom in the 21st century.

CHAPTER I

THE CHALLENGE TO LIBERAL DEMOCRACY

At the onset of the 21st century, al Qaeda introduced the idea of terrorism to the American people in an unprecedented act of brutality and mass murder. Most Americans had never heard of the group or even considered terrorism to be a first-order threat. That soon changed and, with it, the character of American democracy. The 9/11 suicide attacks on the Pentagon and the World Trade Center catapulted America into a new era, an age in which the overreaction to terrorism and the tools created to fight it threaten to undermine the fundamental values of modern liberal democracies everywhere. It is most pronounced and visible in the United States, the United Kingdom, France, and Australia, but this subversive ideology can be detected in all of the major modern liberal democracies of the world.

Liberal democracy—the form of government framed by 18th-century political philosophers and made manifest by the

American and French Revolutions—is bounded by time, political philosophy, and demographics. It comprises most of the populations of North America and Western Europe, and a small percentage of Asia, emerging sometime between the Peace of Westphalia (1648) and the Declaration of the Rights of Man (1789), a period broadly construed as the Enlightenment. In the sweep of history, this movement is still relatively new. It might even be considered an experiment—one in which the rights of individuals are elevated in relation to the prerogatives of kings and the powers of governments. Because of the military dominance and wealth of the West, it is easy to forget that the modern democratic state exists on a narrow band in history, encompasses only a small part of humanity, and may be more fragile than many of its adherents suppose.

In the wake of our new perception of terrorism, we have created a secret security establishment that operates outside the normal constraints that democracy and rule of law impose on our leaders. It is closely linked to state and local law enforcement internally, and internationally, to foreign intelligence agencies and policing organizations. This sector of the government employs hundreds of thousands of officials whose work is classified and unavailable to the public.

I call it the Security Industrial Complex. It is tightly coupled with the digital sector of the economy, and analogous to the Military Industrial Complex. But it focuses instead on civil society—tracking the movements, associations, habits, communications, finances, and faces of ordinary people. In response to the threat of mass-casualty terrorism, the United States built a surveillance security state-within-the-state, funded to the tune of more than $120 billion a year, whose activities are secret, often proscribed, yet tolerated and even venerated by political elites.

This security colossus is aided and abetted by companies in the digital sector that provide access to vast stores of data as well as surveillance software and equipment. The purpose and precise activities of the security establishment, and the extent of its operations, are unknown—to the public, to members of Congress, to the cabinet, and sometimes even to the president of the United States. It is a state-within-the-state whose surveillance technology and operatives penetrate, monitor, and influence vast areas of the government, civil society, and foreign affairs. Its tentacles reach deeply into the Internet, our daily correspondence, and the digital sector of the economy.

The rise of international terror and a corresponding surveillance security state coincided with the digital transformation of the media, the workplace, education, communications, entertainment, medicine, energy infrastructure, government, and of course, society in general. It may be that the threat of terrorism is not the only cause of universal surveillance. Indeed, many people voluntarily or unwittingly[1] cede their privacy to government and the private sector, even in the absence of the threat of international terrorism. The allure of digital devices and the capabilities and efficiencies they bring to life is certainly compelling. But to be clear, the compromise of our liberal ideals, the condition of Secure Democracy, would not have been possible in the absence of the digital revolution. The Internet and the companies it spawned make vast amounts of personal information available in commerce and to the state.

This combination of enhanced state security operations and the headlong growth of the digital sector of the economy constitutes an unprecedented threat to the privacy and civil liberties of ordinary people. Heretofore, most historians and political analysts concerned with freedom focused on what appeared to be isolated examples of unrestrained government power. They wrote about the 1919 "red scare" and "slacker raids" associated with Attorney General A. Mitchell Palmer and his deputy, J. Edgar Hoover. Or the discussion might have turned to the legal basis for internal security in the United States, first enunciated in two memoranda issued by President Franklin D. Roosevelt in 1936 and 1939.[2] Five years later, the Supreme Court decided the *Korematsu* case. It held that "exclusion" leading to the internment of 127,000 Japanese Americans during the Second World War was constitutional. It is still the subject of contemporary analysis. (As Justice Stephen Breyer wrote, the *Korematsu* decision is "so thoroughly discredited that it is hard to conceive of any future court referring to it favorably or relying on it."[3]) There is also an extensive literature on McCarthyism, the loyalty-security boards, and the Internal Security Act of 1950. Scholars and journalists have also analyzed the aggressive domestic "Cointelpro" programs carried out by the Federal Bureau of Investigation in the late 1950s through the early 1970s. Reaching back, one could invoke President Abraham Lincoln's suspension of *habeas corpus* for suspected Confederate spies and saboteurs (as well as the Legislature of Maryland) during the American Civil War, which he considered necessary to preserve the Union. U.S. history even records the passage and repeal of the Alien and Sedition Acts of 1798, a misguided attempt by the Federalists to weaken the Bill of Rights and the Democratic-Republican Party, founded by Thomas Jefferson and James Madison.

These events are often and perhaps rightly depicted as temporary deviations from the liberal tradition in the United States, a response to war or another emergency, to which stable democratic institutions provided an enduring counterbalance. We always returned to our liberal ideals once the crisis had passed.

The Enemy Within

What I have called Secure Democracy embraces large-scale internal security operations within government, where challenges to their legality and legitimacy are unlikely to succeed. But it has not always been that way. Beginning in the late 1940s, there was a slow accretion of largely unaccountable power within the Federal Bureau of Investigation and other U.S. intelligence agencies.[4] By the early 1970s, perhaps in reaction to the Vietnam War and widespread social disorder of the 1960s, a hard core of a state-within-the-state had formed, which was inimical to freedoms Americans had come to expect. The impetus for reform came after March 8, 1971, when a group of anti–Vietnam War activists, whose identities only recently came to light, broke into the FBI field office in Media, Pennsylvania, and carried off a trove of top-secret files.[5]

And what a trove it was.

It must be conceded that these documents included very little data by today's standards. Indeed, the burglary took place prior to the advent of personal computers, the Internet, and large-scale data-mining operations. The purloined files nevertheless documented many programs under which the Federal Bureau of Investigation infiltrated civil society and illegally attempted to stifle nonviolent protest in the United States. When all this was revealed in the pages of *The Washington Post* and *The New York Times*, Congress and the American people were outraged. U.S. Senators Frank Church and Walter Mondale, and their counterparts in the House of Representatives, conducted an extensive Congressional investigation that reined in rogue elements of the intelligence community.[6]

At the end of the Cold War, accordingly, in the concluding decades of the 20th century, Americans could feel reasonably well assured that their liberty and privacy interests were protected from overzealous politicians and the internal security police by the U.S. Constitution and the liberal tradition in America.[7] A balancing mechanism appeared to ensure that typically war-related departures from rule of law would recede when the war emergency ended. And so it is that Americans have tended to acquiesce in whatever internal security measures are put forward by their elected representatives and unelected intelligence officials, protestations of the American Civil Liberties Union to the contrary notwithstanding.

Is such a course correction possible today under conditions of Secure Democracy, where bloated intelligence agencies routinely spy on Americans, amassing data on their activities, affiliations, and ideas?

On June 6, 2013, an important test began. The *Guardian* newspaper released classified information about mass surveillance programs of the National Security Agency, many operated in collaboration with its British counterpart, the Government Communications Headquarters. On that date, former National Security Agency contractor and whistleblower Edward Snowden initiated the sustained release of tens of thousands of secret intelligence documents.[8] They confirmed what careful observers had long since detected: the rise of a comprehensive, high-powered internal and foreign surveillance system, an enemy to liberal democracy, embedded in countless programs and large data-intensive operations across many elements of an outsize U.S. Security Industrial Complex and several of its counterparts abroad.

There was a surge of public indignation, as evidenced in many stories in major media outlets. Over the next three years, the Snowden documents continued to appear, describing many secret programs conducting questionable and arguably illegal surveillance. The U.S. government immediately staked out an adversarial position, with the White House defending ubiquitous surveillance from the outset, as usual, promising to protect both freedom and the national security.

So how did we get here? How do we find ourselves on the cusp of betraying our liberal tradition? It has, no doubt, been coming for years: steadily encroaching surveillance technology, the explosion of data systems, and the militarization of both government and the police. It is a condition that even a prominent international whistleblower could not derail. No doubt, the psychological shock of 9/11 is a critical factor. In its aftermath, the government engaged in a headlong rush to ensure it would never happen again. Congress passed and the president signed the USA Patriot Act in record time—only six weeks after the 9/11 attacks, on October 26, 2001.

But the Patriot Act is little more than a 342-page compilation of all the antidemocratic proposals that had previously been rejected. In every succeeding year, Congress appropriated vast sums to build up the Security Industrial Complex and prosecute the Counterterror Wars in Iraq and Afghanistan, the longest military engagement in the history of the United States. The government also demanded the assistance of the newly established and emerging Internet-based corporations, and most were eager to comply.

And so we find ourselves of the verge of a new era. One with frightening implications for the future of democracy, and it all begins with one simple question.

What if the threat never ends?

What if the 21st century, with its deep fear of terrorism and overreactions to it, has ushered in a state of permanent emergency, one that thrives in the face of an acquiescent society? In the United States, we can see its base in the creation of the Security Industrial Complex. This complex comprises 17 agencies forming an "intelligence community," integrated military components, information-technology companies, ubiquitous surveillance, and official as well as proprietary secrecy. The imposition of pervasive internal security is now considered by many to be a necessary and legitimate function of government. In our contemporary era, democracy is under assault from subversive intelligence agencies that seek nothing less than an end to privacy and the annexation of the Internet.

Public intellectuals and prominent journalists sometimes dismiss of minimize the importance of the Security Industrial Complex. Some argue that government surveillance programs are necessary to discover and defeat terrorist organizations in Afghanistan, Iraq, Libya Nigeria, Pakistan, Somalia, Syria, and Yemen—among other places—that would otherwise attack the United States and Western Europe. In the extreme, or so the argument goes, if terrorists successfully executed another 9/11-type event, it would mean the end of the open society as we know it, an end to tolerant and responsive government that is flexible and transparent. Even if ubiquitous government surveillance is repugnant to modern liberalism, they believe, it is also a necessary evil.[9]

While this argument has gained some traction in the media, and is embraced by CEOs of big private security firms, it rests on questionable assumptions. The first is that a limited "surveillance state," what these writers believe to exist in the United States, is capable of stopping terrorists from inflicting terror on society.[10] As every counterterrorism analyst and operative knows, however, persons and organizations capable of perpetrating international terror can be extremely agile, determined, and competent in the use of digital technology. This means that ubiquitous, big-data surveillance that indiscriminately sweeps up everything is probably not the right approach. After all, there is a constant stream of intelligence failures, stretching from the bombing of the U.S. embassies in East Africa in 1998 through 9/11 to the attacks in 2016 by so-called self-radicalized Islamist militants on a recreation center in San Bernardino and a nightclub in Orlando. We hear a constant refrain from security analysts and the media that the United States played a losing hand in the "propaganda war" with the Islamic State and allied groups—that they have captured the loyalty of young people and will turn them against us. There is, to date, no evidence to support this claim in the United States.

A second assumption is that we can live with the surveillance state because its dimensions are well defined, and if necessary, it can be dismantled or contained within established legal and normative structures. While this perspective may be comforting, it underestimates the resources and powers of Secure Democracy. The secret state employs a multitude of security analysts and agents, occupies 10,000 facilities across the United States, and is funded at a level exceeding half a trillion dollars over the past five years. It will be difficult if not impossible to reconcile such an expansive security apparatus with the core values of liberty and constitutionalism. As the internal security police gain numbers, influence, and power in Washington, London, and Paris, at some point it becomes impossible to characterize the resulting governments as liberal democracies and the corresponding societies as open. Indeed, the surveillance security state begins to define a new, tougher form of democracy.

When we contrast liberalism with the underlying characteristics of Secure Democracy, the differences are significant. The first and most essential feature of modern democratic governance is *rule of law.* But how can rule of law prevail when large elements of the government operate in secrecy and conduct economy-wide, warrantless surveillance that is not disclosed to the public or even officially acknowledged? The 21st-century surveillance security state supports a more repressive form of democracy. Here, rule of law becomes a principle honored in the breach, an ideal to which every agent doffs his hat, but which is flouted time and again in the secret world of terror and counterterror that must not be divulged on pain of imprisonment, or worse.

Under conditions of Secure Democracy, presidents and prime ministers can order surveillance programs that circumvent the law, collecting and storing data on untold millions of people. In 2001 through 2007, for example, President George W. Bush appoved the highly classified "President's Surveillance Program" in a secret executive order. It authorized the National Security Agency, the Federal Bureau of Investigation, and the Director of National Intelligence to circumvent the law by intercepting the electronic communications of Americans without a warrant, without reasonable suspicion, and certainly without probable cause.

Unscrupulous politicians and ambitious intelligence professionals nevertheless continue to hype the threat of terrorism. As Americans, they say, we must forgo forever the luxury of American history, with its protective geography and manifest destiny, to worry instead about a broad and ill-defined threat of terrorists blowing up airplanes or attacking schools and shopping malls. Because the threat is made to appear far more immediate, widespread, and dangerous than it actually is, reform of the intelligence community is highly unlikely. Moreover, the media are largely complicit; they run hundreds of stories every time a mass shooting or bombing occurs, especially if the Federal Bureau of Investigation or the president calls it "terrorism."

The buildup of greater and greater intelligence and surveillance assets raises a simple question: Even if we favor security over liberty and privacy, does it work? Does it stop terror? But the answer is anything but straightforward. According to one authority, the attempt to secure immigration has "seriously damaged the delicate balance between the need to control security threats on the one hand, and the respect for civil liberties and human rights on the other," both in the United States and Europe.[11] Nevertheless, every national security chief will patiently explain to Congress or the parliaments of Europe that intelligence activity has stopped many terrorist plots. But they cannot provide details because it might compromise sources and methods, putting agents, operations, and society at risk. Their mission is sacrosanct.

Mr. Snowden made every effort to promote his cause from asylum in Russia. No doubt he hoped to catalyze profound change and censure of the intelligence agencies, perhaps in the same manner as the antiwar activists who broke into the FBI offices in Media, Pennsylvania, 40 years earlier. But the institutions of internal security had become too deeply entrenched within America's new Secure Democracy. Despite stories in major media outlets, numerous video appearances, interviews, documentaries, and a Hollywood movie directed by Oliver Stone featuring Snowden, his revelations gradually receded from the public view. In the United States, there was no faction in government to take it on, and only a guarded executive response, and so the intelligence agencies continued their brazen activities largely unabated. Such is the authority and influence that the agents of internal security wield in the corridors of power in Washington. They do not fear the lawmakers or the press and least of all the American people.

And why should they? In a poll taken several days before Congress passed the USA Freedom Act (which amends and tempers parts of the Patriot Act), 61 percent of respondents thought that Congress should renew "the law allowing the National Security Administration [*sic*] (NSA) to collect and analyze information on the phone calls of most Americans in order to locate suspected terrorists."[12] Indeed, opinion polls consistently show that warrantless surveillance programs of the National Security Agency and the Federal Bureau of Investigation retain the support of a majority of the people, even when such programs are exposed in the press on numerous occasions. When asked if it was more important to investigate terrorist threats or not to intrude on privacy, about two-thirds of the sample affirmed "it is more important for the federal government to investigate possible terrorist threats, even if that intrudes on personal privacy."[13]

This is a consistent refrain in polls taken in 2002, 2006, 2010, and 2013—even after the existence of the formerly secret National Security Agency surveillance programs was widely publicized.[14] Moreover, when told the "NSA has been investigating people suspected of terrorist involvement by secretly listening in on phone calls and reading emails without court approval," a slim majority of 51 percent of respondents found this activity to be "acceptable" whereas 47 percent responded "not acceptable."[15] Perhaps the wording of the questions influenced the results. And indeed, the questions display a kind of naïveté about the descent of modern liberal democracy into the quagmire of excessive internal security.

In another poll conducted in January 2014, respondents were asked about "the government's collection of telephone and internet data as part of anti-terrorism efforts." Fifty-three percent disapproved and 40 percent approved. If the prompt had been phrased differently, and the respondents had been told that the "NSA is investigating millions of people by secretly collecting data and listening in on phone calls and reading emails without court approval," the poll might have elicited different opinions.[16] And this wording would have been more accurate: We know the National Security Agency and other intelligence units indiscriminately sweep up billions of records and electronic papers of ordinary Americans, even when there is no reason to think they have any connection to terrorism or any other kind of criminal activity.

Terror, Counterterror, and More Terror

Secure Democracy has established deep roots in our system of governance and is changing significantly the nature of our democracy. One of the most vital ways this new form of governing perpetuates itself is tied directly to our reaction to the so-called "war on terror." I call it the terror-counterterror-terror dynamic. This dynamic has been building for a long time, at least since 1990, when the United

States first invaded Iraq and the subsequent al Qaeda bombing of the World Trade Center in 1993—together with several other al Qaeda attacks, culminating in 9/11. Like al Qaeda, the United States sought retribution, engaging in the extended Counterterror Wars in Iraq and Afghanistan, which in turn catalyzed more terror.

In 2014, for example, as President Obama pondered what to do about the expanding, murderous forces of the so-called Islamic State of Iraq and Syria, counterterrorism officials and their friends in Congress argued that if the U.S. military did not stop the Islamic State fighters in Iraq and Syria, the group would mount attacks in the United States and Europe. It is analogous to the fear of Communist conspiracy in the 1950s and early 1960s. We had to stop them in Korea and Vietnam or more dominoes would fall. In the contemporary scenario, security officials warned that European and American Muslims who have traveled to Syria or Iraq would return to commit atrocities at home—fully trained, funded, and directed by the Islamic State.

In one early editorial piece, U.S. Senators John McCain and Lindsey Graham asserted, ". . . its ranks are filled with thousands of radicals holding Western passports, including some Americans. They require nothing more than a plane ticket to travel to United States cities."[17] That same day, Prime Minister David Cameron raised the official U.K. terror threat level from "substantial" to "severe," meaning that "an attack is highly likely."[18] He characterized the Islamic State as a "greater and deeper threat to security than we have known."[19] Such radical hyperbole shows either ignorance or disdain for history; Winston Churchill, who faced the Blitz in World War II, certainly would not have agreed.

In an address from Downing Street, Cameron said, "We need to do more to stop people travelling [to the Middle East], to stop those who do go from returning, and to deal decisively with those who are already here." He planned to revoke British passports of an estimated

250 "jihadis" who were thought already to have returned to the United Kingdom from the Middle East.[20] Six weeks later, in an address to the Australian Parliament that had just passed a tough new terrorism law, he said he would soon introduce a similar counterterrorism bill in the United Kingdom, including "new powers for police at ports to seize passports, to stop suspects travelling, and to stop British nationals returning to the UK unless they do so on our terms."[21] And that is exactly what he did. A new security law, the Counter-Terrorism and Security Act of 2015, confers unprecedented police powers on the British intelligence and security agencies.[22]

And Cameron was soon to take tough action. In September of 2015 the United Kingdom announced that it had carried out targeted killings of Reyaad Khan and Ruhul Amin, two U.K. citizens in Syria who had joined the Islamic State fighters. In a statement to the House of Lords, the British prime minister assured members of Parliament and the public that the operation was "entirely lawful." "We were," he said, "exercising the UK's inherent right to self defense. There was clear evidence of the individuals in question planning and directing armed attacks against the UK." He said there was no government in Syria with whom he could work, and so the only alternative was to make a preemptive strike against the prospective "terrorists." He added, "I can tell the House that our police and security services have stopped at least six different attempts to attack the UK in the last twelve months alone."[23] But he did not provide details or evidence. There is, of course, no conceivable legal basis on which a head of state can unilaterally decide to assassinate its citizens, citing threats of terrorism and other rationalizations to the contrary notwithstanding.

In the days that followed, British Minister of Defense Michael Fallon told the BBC, "We wouldn't hesitate to do it again if we know that there is an armed attack that is likely. If we know who is involved in it, then we have to do something about it."[24] Cameron had followed the lead of President Obama, who ordered the Central Intelligence Agency to assassinate Anwar al-Awlaki, an American citizen, in Yemen on September 30, 2011.

In both the United States and the United Kingdom, foreign-policy decisions are increasingly driven by internal security calculations. This is a radical departure from the past in which foreign-policy fears launched domestic responses: the Palmer Raids in 1919, the passage of the Communist Control Act of 1954, and the insertion of the FBI Cointelpros into the fabric of society and politics in the 1960s. But under conditions of Secure Democracy, the relationship between foreign policy and internal security policy can evidently be reversed. President Obama made a speech to the American people in which he referred to the Islamic State group as a terrorist organization. He said, "Our objective is clear: We will degrade and ultimately destroy [them] through a comprehensive and sustained counterterrorism strategy." The United States, he said, must lead a coalition against the militants in part because "our Intelligence Community believes that thousands of foreigners—including Europeans and some Americans—have joined them in Syria and Iraq. Trained and battle-hardened, these fighters could try to return to their home countries and carry out deadly attacks."[25]

It is likely the president was channeling misinformation fed to him by his security chiefs, possibly John Brennan (CIA), James Clapper (DNI), James Comey (FBI), or another intimate in his circle of security advisors. Three days after Islamic State–inspired terror descended on Paris killing 129 persons in November of 2015, Brennan seized the opportunity to debunk efforts to rein in surveillance activity. He told a conservative think tank in Washington:

In the past several years because of a number of unauthorized disclosures and a lot of handwringing over the government's role in the effort to try to uncover these terrorists, there have been some policy and legal and other actions that are taken that make our ability collectively internationally to find these terrorists much more challenging. And I do hope that this [the terror attack on Paris] is going to be a wake-up call.[26]

"Handwringing"? These remarks circulated widely in the print media and on the web. But the editorial board of *The New York Times* would have none of it. "It's a wretched yet predictable ritual," they wrote, "after each new terrorist attack: Certain politicians and government officials waste no time exploiting the tragedy for their own ends. The remarks on Monday by John Brennan, the director of the Central Intelligence Agency, took that to a new and disgraceful low."[27] But former CIA Director R. James Woosley did Brennan one better. He said, "I'm no fan of the changes that were made after [NSA contractor Edward] Snowden's leaks of classi-fied information. . . . I think they've seriously reduced our abili-ties. I think Snowden has blood on his hands from these killings in France."[28] Clearly an absurd proposition, in which the former CIA chief attempted to deflect criticism by blaming the messenger.

Whether "trained and battle-hardened" Islamic State fighters return to the United States to commit atrocities is for history to say. If they do, it will be part of a continuing terror-counterterror-terror dynamic. Both the president and his CIA director made many comments about the Islamic State, but they failed to rec-ognize that U.S. counterterrorism policies played a pivotal role in its rise. We know for certain that the Islamic State is a child of the American and British occupation of Iraq, part of a secu-rity dynamic that has been playing out for a very long time. In 2003, Abu Bakr al-Baghdadi, who would become the leader of the Islamic State and self-proclaimed caliph of the Muslim world, was a religious student and cleric at the Imam Ahmad ibn Hanbal Mosque in Samarra.[29] From February through December 2004, he was imprisoned as a "civilian internee" at Camp Bucca, a notorious U.S. military detention facility in the vicinity of Umm Qasr, where torture and humiliation of detainees is reported to have been commonplace. After his release, he became progressively more involved in militant insurgency, a rising leader of al Qaeda in Iraq. It is ironic, indeed, that the al Qaeda group *did not even exist* in Iraq prior to the U.S. invasion in 2003.

In 2010, al-Baghdadi broke with al Qaeda to establish and assume the leadership of the Islamic State, mounting a military campaign to oust remnants of the U.S. occupation and overthrow the governments of Iraq and Syria. In a stunning series of victories in 2014 and 2015—notable for mass executions, rape, beheadings, crucifixions, immolations, and sophisticated (if often morbid) propaganda—the group gained control of a large swath of Iraq, including Fallujah, Mosul, and sections of Ramadi. It seized several key oilfields and infiltrated or occupied many towns in Syria and along the Iraqi border with Turkey—provoking President Obama to resume U.S. air strikes in Iraq and commence them in Syria and Libya. In time, Russia, Turkey, France, the United Kingdom, and other states joined the offensive—although for different reasons and often working to different ends.

As it turned out, the threat appeared not to come from returnees but from persons who had become "self-radicalized" while viewing materials on the Internet. In several prominent cases, those perpetuating the terror did not travel to the Middle East or have direct contact with Islamic State or other recruiters. In some cases, no connection to any terrorist group or propaganda could be found, as in the case of the June 2016 Orlando massacre in which Omar Mateen—a social misfit—staged an attack at a gay nightclub, killing 49 persons and wounding 50. He legally bought two guns from a store in Florida about a week before the rampage. One was a Sig Sauer MCX .223-caliber semi-automatic assault rifle with a magazine capacity of

30 rounds. He also carried a Glock 17 9mm semi-automatic pistol. It has a magazine capacity of 17 rounds and is widely used by law-enforcement officers.

In Chattanooga, Tennessee, Muhammad Youssef Abdulazeez appears also to have been self-radicalized. In July 2015, he opened fire on a Navy reserve facility, killing four U.S. Marines and a sailor. He was also an outcast and is reported to have suffered from drug and alcohol abuse, depression, and bipolar disorder. FBI Director Comey characterized the motivation: "There is no doubt that the Chattanooga killer was inspired, motivated by foreign terrorist organization propaganda." Although, he added, it was not possible to determine which terrorist group may have inspired Abdulazeez.[30] Surely the FBI director was punting if he could not identify the motivating group or the propaganda in question. But such undocumented suppositions often pass for facts when relevant documents and the investigation are classified and unavailable to the media and the public.

Director Comey's self-radicalization theory was also applied to the San Bernardino incident, in which Tashfeen Malik and her husband, Syed Rizwan Farook, killed 14 and injured 21 at a county recreation center. Investigators were unable to find a direct connection to any terrorist group. Right on cue, the Islamic State group took credit, as it did for the July 2016 truck that rampaged through a crowd in Nice, France, killing 84 persons who were celebrating Bastille Day. But the driver, Mohamed Lahouaiej Bouhlel, did not appear to have connections with any violent group or to have been influenced by anti-Western propaganda. If the Islamic State group ever does send soldiers and order acts of terror in the United States or the United Kingdom, it will be another episode of the cycle of terror and counterterror, a dynamic that is too often used to justify the increase of internal security measures and budgets in democratic societies.

"I Cannot Choose but Laugh"

Great harm is, of course, inflicted on society and our psychology every time a lone wolf picks up an assault rifle and kills innocent people, especially police officers, as happened in Dallas, Texas, and Baton Rouge, Louisiana, in July 2016. It is terrorism, pure and simple, even if it evolves in the mind of a single person. And the fear of such acts, especially scaling up to 9/11 and mass-casualty terrorism, has propelled the ascendance of security over liberty in the 21st century. Because we fear terror, it is tempting to excuse or overlook the loss of privacy and the assault on civil liberties.

It is sometimes argued that while governments may be conducting extensive warrantless surveillance and otherwise building up internal security assets, innocent people are not hurt by it, and so there's no harm, no foul. If there is harm, it consists of exposing critical activities of the Security Industrial Complex—its extent, agents, activities, funding, sources, and methods. This reasoning, however, ignores the injustice inflicted on minorities, who are disproportionately targeted by intelligence and police units, and who rarely have the resources to defend themselves. It undermines the core values of liberal democracy: privacy, the right to confront one's accuser, the right against self-incrimination, freedom of speech, and perhaps most important, the elevation of the individual and rule of law in the face of overwhelming powers of arbitrary governance—surveillance, investigation, infiltration, intimidation, prosecution, incarceration, and torture. If there is another 9/11 or an act of catastrophic terror, many civil libertarians believe that it would provoke a draconian response, perhaps even an end to the open society as we know it.

But what if we have already reached a middle ground, a society in which the powers of a secret government exert a chilling effect on human relations and the willingness of individuals to write what they think and to speak their minds? Most digitally savvy people already assume their communications are monitored, and many adjust their text or speech. It is a kind of self-censorship. Perhaps John Adams got it right when he wrote to Thomas Jefferson in 1817, four decades after signing the Declaration of Independence:

> When people talk of the freedom of writing, speaking, or thinking, I cannot choose but laugh. No such thing ever existed. No such thing now exists; but I hope it will exist. But it must be hundreds of years after you and I shall write and speak no more.[31]

This is where internal security plays a trump card. It is not necessary to obliterate the open society and transform it into a police state. Secure Democracy is far subtler in its application. It mimics the form and processes of democracy but gradually drains it of content and freedom.

In the wake of the disastrous attacks of 9/11, the Security Industrial Complex expanded precipitously, as did the institutional and legal base that supports secret government surveillance and incursions on the rights of citizens, particularly in the arena of counterterrorism. A cabinet-level agency, the Department of Homeland Security, reaches deeply into the structure of state and local governance. It provides equipment, military-grade weapons, surveillance technology, training, and intelligence to state and local police departments, and funding for counterterrorism. In sum, following the attacks of 9/11, vast elements of the internal security apparatus were installed within all levels of government in the United States—federal, state, and local—such that it is highly unlikely that a private individual could present more than a symbolic challenge to internal security activity.

During the presidencies of George W. Bush and Barack Obama, enforcement of the Freedom of Information Act became increasingly lax. According to an analysis of federal data by the Associated Press, the "Obama Administration set a record again [in fiscal 2014] for censoring government files or outright denying access to them."[32] Requests for information were delayed or denied on national-security grounds, and information released under the FOIA was often heavily redacted. Although Obama pledged greater transparency on numerous occasions, the results were less impressive. Jill Abramson, executive editor of *The New York Times*, described the situation. "The Obama years," she said, "are a benchmark for a new level of secrecy and control. It's created quite a challenging atmosphere for *The New York Times*, and for some of the best reporters in my newsroom who cover national security issues in Washington." She also said that criminal investigations of leaked information had ". . . put a chill on reporting about national security issues in Washington."[33]

It is here that the secret government collides with the First Amendment of the U.S. Constitution. While lower courts will sometimes attempt to safeguard a reporter's "confidentiality privilege," the Supreme Court often defers to the executive in national-security cases. One of the cases to which Abramson alluded involved the refusal by national-security reporter James Risen to disclose a source for his book *State of War*, which revealed classified information about a CIA operation, code-named Merlin, to disrupt the Iranian nuclear program. After a six-year struggle featuring Risen and *The New York Times* on one side with the CIA and the Justice Department on the other, the U.S. Supreme Court declined to hear the case without comment, letting a lower court opinion stand. At the discretion of the prosecutor, Risen ultimately was not called to testify, but he lived under the threat of imprisonment for six years.[34]

Now the First Amendment is forceful because it is unequivocal. It says, "*Congress shall make no law . . . abridging the freedom of speech, or of the press. . . .*" Clearly in the Risen case, which can be generalized to the larger society, national-security speech as well as the right of the press to publish it is predictably "abridged."

Penetration of Civil Society

As technology has evolved, the intelligence agencies have engaged in widespread invasion of computers: hacking into personal, public, and private networks and machines, embedding pernicious surveillance viruses that cannot be detected by available antivirus software programs. In essence, the U.S. government conducts a massive cyber-spying program, at times using the alias of the Equation Group, a secretive cyber-espionage organization operated by the National Security Agency. According to Kaspersky Lab, which analyzed the Equation Group, the group's spyware is a "highly sophisticated threat actor that has been engaged in multiple computer network exploitation operations dating back to 2001, and perhaps as early as 1996."[35] Indeed, using this technique, the National Security Agency is "able to embed spyware in computers that gives it total control over them, even after the hard disk has been erased and the operating system reinstalled."[36] The Equation Group was also allegedly responsible for the "infamous Regin and Stuxnet attacks." In a bizarre twist, a group calling itself the Shadow Brokers held a Bitcoin auction in August of 2016, offering to sell Equation Group codes to the highest bidder, codes allegedly used to infiltrate companies such as Cisco, Juniper, and Fortinet.[37]

Here and in the less high-tech domain, government infiltration of the groups and associations that comprise civil society is emblematic of Secure Democracy. The phenomenon was clearly demonstrated in the United States during the 1960s. The Federal Bureau of Investigation launched dozens of secret surveillance programs, placing informants in all walks of American society. J. Edgar Hoover appears to have initiated most of these efforts, without enabling legislation or judicial review, and with little or no oversight. History records these events as aberrations in our traditions of freedom and liberalism. McCarthyism too—with its star chambers, Hollywood blacklists, and loyalty-security boards—is likewise seen as a dark time.

Following the Church Committee investigations, it was widely believed that the Federal Bureau of Investigation and other intelligence and law-enforcement agencies had been brought to heel by superior power emanating from the U.S. Congress. But that discipline dissipated after 9/11, when reckless spending on war and intelligence became the new normal at the dawn of Secure Democracy. In a telling example, several U.S. government agencies permit their "confidential informants" to conduct "otherwise illegal activity." The bureau authorized its informants to break the law 5,658 times in 2011[38] and 5,939 times in 2012, an increase of 5 percent.[39] Other agencies, including the Drug Enforcement Administration and the Bureau of Alcohol, Tobacco, Firearms, and Explosives, also permit informants to break the law but do not know how frequently that permission is given.[40] The Drug Enforcement Agency "has approximately 4,000 active confidential sources at any given time"[41] and the Federal Bureau of Investigation operates about 15,000.[42] The bureau maintains that the use of confidential informants in the commission of "otherwise illegal activity" is tightly controlled but admits that in "an investigation relating to a threat to the national security or foreign intelligence collection" the standard is considerably relaxed.[43]

Federal penetration of civil society goes hand-in-hand with the hardening or militarization of local police, a clear indication that internal security is supplanting liberal democracy. We are in the midst of a major transition in which the distinction between the military and the police is breaking down, weakening the historical prohibitions against deploying the military and the use of military force at home. This is evident in the embrace by local police of military-grade weapons and tactics. It can be seen in the adoption of police-type procedures by the military in Iraq and Afghanistan. As one criminologist succinctly put it in 2007, "The on-going war on terrorism is . . . blurring [the] distinction between the police and military, between internal and external security, and between war and law enforcement."[44]

Under conditions of Secure Democracy, investigatory and police powers are greatly enhanced and directed at vulnerable subsets of the population. Consider the 8,000 men from Arab and Muslim countries who were subjected to counterterrorism "interviews" by the U.S. Department of Justice and local law-enforcement agencies following 9/11.[45] A subsequent initiative by the Immigration and Naturalization Service was designed to "track down and deport 6,000 noncitizen males from (unnamed) Middle Eastern countries who had been ordered deported by an immigration judge but had never left the U.S."[46] Another area: extraordinary rendition, in which suspected terrorists are transported to facilities outside the United States to be interrogated either by U.S. agents or agents of another country, who are not held to standards of due process, *habeas corpus,* or prohibitions against torture. This practice began in the administration of President Bill Clinton but accelerated dramatically after the attacks of 9/11.[47] Another source indicates "the CIA gained expansive authority to engage in 'extraordinary rendition,' defined here as the transfer—without legal process—of a detainee to the custody of a foreign government for purposes of detention and interrogation." Approximately 54 countries accepted prisoners from the United States under this mechanism.[48]

Excessive police powers are also found in the administrative warrants issued by the Federal Bureau of Investigation that do not require a court order. For the three-year period 2003–2005, the bureau issued 143,074 national-security letters.[49] These letters compel recipients such as financial organizations, telecommunications companies, and institutions of higher education to provide information on clients, customers, or professors, and to do so in secrecy. Criminal penalties attach to bank or university employees if they reveal the existence of the investigation to the person about whom they are providing information. In a positive development, these letters may be subject to some judicial oversight by the USA Freedom Act of 2015. Only time will tell how the act is interpreted and if it can be enforced.

Police powers have increased at the local level as well. Militarization of the police is evident in the spectacular rise in the number of paramilitary units, better known as "special weapons and tactics," or SWAT, teams, and the transfer of unprecedented amounts of military equipment to them. No one knows precisely how many SWAT teams exist or exactly what they do. The U.S. government does not publish statistics, and only one state, Maryland, requires detailed reports on SWAT operations. There were 1,689 SWAT raids in Maryland in 2014, of which 453 took place in Prince George's County, in predominately African-American communities.[50] One study found that African Americans were far more likely to be "impacted" by SWAT deployments than whites. In Allentown, Pennsylvania, for example, "Blacks were nearly 24 times more likely to be impacted by a SWAT raid than whites were." That number was 37 for Huntington, West Virginia, and in Ogden, Utah, it was 40 times.[51]

The Department of Homeland Security provides grants to local governments and police units to enable them to transport and maintain military-grade equipment, which comes to them at deeply discounted costs from Washington. Indeed, under the auspices of Secure Democracy, there has been a sea change in the level of support flowing from the federal government to local police forces across the nation. In every respect, the Department of Homeland Security has assisted and fortified state and local police units, disbursing $35 billion in grants to them between 2002 and 2011.[52]

Our condition of Secure Democracy has more subtle manifestations as well. Most people, for example, have been acculturated to obey security officers, first at airports, then in the workplace, movie theaters, and other commercial establishments, and subsequently at many social functions such as college reunions, concerts, and meetings of private associations. Although many citizens do not exercise the right to vote, most if not all are able to do so. In the main, professors can say what they like in the classroom and in the media, but few speak up about the swollen intelligence agency budgets or the emergence of Secure Democracy. Most professors of international relations are eager to place their students in security and intelligence jobs. The few who speak truth to power find themselves under pressure to conform to academic norms by colleagues and university administrators. Indeed, Secure Democracy retains much of the form and appearance of its more liberal cousin, the open society, while violating its core principles of privacy and individualism.

And so it was at the turn of the 21st century that many of the liberal democratic states found inflection points—such as 9/11 in the United States, the 7/7 bombings of the London subway (2005), and other terrorist events in Europe and East Asia. This enabled the construction of a bureaucratic, legislative, operational, and ideological infrastructure that undermines and subverts liberal democracy. The most blatant manifestation was the creation of a Security Industrial Complex in America.

CHAPTER II

DIMENSIONS OF THE SECURITY INDUSTRIAL COMPLEX

On January 17, 1961, President Dwight D. Eisenhower addressed the people of the United States as their leader for the last time. On that occasion, the commander in chief issued a prescient warning. "In the councils of government," he said, "we must guard against the acquisition of unwarranted influence, whether sought or unsought, by the military industrial complex. The potential for the disastrous rise of misplaced power exists and will persist. We must never let the weight of this combination endanger our liberties or democratic processes."[53]

It is likely Eisenhower thought the expanding influence of the military and industry could combine to shift the character of the state to a more authoritarian form. By 1961, the U.S. defense budget exceeded $400 billion (in constant 2016 dollars), which would turn out to be a peacetime baseline for military spending.[54] Although he did not address the subject, he must also have been acutely aware of the activities of the intelligence services, both civilian and military. But because his remarks antedate the digital revolution, he could not have foreseen the advent of a 21st-century constellation of intelligence agencies, working closely with law enforcement and the information-technology industries, capable and willing to track and trace the communications and locations of hundreds of millions of ordinary citizens.

His warning is nevertheless prophetic because a version of what he feared has come to pass, to differing degrees, in the most populous modern liberal states of the world. In the decade following the attacks of 9/11, the United States steadily built up the structural elements of its Security Industrial Complex at an extraordinary rate, both within government and in the private sector. Industry joined forces with the internal security state to acquire "unwarranted influence" and "misplaced power" that corrupts essential elements of government and the open society.

The United States transitioned to Secure Democracy mainly during the presidencies of George W. Bush and Barack Obama. This can be seen in the expansion of funding for internal security and counterterror programs in the 17 U.S. intelligence agencies, the Department of Homeland Security, and elements of local and state police units. It is also apparent in the rise of hundreds of associated digital-technology firms, together with surveillance-software developers and equipment makers. Prominent information-technology companies have for many years participated in government spying.[55] These companies are even more likely to play a central role in government surveillance programs as cybercrime and cyber-warfare are accorded escalating importance in national intelligence and defense circles.

The Security Industrial Complex is similar in structure to the Military Industrial Complex (indeed there are several common elements) as shown in **FIGURE II.1**, which depicts the iron

MILITARY AND SECURITY IRON TRIANGLES

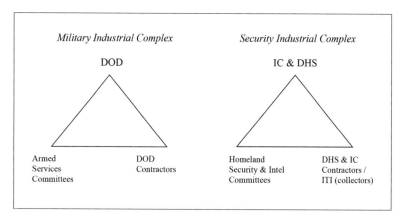

triangles for both *military* and *internal* security. There is, moreover, a significant overlap among the defense and security elements of government, associated contractors, and other special interests aligned with the departments of Defense and Homeland Security. According to Representative Bennie Thompson, who was then chair of the Committee on Homeland Security, "In 2006 alone, DHS spent about 40 percent of its $31 billion budget on contracts for goods and services—making DHS the third largest purchaser in the Federal sector."[56] It appears that Representative Thompson understated the budget allocation of the Department by more than half; the actual outlay in 2006 was $69 billion.[57]

The structural elements of the triangles in **FIGURE II.1** are strikingly similar—a cabinet-level agency, dedicated committees of Congress, overlapping sets of interest groups/contractors, and rotation of elites among the institutions that form the triangles. This configuration does resemble other segments of the government. There could be a similar triangle for the agricultural sector, for instance. But significant differences set the security triangles apart. The triangle on the right includes many agencies of government. In addition to the contractors, the information-technology industries and big-data analytics corporations are deeply imbedded in the Security Industrial Complex—not only as equipment suppliers but also as an integral part of the complex itself. These companies historically have collected, stored, and provided digital records for intelligence agencies, both bulk metadata and the content of phone calls, emails, documents, and many other digital items. They are part of what might be called the algorithm economy. As Representative Thompson pointed out, security commands the lion's share of procurement in government. But more important, security—both military and "homeland"—represents the hard core of the state, its most coercive instrumentality. Fundamentally, the security triangles are based on fear: fear of hostile militaries and fear of terrorism at home and abroad.

The Security Industrial Complex is similar to its military counterpart because the government and civil sectors are economically and ideologically intertwined. The leadership structure of the Security Industrial Complex mirrors the revolving door of the military, where members of Congress, contractors, retired general officers, and executive appointees move between government and industry, depending on the political winds. Just as a vast industry sprang up and was cultivated to build weapons and serve the military buying commands, the corresponding security sector of the commercial economy is booming. The cybersecurity market reached $75 billion in 2015 and is expected to expand to $170 billion by 2020.[58] The video surveillance market was forecast to exceed $71 billion in 2022 and is expected to do so with a compound annual growth rate of 15.56 percent.[59] And information security spending was projected to grow 4.7 percent in 2014, reaching $75.4 billion for 2015.[60] While it is not possible to disaggregate these numbers into the public and private spheres, they do give us an indication of the rise of a commercial security sector that is powerful and unprecedented.

But there is another common factor as well. The budget for the military has "normalized" at between $400 billion and $750 billion for more than 60 years as shown in **FIGURE II.6**. It did not decrease after the end of the Cold War and shot up after 9/11, the period of the Counterterror Wars in Iran and Afghanistan. Similarly, the budget for internal security and counterterrorism increased by a factor of 4 in the 15 years following 9/11, even though the number of terrorist attacks and fatalities in the United States was miniscule (see **FIGURES II.3** and **II.5**). Security budgets may in fact have stabilized at approximately $120 billion a year, far below the military budget, but still a staggering number. Moreover, the impact of vastly enhanced internal security on the structure of society and the nature of the polity is even more profound than that of the military, because internal security measures directly touch the lives of ordinary people. Indeed, one of the most telling features of the Counterterror Wars following 9/11 is that they were prosecuted even in the face of the Great Recession. Most people lost interest in them as the wars dragged on—as the recession took its toll on the average American—even as the wars in Iraq and Afghanistan became the longest, and apart from the World Wars, the costliest in U.S. history.

Internal security can be seen in increasingly elaborate and intrusive screening procedures at airports, the excessive use of national-security letters requests in three years by the Federal Bureau of Investigation, warrantless wiretapping and monitoring of billions of domestic and international communications, and the increasing use of government agents to infiltrate private and political organizations.[61] This kind of intelligence activity is not entirely new in the American experience. Most careful observers of U.S. history are well aware of the illegal programs of the Federal

Bureau of Investigation and other intelligence agencies, especially during the 1960s. The new part is the scale, the scope, and the technological sophistication of internal security operations. As a consequence, there are, for example, major differences between the bureau of J. Edgar Hoover (1924–72) and the bureau of Robert S. Mueller III (2001–13) and his successor(s).

Hoover's bureau was mainly concerned with fighting crime and took great pains to insulate itself from other intelligence agencies; today's bureau is focused more on counterterrorism. It shares intelligence extensively with other federal, state, and local units, with foreign intelligence agencies, and with police organizations. The old bureau physically tapped into phone lines and made hard copies of records or conducted "black bag jobs" to copy or steal private papers and correspondence. The new bureau conducts extensive electronic surveillance and receives digital copies of emails, phone conversations, text messages, and other communications from the National Security Agency, other intelligence agencies, and companies in the digital sector of the economy.

The old bureau conducted clandestine activities, which were considered *prima facie* to be illegal and unconstitutional, and was subsequently brought to heel by the Church Committee in Congress. Today's bureau is a component of a much larger and more powerful intelligence sector, which is unlikely to be investigated much less dismantled by any committee of Congress. As we shall see, Congress can exert only token guidance over the minions who form the Security Industrial Complex, including the torture programs of the Central Intelligence Agency and subsequent reporting about them. Perhaps most important, the iron triangle depicted in **FIGURE II.1** now incorporates the Federal Bureau of Investigation as one among many interconnected intelligence agencies and operations that pose a threat to liberty in the 21st century.

Washington Antics and the Snowden Effect

Academics and journalists long suspected and partially documented the existence of large-scale and illegal digital surveillance by the intelligence agencies, even prior to the revelations of Edward Snowden.[62] But he confirmed their suspicions by releasing tens of thousands of secret papers chronicling the illegitimate activities and programs of significant portions of the Security Industrial Complex. In fact, the materials detail the existence and character of numerous economy-wide and global surveillance programs. Many are operated by the National Security Agency, in cooperation with telecommunications and Internet companies, European governments, and the "Five Eyes" surveillance alliance. Five Eyes is an agreement to share signals intelligence (which can include bulk metadata) among five English-speaking countries—Australia, Canada, New Zealand, the United Kingdom, and the United States—dating back to the Second World War in one form or another.

The Snowden affair is chilling—not only the programs that were revealed but also the way in which knowledge of them has been received. In a modern liberal democracy, one would expect major corrective action because these surveillance programs—and the actions taken as a result—present fundamental challenges to the rights and liberties that define liberal democracy. Government officials should make major changes to terminate (or at least create a legal foundation for) these programs or else expect to be drummed out of office.

But President Obama did not see it that way. He made a passionate plea in his weekly address to the nation, urging Congress and the American people to support passage of the USA Freedom Act. As briefly noted in Chapter I and analyzed here and in Chapter VIII, the USA Freedom Act modified some elements of the USA Patriot Act, in part transferring the storage of bulk metadata from the National Security Agency to the telecommunications companies that collect it in the first place. Although the president painted the issue with broad-brush strokes, his major concern appears to have been to continue the authority of the intelligence agencies to acquire business records, conduct roving wiretaps on suspected terrorists, and to tap the phones of alleged "lone wolves."[63] The USA Freedom Act, which is technically an amendment to the Foreign Intelligence Surveillance Act of 1978, was the answer.

But the president did not address the most critical issue: The Federal Bureau of Investigation and the National Security Agency violated the law when they collected information under the authorities he was trying to preserve. Acting on a request from the bureau, Judge Roger Vinson of the U.S. Foreign Intelligence Surveillance Court issued a four-page order labeled "TOP SECRET//SI//NOFORN," which has since been declassified. It directed Verizon to provide the intelligence agencies with "all call detail records or 'telephony metadata' created by Verizon for communications (i) between the United States and abroad; or (ii) wholly within the United States, including local telephone calls."[64]

But the controlling section of the Foreign Intelligence Surveillance Act (50 USCA Section 1861) does not permit collection of such information. Under this section, the FBI director may apply for an order requiring the production of "any tangible things (including books, records, papers, documents, and other items) for an investigation to obtain foreign intelligence information not concerning a United States person." In the alternative, the application must include a showing that the information is relevant to an investigation to protect against international terrorism or clandestine intelligence.[65] The fact is that the Foreign Intelligence Surveillance Court (FISC) had become a rubber stamp. According to the solicitor general of the United States:

> As of October 1, 2013, fourteen different judges of the FISC, on thirty-four separate occasions, have approved Section 1861 orders directing telecommunications service providers to produce records in connection with the Telephony Records Program.[66]

The United States Second Circuit held that the NSA's Telephony Records Program was illegal in 2015,[67] but the inescapable conclusion is that the intelligence agencies have for many years violated the law with the direct complicity of the Foreign Intelligence Surveillance Court—a complicity that was only possible because the court operates in secrecy.

The USA Freedom Act appears to remedy a few of the most blatant infirmities of the Foreign Intelligence Surveillance Act as amended. But it is clearly no panacea. Under the new statute, the court continues to operate as a secret, *ex parte* proceeding and is subject to all kinds of caveats and abuses. Secret courts normally have no place in liberal democracy. Justice is supposed to be even-handed or "blind" but not hidden from public view. The USA Freedom Act provides for an *amicus curia*, or friend of the court, to assist in resolving issues fairly, but only at the discretion of the court. Another section of the act states that major decisions of the court or summaries of them must be published. But it also gives the Director of National Intelligence the power to redact information or prohibit publication, in which case the proceedings again go dark. This was a major misstep that further erodes the legitimacy of the court.

Not only is the Foreign Intelligence Surveillance Court largely secret, but it is also a court that operates independently of most of the rest of the federal judiciary. It is difficult to gain standing, but in rare instances when a case is appealed, it goes to a special Foreign Intelligence Surveillance Court of Review, so that cases are kept out of the Article 3 courts established by the Constitution. This means that only one group of judges construes the law, and the malfeasance of those judges is now well documented. Moreover, an appeal of a Foreign Intelligence Surveillance Court opinion can only reach the U.S. Supreme Court if it is "certified" by the Foreign Intelligence Surveillance Court of Review—an extremely unlikely event.

But perhaps most important, the FISA court hears from only one party to the case and that party is the U.S. government, typically representatives from one of the intelligence agencies or the Department of Justice. Opposing attorneys or independent experts are rarely, if ever, present at the proceeding. This constitutes a profound structural fault: it means there is no mechanism to challenge the assertions of the government, other than the judges of the court. And because the FISA court judges are drawn from the federal judiciary, and rotate for weekly sittings from their federal district and appeals courts and then return to them, they cannot be expected to be expert in surveillance jurisprudence. Even knowledgeable judges with the best of intensions would find it hard to make good decisions under these limiting circumstances. This conclusion is born out by the fact that the FISA court has functioned as a rubber stamp, declining only 11 of more than 33,900 government requests for surveillance over three decades.[68]

Moreover, because the deliberations of the court take place in secret, and it is a criminal offense to disclose classified information, no public record is made, and so there is no public debate or discussion of most cases in the media or anywhere else for that matter. Accordingly, the actions and decisions of the court cannot be held to constitutional standards. Finally, it would appear that the way in which the FISA judiciary is appointed has resulted in a politically skewed distribution among the judges. Chief Justice John G. Roberts Jr. has taken a partisan approach to Foreign Intelligence Surveillance Court appointments. Of the 16 judges he has appointed, 81 percent are Republicans and 50 percent served in the executive branch. This compares with the more centrist record of his conservative predecessor, Chief Justice Warren E. Burger, who appointed 20 judges—60 percent Republicans and 40 percent who served in the executive.[69]

In his appeal for passage, President Obama presented the USA Freedom Act as a remedy to past excesses of the intelligence agencies and government spying, a kind of balance between liberty and security. But in the end, it is difficult to see how balance can be achieved. Indeed, if the court refuses to follow the statute and impose the new legislative restrictions on the intelligence agencies, as it did in the Verizon case, liberal democracy will have been dealt another significant blow.

In his speech urging passage of the USA Freedom Act, President Obama appeared not to notice the fundamentally undemocratic nature of the Foreign Intelligence Surveillance Court system or the leverage that the USA Freedom Act gives to the intelligence agencies. He did not seem to grasp that wiretaps on "so-called lone wolves— suspected terrorists who may not be directly tied to a terrorist group"—are little more than fishing expeditions. The wiretaps have failed to net a single terrorist, although agents of the Federal Bureau of Investigation shot and killed a "lone wolf" who was under surveillance in Boston during the Senate debate of the USA Freedom Act.[70]

But perhaps as important, the president contended that these "tools are not controversial."[71] Nothing could not be further from the truth. The tools are, in fact, so controversial that attempts to make even modest changes caused Republic members of Congress to make common cause with more liberal members, briefly delaying passage of the USA Freedom Act.

This filibustering tactic forced the Senate into a rare Sunday session at the end of a recess, but the USA Freedom Act passed easily in the days that followed. Even though the act changes the way in which business records are collected and stored, the intelligence

agencies could easily find workarounds.[72] In the weeks following the passage of the act, the Federal Bureau of Investigation
changed its policy from surveilling "lone wolf" suspects to arresting them. Chairman Richard Burr of the Senate Select Committee
on Intelligence provided the rationalization. He commented that
arrests of "lone wolves" by the FBI are "an indication that the
increased number of threads of threats . . . is at the highest level
that most of us have seen since 9/11."[73] One can only guess at the
meaning of the phrase "threads of threats" or who "most of us"
might be. All in all, the USA Freedom Act made very little difference in terms of the overall surveillance architecture and activities
of the Security Industrial Complex.

There is little doubt that the trove of secret NSA documents
released by Edward Snowden influenced the American and
European publics and their legislatures. He revealed the existence of
more than 20 secret surveillance programs. He made video appearances and received awards at venues including the Cato Institute,
Swedish Television News, Amnesty International in France, the
Festival of Liberty in Brussels, and at Princeton University—among
many others. But on balance, when we examine the structure and
magnitude of the Security Industrial Complex—its insubordination
to rule of law and its mushrooming presence in terms of authority,
budgets, and sheer numbers of agents—it is prudent to conclude
that the Snowden affair is largely noise in the signal. With respect
to the USA Freedom Act, the debate came down to three items: the
collection of metadata, roving wiretaps, and electronic tracking of
suspected "lone wolf" terrorists. All of these techniques were preserved in one form or another.

We should nevertheless pay attention to what Snowden did
reveal, because surveillance programs are emblematic of the rise of
Secure Democracy. Most of the Snowden disclosures focus on the
National Security Agency, which is just one cog in the machinery of

the Security Industrial Complex. Many of the NSA's data retrieval, storage, infiltration, and analysis systems interface with one another, and data can often be shared among them. In addition, the NSA selectively shares data with its foreign partners and other elements of the U.S. Security Industrial Complex. It has a physical and highly secure presence across the United States and in many countries of the world. The group of surveillance programs discussed here is by no means exhaustive. In June 2013, Snowden provided a trove of tens of thousands of secret NSA documents to journalists Glenn Greenwald, Laura Poitras, and Ewen MacAskill, and thereafter reportedly deleted his own access; leaving it to the reporters and their editors to sift and sort, and tell the NSA story as they saw it.

Although it took months for journalists to make sense of them, and there were some mistaken reports, these documents revealed much about the inner workings of the NSA, most famously "PRISM" (aka, SIGAD US-984XN). It is a massive Internet data-mining system deployed in 2007 by the National Security Agency in collaboration with its U.K. counterpart, the Government Communications Headquarters, or GCHQ. The National Security Agency elicited and/or compelled the cooperation of nine major information-technology companies including Apple, Facebook, Google, Microsoft, and Verizon, initially paying some for their participation.[74]

PRISM is National Security Agency's most important source of raw intelligence, which is interpreted by analysts and incorporated in their secret reports. Although NSA officials and politicians contend that PRISM is narrow and directed only against foreign "targets," it can easily be used to spy on Americans. PRISM indiscriminately sweeps up metadata as well as the contents of emails, chats, videos, voice messages, photos, social media, and other information. Metadata is defined as data that describes other data such as call logs, library catalogs, the numbers of clicks on YouTube videos, Internet browsing records, and the locations of phones.

"Boundless Informant" is a metadata tool that analyzes and visually portrays information collected globally by the National Security Agency and its various partners.[75] "The focus of the internal NSA tool is on counting and categorizing the records of communications, known as metadata, rather than the content of an email or instant message." Over a thirty-day period, the program collected nearly three billion pieces of information.[76] Boundless Informant configures the data to create global "heat maps." These portray how many records are obtained from any particular NSA unit. The information can be displayed visually, indicating the volume and kinds of information that are collected "against" each country and region of the world. The National Security Agency has data collection and storage units located throughout the world. Boundless Informant helps to keep track data collected by these far-flung operations.

Another NSA program, "Mainway," consists of metadata from 100s of billions of phone calls that pass through the four largest U.S. telecommunication companies—AT&T, SBC, BellSouth, and Verizon. In 2011, the program collected some 700 million phone records each day. Its function is to chain-link email addresses and phone numbers for metadata compilation, and to record detailed telephony information. Mainway contains of trillions of records, which are used in traffic and social network analyses. It has been deployed illegally "to create sophisticated graphs of some Americans' social connections that can identify their associates, their locations at certain times, their traveling companions and other personal information."[77]

Its counterpart for the Internet is codenamed "Marina." Marina collects and stores massive amounts of metadata harvested from the Internet, typically through an array of NSA programs. The data is amassed and is stored for up to a year, regardless of whether the individual is of interest to the NSA or the U.S. government. "The material [is] used to build 'pattern-of-life' profiles of individuals," which are essentially detailed pictures of a person's habits and life activities.[78]

"Tempora" is the codename for a data-interception program operated by the U.K. Government Communications Headquarters and shared with the National Security Agency. It attaches directly to the fiber-optic backbone in the Internet to collect vast amounts of data on individuals and their communications. Its database contains both metadata and content of private communications. Content is stored for three days and metadata for thirty.[79] Approximately 300 GCHQ analysts and 250 NSA analysts work on the program. Tempura sweeps up data indiscriminately so that the "GCHQ and the NSA are consequently able to access and process vast quantities of communications between entirely innocent people, as well as targeted suspects."[80]

The "XKeyscore" program also came to light. It is a massive, user-friendly repository, a complex data storage and retrieval system that permits NSA analysts to search, query, and task various existing databases derived from the Internet and a variety of other sources. That is, XKeyscore gives NSA analysts and officers access to previously collected metadata as well as the content of Internet and telephony communications.[81] From an interview with Edward Snowden, XKeyscore appears to operate as a near real-time surveillance tool of extraordinary range and power. Snowden characterized it as a broad-based, extremely flexible surveillance platform. In his words:

> You could read anyone's email in the world. Anybody you've got email address for, any website you can watch traffic to and from it, any computer that an individual sits at you can watch it, any laptop that you're tracking you can follow it as it moves from place to place throughout the world. It's a one stop shop for access to the NSA's information. And what's more you can tag individuals using "XKeyscore."[82]

Another secret NSA surveillance activity, the "Bullrun Decryption Program," is designed to collect and decode encrypted information, including data from virtual private networks. It inserts "vulnerabilities" into commercial encryption systems, information-technology systems, networks, and endpoint communication devices such as cell phones and tablets. These vulnerabilities may consist of code or other sets of instructions that are bypass encryption and expropriate or surreptitiously copy the data. Its counterpart program in the United Kingdom is codenamed "Edgehill." Both programs are "aimed at defeating online privacy by decrypting email, online banking and medical records." The Bullrun program is one of the most expensive in the NSA arsenal, costing over $800 million in 2011 through 2013.[83]

The U.K. Government Communications Headquarters and the NSA jointly operate "MUSCULAR," a program designed to break into Yahoo, Google, and similar encrypted company links that connect data centers around the world. "A top-secret memo dated January 9, 2013 says that the NSA gathered 181,280,466 new records in the previous 30 days. Those records include both metadata and the actual content of communications: text, audio, and video."[84]

The National Security Agency also runs "FASCIA," another large-scale database. It consists of trillions of device-location records that are analyzed by the "CO-TRAVELER" tools. These attempt to uncover new suspects by mapping their physical movements in relation to known suspects. Essentially, CO-TRAVELER is designed to mine the FASCIA database "to look for unknown associates of known intelligence targets by tracking people whose movements intersect."[85] Inevitably, CO-TRAVELER and FACIA scoop up location data on almost everyone who carries a mobile phone the world over.[86]

The U.K. Government Communications Headquarters used NSA tactics in "Operation Socialist" to hack into a Belgian telecommunications company, Belgacom, which is responsible for the smart phones used by the European Commission, the European Council, and the European Parliament. By using malware to collect information from certain high-level employees, the GCHQ attempted to gain access to the smart-phone user information located on the Belgacom servers. But Belgium authorities discovered the attack before any serious leaks occurred. It is possible, although not definite, that the attack was initiated using the NSA program codnamed "Quantum."

Quantum has essentially "weaponized" the Internet with its capacity to embed software into remote computers, giving the perpetrator the ability to reprogram or even destroy the target computer. In one application, it uses old-fashioned radio waves to penetrate computers. In somewhat more technical language, Quantum "allows the NSA to hijack both IRC and HTTP-based criminal botnets, and also includes routines which use packet-injection to create phantom servers."[87] The NSA works closely with the U.S. Cyber Command and claims that the Quantum program is used as "'active defense' against foreign cyberattacks," often against Chinese or Russian hackers, not for industrial espionage, and never in the United States.[88]

"Operation Mullenize" brought the National Security Agency together with the GCHQ in an attempt to hack into Tor, an online anonymizing service. In this operation, the GCHQ stained a traceable code into individual computers running Tor via the Firefox web browser to re-create a browsing system. They were able to inject over 200 stains within a two-month period in 2012.[89]

Britain's formerly secret Joint Threat Research Intelligence Group (JTRIG) also came to light. It employs "'dirty tricks' for use against nations, hackers, terror groups, suspected criminals, and arms dealers. The Group's activities include releasing computer viruses, spying on journalists and diplomats, jamming phones and computers, and using sex to lure targets into 'honey traps.'"[90]

The JTRIG most closely resembles the Cointelpro operation of the late 1950s though the early 1970s conducted in the United States by the Federal Bureau of Investigation. The programs were initiated under the authority of then director, J. Edgar Hoover. They were revealed by the "Church Committee," formally known as the U.S. Senate Select Committee to Study Governmental Operations with Respect to Intelligence Activities, in the middle 1970s. It will be interesting to see if the U.K. Parliament has the power and political will to confront and curtail the illegal activities of the Joint Threat Research Intelligence Group.

The "Dishfire" database is operated by the National Security Agency. With the help of an analytical tool called "PREFER," Dishfire captures and catalogues some 200 millions text messages every day by tracing cell phones that are used for international communications. In theory, texts from American citizens are deleted from the system, but international phones are fair game. Dishfire information is shared with U.K. intelligence. "Squeaky Dolphin" is a British surveillance system that collects and analyzes data from social media in real time. Finally, the Optic Nerve program is a joint U.K.-U.S. mass surveillance operation that gathers Yahoo webcam videos, accessing approximately 1.8 million Yahoo user accounts in a six-month period.[91]

Although this account is certainly incomplete, it is still a dazzling array of secret surveillance programs.

TABLE II.1 indicates which programs collect metadata about communications and which programs collect the content of communications, including text, voice, and video. Almost all of these surveillance programs rely on gaining access to Internet data, which is often held in the servers, transmission corridors, and data repositories of private-sector corporations. The number and scope of the programs also indicates that elected officials are either misinformed or lying when they assert that the U.S. or U.K. governments do not surveil the content of emails and other

TABLE II.1:

SELECTED SURVEILLANCE PROGRAMS BY TYPE OF DATA COLLECTED

Metadata	Content Data	Metadata & Content Data	Neither—"Dirty Tricks"
PRISM	Bullrun	XKeyscore	JTRIG
Boundless Informant	Quantum	MUSCULAR	Operation Socialist
Mainway	Dishfire	Squeaky Dolphin	
FASCIA	CO-TRAVELER	Optic Nerve	
Marina	Operation Mullenize	MYSTIC	
		Tempora	

private communications. Indeed, as President Obama prepared to exit his office, he took steps to expand the number of intelligence officers and agencies with direct access to the content of phone calls and emails scooped up by the National Security Agency.[92]

TABLE II.2 indicates whether or not companies voluntarily cooperated with the intelligence agencies or if their information was "hacked" (stolen) by the agencies. It is clear from the table that many corporations enter into secret agreements with the National Security Agency to share data from unwitting organizations and individuals whose privacy is compromised. Some companies chose to cooperate with the National Security Agency in secret and had done so for many years. Some were even paid. But it is also clear that many other companies were the unwitting victims of government scrutiny and could not protect their customers from intrusive government surveillance.

There have been two consistent reactions to the Snowden affair. One group asserts that Snowden, like Private Bradley Manning (who provided classified documents to WikiLeaks), has irrevocably damaged the "national security interests" of the United States and its surveillance partners, especially the United Kingdom. Even

TABLE II.2:

SELECTED SURVEILLANCE PROGRAMS
CORPORATE COOPERATION VS. INVOLUNTARY PARTICIPATION

Cooperation with Corporate Consent	Involuntary/"Hacked" Corporate Participation
PRISM	Bullrun
Boundless Informant	MUSCULAR
Mainway	Dishfire
Tempora	Squeaky Dolphin
FASCIA	Optic Nerve
Corporate Partner Access	Quantum
XKeyscore	Operation Socialist
	Operation Mullenize
	Mystic
	Marina

though they have not specified what that damage is, they insist he is a criminal who must be brought to justice. And this will very likely happen if Snowden returns to the United States or travels to a country with which there is an extradition treaty. In this view, blame has been misdirected, not against Snowden as it should be, but against the government and its intelligence agencies. In this view, "transparency" is favored over privacy.

The second view sees Snowden as a kind of culture hero. His intention, they believe, was to unmask spying activity that is inimical to liberal democracy. He apparently did so as a matter of conscience and at great peril. By this assessment, Snowden stands in bold contrast to the minions who populate the Security Industrial Complex, who have built a vast internal security apparatus within the state, based on fear-mongering and personal ambition, indifferent to democratic principles and the privacy rights to which a free people are entitled. They believe the programs constitute a significant incursion on liberal democracy and the rule of law. Snowden is seen in these circles as a defender of democracy and a whistleblower of great integrity. The American Civil Liberties Union engaged in a major effort to convince President Obama to pardon him.

There can be no doubt that Snowden brought many unsavory and illegal government surveillance programs and tactics to the attention of the news media and public at great personal sacrifice. As of this writing he is a fugitive, living in Russia because the U.S. government revoked his passport. After leaving office, Attorney General Eric Holder embraced both sides of the debate. He said that Snowden's actions were "inappropriate and illegal" and had "harmed American interests," but at the same time he grudgingly conceded that Snowden "actually performed a public service by raising the debate."[93]

But here it must be added that the debate within the government was largely one-sided. It did not challenge surveillance policy in any significant way—the murky USA Freedom Act to the contrary notwithstanding—because it did change the structure or powers of the Security Industrial Complex in America. Even though Snowden's disclosures confirmed an aspect of the complex, the emergence of a surveillance security state-within-the-state, it was largely confined to two agencies—the National Security Agency in the United States and the Government Communication Headquarters is the United Kingdom. Patient and interested observers had long suspected the existence of such operations at home and abroad.

Many of the particulars are new. The surveillance of three French prime ministers and other elites was taken in relative stride by French authorities after President Obama apologized. The tapping of German Chancellor Angela Merkel's cell phone was another matter. It was greeted by outrage from the Office of the Chancellor and the German media. It caused legal action against the unnamed perpetrators and a temporarily souring of U.S.-German relations.[94] As we shall see, the German public is somewhat more resistant to foreign and government surveillance than the American, French, and British publics. What Snowden did was to cause angst among many of the agents, constructors, contractors, and various elite beneficiaries of the surveillance security state, and indignation among world leaders and a segment of the American and other publics.

He also catalyzed pushback from some Internet service providers like Apple, Facebook, Google, and Microsoft, who feared that their collaboration with and vulnerability to government surveillance would sully their corporate images, conferring competitive advantage to their more upright European competitors. But there is much more here than meets the eye. Snowden, who sacrificed his career and freedom, is only a minor player on this stage. Unless Americans and the citizens of other modern liberal nations are willing to defend privacy, democracy, and freedom at home and abroad, most of what he revealed will soon be forgotten, mere shards of the broken crystal of liberty in history.

Contours of the Secure State

The Security Industrial Complex, this murky surveillance state-within-the state, is far more opaque than other functions of government because it is shrouded in official secrecy. While not a perfect overlay, we can get some insights into the magnitude of its operations by examining the budgets of the Department of Homeland Security together with those of the intelligence agencies. **FIGURE II.2** presents a formulaic diagram of the intelligence community as a constellation of agencies centered on the Office of the Director of National Intelligence. This diagram suggests a logical and interrelated ordering of agencies, but the reality is somewhat more chaotic. In fact, as the media and policy analysts

FIGURE II.2:

THE U.S. INTELLIGENCE COMMUNITY*

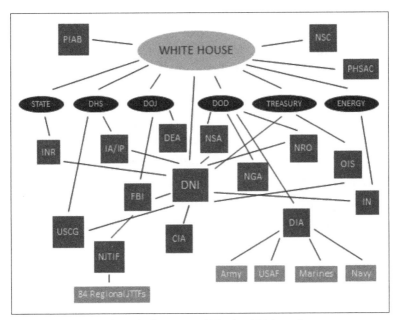

* Source: Update of Ben Temchine and Erika Trautman, PBS Frontline, 2003. Accessed at
http://www.pbs.org/wgbh/pages/frontline/shows/sleeper/homeland/chartintelligence.html on May 6, 2014.

repeatedly point out, the various components of the intelligence community lack cohesion, have overlapping responsibilities, conduct turf battles, and very often fail to communicate effectively with one another. These facts routinely surface in the wake of intelligence failures. But there is a more important story to be told.

In June of 2010, *The Washington Post* concluded a two-year, in-depth investigation of the U.S. intelligence community. It published a series of exhaustive reports that won the Pulitzer Prize. The news organization found that the U.S. government's response to the attacks of 9/11 was far-reaching; indeed, it was "so large, so unwieldy, and so secretive that no one knows how much money it costs, how many people it employs, how many programs exist within it, or exactly how many agencies do the same work." Despite pervasive secrecy in the intelligence world, the *Post* reporters surmised: "Some 1,271 government organizations and 1,931 private companies work on programs related to counterterrorism, homeland security, and intelligence in about 10,000 locations across the United States." Moreover, they found: "An estimated 854,000 people . . . hold top-secret security clearances." This figure is quite conservative as official documents put that number at more than 1.5 million in 2012.[95] Intelligence analysts, the paper said, write over 50,000 reports each year, most of which are ignored. The *Post* reporters concluded that so many new secret facilities have been built since 9/11 that they now cover approximately 17 million square feet, or about the same space as three Pentagons.[96] But even these journalistic investigations fail to capture the magnitude of the Security Industrial Complex in America.

FIGURE II.3 shows the fiscal outlays of the U.S. Department of Homeland Security from FY1989–2014 projected through FY2019. (The use of the word "homeland" is interesting in itself, as it evokes the German reverence for their "homeland" in the run-up to World War II.) It is clear from the graph that spending was relatively stable, averaging roughly $10 billion annually until 2001, the year of the 9/11 terrorist attacks. The Department of Homeland security was formed in November of 2002 by haphazardly clumping together all or part of 22 existing federal agencies and offices into a new department. After its establishment, the budget for the Department of Homeland Security accelerated by a factor of seven to reach $69 billion in 2006 and is projected to stabilize again, somewhere between $40 billion and $50 billion annually.

As the organization chart in Figure II.2 indicates, the intelligence community is made up of many agencies of government, including the Federal Bureau of Investigation, the National Security Agency, the Defense Intelligence Agency, and others that

FIGURE II.3:

OUTLAYS OF THE DEPARTMENT OF HOMELAND SECURITY 1898-2019*

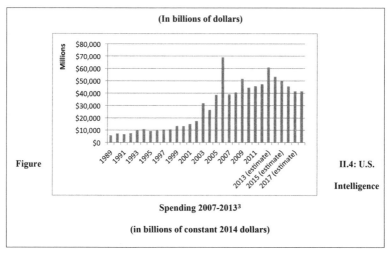

(In billions of dollars)

Figure   II.4: U.S.

Intelligence

Spending 2007-2013[3]

(in billions of constant 2014 dollars)

---

* Executive Office of the President of the United States, Fiscal Year 2914 Historical Tables, Budget of the U.S. Government, Office of Management and Budget, Table 4.1—Outlays by Agency: 1964-2`18, pp. 86-87. Accessed at http://www.whitehouse.gov/sites/default/files/omb/budget/fy2014/assets/hist.pdf, on June 4, 2014.

may be somewhat less familiar to the uninitiated. The Department of Homeland Security is listed as one of six cabinet-level agencies with intelligence operations. It is deeply involved in internal security and funds many programs at the state and local levels.

But as the organization chart shows, homeland security is just one component of the sprawling intelligence and security apparatus that composes the Security Industrial Complex in America. It claims only about one-third of the federal budget allocated to counterterrorism, intelligence operations, and other secret government activities. And this excludes hundreds of billions of dollars allocated to fund military counterterrorism activities in Iraq and Afghanistan. Intelligence budgets speak eloquently and without hyperbole. As can be seen in Figure II.4, the budget of the "National Intelligence Program" (the middle line) is comparable to that of the Department of Homeland Security.

FIGURE II.4 presents spending levels for both the "civilian," or "national" (NIP), and "military" (MIP) intelligence programs and agencies. Civilian intelligence agencies include household names like the Central Intelligence Agency and the Federal Bureau of Investigation, which technically fall under the jurisdiction of the Office of National Intelligence. However, the distinction between civilian and military intelligence programs and activities is cloudy at best. The Central Intelligence Agency, for example, is considered to be a civilian organization, but it supports military activities, including those associated with SEAL Team 6[97] and conducts deadly drone operations abroad. Many of these come under the authority of its National Clandestine Service, which is "the national authority for the coordination, de-confliction, and evaluation of clandestine operations across the Intelligence Community of the United States."[98] Moreover, in a 2015 reorganization, the agency "stood up" a new Directorate of Digital Innovation, the equivalent of the military's Cyber Command, and sought to emulate "the Defense Department's structure of having a single military commander in charge of all operations in a particular region—the way a four-star commander runs [the] United States Central Command."[99] Conversely, the National Security Agency is classified as a military unit, but as we have seen, it was deeply enmeshed in the PRISM program, the President's Surveillance Program, and many other operations that are unrelated or only tangentially linked to military activity. As can be seen in Figure II.4, U.S. intelligence spending averaged approximately $80 billion per year over the seven-year period 2007 to 2013.

While it is possible to disaggregate and assess the magnitude of military and national intelligence in the abstract, in practice, very few budgetary data are released to the public. There is no credible reason for this opacity. Every intelligence chief will claim that divulging precise agency and program budgets would harm the national security (itself an abstract term), indicating the size

U.S. INTELLIGENCE SPENDING 2007-2013*

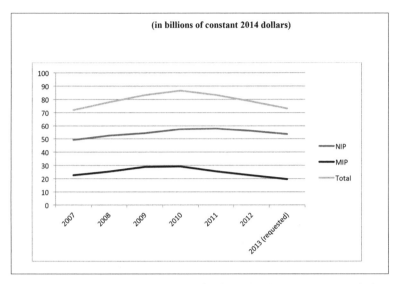

(in billions of constant 2014 dollars)

Source: Congressional Research Service, derived from Office of National Intelligence and Department of Defense press releases.
• Marshall C. Erwin and Amy Belasco, "Intelligence Spending and Appropriations: Issues for Congress," Congressional Research Service, September 5, 2013, p. 2. Accessed at http://fpc.state.gov/documents/organization/214426.pdf on February 18, 2015.

and scope of operations to the nation's adversaries, and possibly even reveal "sources and methods." But this is certainly a spurious argument because this information—even though it is classified— is already available to anyone with an Internet connection. When intelligence spending is actually disclosed, either through leaks or by official press releases, little or no harm has come of it.

The damage occurs when intelligence officials and agents carry out programs that are not in the national interest, foment international discord, threaten the integrity of the legal system, and/or degrade the rights of the people. Secret budgets mean that the agencies and those who run them can more easily engage in waste, fraud, and abuse of the public trust because the system of checks and balances is largely disabled. This lack of transparency stifles debate since the public is not given access to the information. Critics of the intelligence establishment must omit classified data and use publicly available estimates, as revealing the data can be a criminal offense.

As is well known from the dawn of history, money is power and the more unaccountable and absolute power is, the more corrupt those who wield it have become. Detailed classified budgets have leaked and are available online, and these more accurate data appear to be largely consistent with the data presented in this chapter.[100] Nevertheless, a more accurate picture of the cost and extent of the Security Intelligence Complex emerges when civilian and military intelligence budgets are combined—as they are by the Congressional Research Service in **FIGURE II.5**.

The trend lines in the figure are instructive. In 1980, intelligence budgets reached approximately $20 billion. After 1980, however, they rose steadily through 1989, apparently in lockstep with the Reagan military spend-up, peaking at about $47 billion, an increase of about 135 percent. Following the end of the Cold War, intelligence budgets began to decline. In the five years leading up to 2001, U.S. intelligence spending was stable at roughly $38 billion per year. But after 9/11, spending rose steadily, more than doubling to roughly $86 billion in 2010. If we combine the average annual budgets of the intelligence agencies (~$75 billion–$80 billion) and the Department of Homeland Security (~$45 billion) over the past seven years, the security outlay is something on the order of $120 billion a year.

These data also give some perspective as to why it was possible for Congress to exercise its oversight authority in the Church Committee investigation in the mid-1970s and likely impossible to do so in the 2010s. In truth, the intelligence agencies were more respectful of the Congress when they were smaller and less institutionalized. Forty years later, in a far more limited Congressional

ESTIMATED AND ACTUAL TOTAL INTELLIGENCE SPENDING 1980-2012*

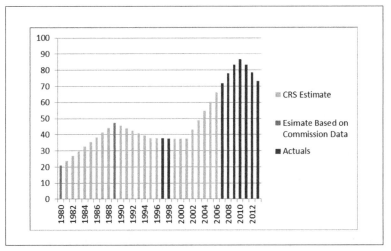

Source: Congressional Research Service
• Op. Cit., Erwin and Belasco, p. 5.

review and oversight of the torture programs of the Central Intelligence Agency, the agency was able to set the conditions under which the Senate Select Committee on Intelligence could examine documents, and in the end, to suppress 90 percent of the committee's report. The ability of the Central Intelligence Agency to resist the Congress is a key measure of the power of the surveillance security state in the 21st century.

The ascendance of the Security Industrial Complex in the United States can best be understood in the context of its counterpart, the Military Industrial Complex. Although the two entities are conceptually and sometimes institutionally distinct, they share many attributes. Both are concerned with national security, broadly construed. The intelligence community straddles the civilian government and the military—with elements located in the military service intelligence units (Army, Navy, Air Force, and Marines) as well as the Defense Intelligence Agency and the National Security

Agency. Increasingly the Intelligence Community complements the military in counterterrorist activities conducted in foreign nations.

The Central Intelligence Agency, for example, and the military's Joint Special Operations Command both conduct assassinations in foreign countries through lethal drone programs against the same people and organizations, although they do so under different authorities using different chains of command. One explanation for this duplication is that it provides "plausible deniability" to defuse public and international pressure against armed drone operations, because "the U.S. government cannot legally acknowledge covert actions undertaken by the CIA."[101] Indeed an underlying rationale for the U.S. military occupation of both Iraq[102] and Afghanistan was to defend the internal security of the United States from foreign terrorist organizations, several of which—the intelligence agencies asserted—were associated with al Qaeda and assumed to be planning strikes on the United States. Moreover, the military's global internal security operations—including the Counterterror Wars and Special Forces operations—help to explain the extraordinary and parallel expansion of intelligence and defense budgets in 2001–14.

The Counterterror Wars in Context

The United States has maintained its Military Industrial Complex in a permanent state of wartime readiness for more than 60 years, beginning with the onset of the Korean War, and burgeoning in the context of the Cold War—with every kind of mischief—extending to the Vietnam War; the 1990–91 Gulf War; the Bosnia and Kosovo wars; the wars in Iraq, Afghanistan, Syria, and Somalia; and others. The existence of the U.S. military and the willingness to use it hold manifold implications for the character of U.S. foreign policy and the structure of foreign relations more generally.

The advent of far-flung military bases and power-projection capabilities during the 1950s and '60s helped to forge a bipolar world order in which the United States and the Soviet Union reached a remarkably stable political and military standoff. But this configuration of power politics, and the vacuum left in its wake, required significant and continuous changes to the American polity, principally the building up of the institutions and legal framework of national security, as well as associated research and development in the educational and industrial sectors to conduct weapons research and supply the "buying commands" of the U.S. military.

Venerable institutions of technical and scientific learning—from Stanford and Berkeley on the West Coast to MIT, Princeton, and Carnegie Mellon in the East to Texas A&M and Georgia Tech in the South—became deeply enmeshed in a scientific enterprise fashioned to support military research and development. Because MIT was at the center of military innovation, it became the quintessential Cold War institution, deeply engaged with all elements of the Military Industrial Complex. The U.S. innovation system, a triad of great technical universities, private-sector industrial laboratories, and government research and development facilities—all sponsored and/or funded by the U.S. government—remains the envy of the world, propelling constant invention, advancement, and improvement of technology in both the military and civil sectors.[103] Even though the commercial applications of these dual-use technologies brought digital sophistication and prosperity to the West and many countries in Asia, they first spawned and then institutionalized a vast military industrial enterprise in the U.S. and global economies.

In the 21st century, the U.S. military is characterized less by continuity than by change. Digital technology enhances the capacity and is infused into military platforms from ships to tanks to missiles to satellites to planes and unmanned weapons platforms. An entire class of hypersonic weapons is now under development, as are autonomous weapons systems. Controlling the battle space, as it is now called, depends on several newer dimensions of C⁴ISR, which stands for the integration and fusion of "Command, Control, Computers, and Communications, Intelligence, Surveillance, and Reconnaissance." This reconnaissance-strike capability was first demonstrated on a limited scale in the 1990–91 U.S.-led invasion of Iraq. It has been honed in every subsequent war and military engagement. The result is that the United States military stands in a class of one with no significant competitors and enjoys a budget that approximates the combined costs of the next 10 largest militaries in the world.[104]

FIGURE II.6 depicts a wartime-level military budget for over 60 years. It has swung between a low of $392 billion in 1975 and a high of $760 billion in 2008 in constant 2016 dollars, rising and falling with the onset and end of the Korean War, the Vietnam War, Reagan's Cold War spend-up, and the Counterterror Wars in Iraq, Afghanistan, and the operations of U.S. Special Forces in 134 countries.[105]

Defense spending associated with the Counterterror Wars in Iraq and Afghanistan constitutes the largest increase in military outlays since the Korean War, exceeding $700 billion each year—2007 through 2011. It is worth remarking that such spending coincided with the Great Recession that technically took place beginning in Q3 2008 and ended after Q1 2009, with repercussions lasting well into 2015. The economic damage has been mitigated only by massive Federal Reserve programs to depress interest rates, bail out financial institutions, and issue hundreds of billions of dollars in bonds to restrain inflation and bolster the economy. If the choice had been between guns and butter, it is probable that no amount of fear-mongering could have convinced the U.S. population to continue to fund the Counterterror Wars at these historically unprecedented levels. But the truth is that most people were largely unaffected by these wars or did not comprehend the financial obligations associated with them.

It was in fact a case of smoke and mirrors, involving considerable artifice. Funding for the Counterterror Wars was enacted largely

FIGURE II.6:

U.S. DEFENSE SPENDING 1948-2020*

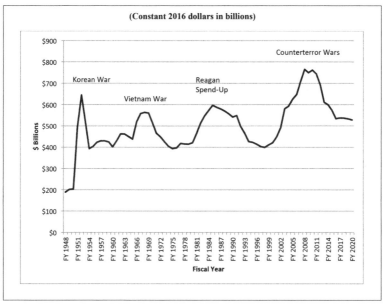

(Constant 2016 dollars in billions)

* Department of Defense, Office of the Under Secretary of Defense (Comptroller) "National Defense Budget Estimates for FY2014," May 2013, Table 6.2, pp. 94-102. Accessed at http://comptroller.defense.gov/Portals/45/Documents/defbudget/fy2016/FY16_Green_Book.pdf on May 27, 2015.

through "supplemental appropriations," which are not presented as part of the defense budget, or prepared under the usual defense appropriations process. These add-ons, known as the Overseas Contingency Operations budget, pass under the radar of most commentators and certainly the vast majority of the American people. Perhaps the transition to an all-volunteer military put the public at arm's length, unlike the Vietnam War years when young men faced the draft, catalyzing considerable social ferment.

Certainly, the Bush and Obama administrations took great pains to orchestrate media coverage of the wars, "embedding" reporters in combat units, creating a psychological bond between soldier and reporter, enhancing the likelihood of sympathetic news. Moreover, embedded reporters were carefully vetted for previous positive war coverage and required to sign documents so they could be summarily dismissed without recourse or appeal.[106] This would appear to be a 21st-century portrayal of a "free press" operating under Secure Democracy. Until February of 2009, the government prevented the media from photographing the coffins of fallen soldiers; and in fact, body armor and new war-fighting technologies combined to decrease the number of fatalities, although the number of casualties rose dramatically, as did media reports over deplorable bureaucratic treatment and medical neglect of dismembered and disabled veterans.[107]

Public opinion polls leading up to the period of the Great Recession of 2008–09 (and the corresponding great defense-budget buildup) show growing indifference to the Counterterror Wars. Indeed, public interest in news from Iraq decreased steadily from a high of about 63 percent in 2003 to a level of only about 19 percent in December of 2010. By the time of the Great Recession, only about 25 percent of the American public closely followed the news from Iraq.[108] Perhaps more important, as military spending related to the Counterterror Wars escalated to unprecedented heights, public support for the Iraq War fell steadily.

Following the commencement of hostilities on March 20, 2003, support for the invasion and occupation among students and the general public soon began to erode. There is no indication that the change in public opinion was linked to the rising cost of the war, as indeed, most people had no idea of what the true costs actually were. Although three-quarters of Americans supported the decision to invade Iraq in 2003, five years later, in 2008, that proportion had fallen to approximately one-quarter. As the war wound down and the troops came home, less than half of those polled in December of 2010 concluded that using military force in Iraq had, after all, been the right decision.[109]

Apparently, people lost interest in the war and withdrew their support, even as military spending increased by 64 percent from

$490 billion in 2002 to $764 billion in 2008. If we return to Figure II.6 (above) for a moment, we can see that the defense budget is projected to fall and then level off in the years 2017–20 to about $530 billion. When we look at the preceding six decades, however, it is clear that a floor of close to $400 billion is characteristic of American military spending and is projected to increase in the future by about $130 billion a year. This floor has less to do with the state of international security than one would think. It does not reflect the end of wars or even the end of the Cold War. It is likely more indicative of the bureaucratic and political power of the Military Industrial Complex, a complex that replicates itself at the $400-plus billion level annually, based not on actual security needs but on highly ritualized perceptions or misperceptions of the threat, as the case may be. The plain fact is that wars and threats have come and gone over the past six decades, but U.S. military spending has averaged $506.5 billion each year in constant 2016 dollars—for a total of $33.9 trillion.

Figure II.6 is critical to this discussion because the United States has established a permanent Security Industrial Complex over the past one and a half decades, similar to and closely linked with the Military Industrial Complex. At the end of the Reagan military spend-up, which paralleled the end of the Cold War, the U.S. military budget began to fall in the pattern established following the Korean War, but this time a remarkable event occurred. Even though the United States invaded Iraq in the first Gulf War on August 2, 1990, there was barely an uptick in the military budget, which continued to fall through the decade of the 1990s. But the "peace dividend" that so many had anticipated failed to materialize. The budget hit the $400 billion floor, passed briefly through it, and then rebounded in 1999 prior to the events of 9/11. Certainly the pattern was well established, but now the lid was blown off by military operations targeting an elusive terrorism abroad to increase security at home, and the budget rose to $764 billion in 2008. It would seem that military and internal security operations are now joined at the hip, that internal security threat perceptions drive military operations abroad. This would certainly help explain the unprecedented explosion in defense appropriations associated with the Counterterror Wars in Iran and Afghanistan after 2002, together with the intelligence spend-up. And it is certainly consistent with the constant rhetorical drumbeat in 2015–17 that the United States and its allies must defeat the militant forces of the Islamic State insurgency or face terrorism from that group and its adherents at home.

In this respect, the terrorist attacks on the Pentagon and Twin Towers forever bound the military to the Security Industrial Complex. Certainly the Counterterror Wars were closely linked to the Bush administration's "global war on terror" and with the general rubric of internal security. While President Obama dropped the "global war" terminology, he retained the policies of the Bush administration. And this is precisely where the distinction between internal security, national security, and international security breaks down. But there was still an important difference: Because the military was prohibited from operating at home, its effect on civil society and constitutional norms was minimized.[110] This is not the case with the buildup of internal security and the associated Security Industrial Complex. Given the magnitude of the threat assigned to al Qaeda by the George W. Bush and Obama administrations, the U.S. government took extraordinary counterterror measures resulting in unprecedented accretion of internal security powers by the executive branch, but importantly, it also increased intelligence and police powers at the state and local levels.[111]

The Buildup of Internal Security Assets

In the years following 9/11, at the federal level, the U.S. government undertook the most extensive reorganization since the New Deal, forming a cabinet-level department, restructuring major elements of the intelligence community (even creating an intelligence czar). It generated new categories of detainees, abrogating the Geneva Conventions, and implemented torture programs, with many attendant legal changes that bear on constitutionally protected rights of citizens and other persons. And it launched the Counterterror Wars in Iraq and Afghanistan, by far the longest and most costly wars since World War II. During and following these counterterror occupations, the United States deployed Special Forces and drones (both surveillance and attack) in many countries of the world, continuing a low-level but constant drive to identify and eradicate terrorist groups, especially their leaders.

At the local level, the cutting edge of police powers expanded in response to mandates from Washington, but also from a deep-seated and typically unnecessary fear of terrorism in many communities, given that there have been few terrorist events in the United States in the past decade and longer.[112] In the area of border security, for example ". . . the federal government and members of Congress have increasingly sought to involve state and local government institutions more extensively and directly in the federal government's immigration enforcement initiatives."[113] The new intelligence and police powers installed at the federal level in the years following 9/11 were also made available to augment policing at the local level.

In New York City, which bore the brunt of the attacks, local police infiltrated many groups and kept dossiers on protestors who sought to organize demonstrations during the Republican National Convention in 2004.[114] In the cause of "homeland" security, and often funded by the department of that name, state and local authorities increased their firepower, their equipment, their intelligence capabilities, and their ability to respond at least to limited local disasters. The New York City Police Department created a new Counterterror Division, with state-of-the-art intelligence facilities including a "Global Intelligence Room," 125 specially selected analysts, language specialists, and police officers. Heavily armed SWAT teams make regular and highly visible appearances at sports events, Wall Street, Times Square, the Empire State Building, the Brooklyn Bridge, and other "high-value targets." New York City police/intelligence officers are also assigned to the New Scotland Yard in London, Interpol in Lyon, as well as counterpart organizations in Hamburg, Toronto, and Tel Aviv.[115] And in November of 2015, following the terrorist attacks on the *Charlie Hebdo* offices and the Islamic State attacks at multiple locations in Paris, New York City authorities announced the creation of a "standing counterterrorism force" featuring 527 officers and "new cars fitted to hold Colt M4 semiautomatic assault rifles."[116]

New York City is not alone in its acquisition of intelligence assets. Many other big-city police departments have pursued a parallel course, including Los Angeles. Together with a large swath of Southern California law enforcement, the Los Angeles Police Department has expanded it surveillance and intelligence capabilities, attempting to merge local law-enforcement expertise with intelligence tools and agency algorithms. As reported in the *LA Weekly*, "The use of military grade surveillance tools is migrating from places like Fallujah to neighborhoods including Watts and even low-crime areas in the San Fernando Valley." For example, "Two dozen police agencies have gathered more than 160 million data points showing the exact whereabouts of L.A. area drivers on given dates."[117] Perhaps more important, the Los Angeles Police Department adopted a counterterror strategy of "convergence," which means that "the time-tested approaches (investigative policing and crime-solving skills) that emphasize prevention must converge with new ones that focus on prediction."[118] As the war in Afghanistan wound down, the Obama administration arranged for an extraordinary transfer of surplus military equipment to local police departments, which began to use it in ordinary law enforcement. Among many other items, the equipment included "tens of thousands of machine guns; nearly 200,000 ammunition magazines; thousands of pieces of camouflage and night-vision equipment; and hundreds of silencers, armored cars, and aircraft."[119]

On the afternoon of August 9, 2014, police officer Darren Wilson shot and killed Michael Brown, an unarmed African-American teenager, in Ferguson, Missouri. Residents of Ferguson protested longstanding police brutality. Heavily armed and armored Caucasian police responded to the crowds with tear gas, rubber bullets, flash grenades, and a display of military-grade equipment acquired from the federal government. Political authorities—including the president of the United States and the governor of Missouri—denounced the violence and initiated investigations into the shooting.[120] But at the same time, they established a no-fly zone covering 37 square miles around Ferguson for 12 days to keep media helicopters from documenting the violence.[121] President Obama hewed a fine line in his comments, suggesting the possibility of differential treatment of blacks and whites, but his main message was to restore law and order. He said:

> While I understand the passions and the anger that arise over the death of Michael Brown, giving in to that anger by looting or carrying guns, and even attacking the police only serves to raise tensions and stir chaos. It undermines rather than advancing justice.[122]

The National Guard was called up to help restore order. As the citizenry awaited word as to whether the police shooter would be indicted, police departments across the United States, including those in Los Angeles, Los Vegas, Albuquerque, Philadelphia, New York, and Boston, among others, made preparations to control protests.[123] There were appeals from diverse quarters to rein in the transfer of military equipment to local law enforcement. President Obama ordered a review of the programs that supply military equipment to local police units, and Congress planned to hold a hearing.[124] The review indicated that many different federal programs supply equipment and weapons to units of local law enforcement. Moreover, it said the programs lacked transparency and coordination and that local police were not given sufficient training in the appropriate use of military-grade equipment in a civilian context. Military equipment continued to flow to local police departments from multiple federal agencies including the departments of Defense, Justice, Homeland Security and Treasury, among others.[110] President Obama promised he would create new standards for the equipment-acquisition programs, but he did not impose restrictions on the program because of its popularity with the U.S. Congress and local police.[111]

Here, we can see that the surveillance security state, or Secure Democracy as I have called it, embodies a certain elasticity that distinguishes it from more authoritarian forms of governance. It may be that political authorities will decide the police are too heavily armed and will reduce the flow of military equipment to them. Perhaps they will not. In Secure Democracy, the internal security state exists side-by-side with voting, elections, political parties, the courts, legislatures, and executive functions—all hallmarks of modern liberal democracy. It is, however, largely differentiated from liberal democracy because excessive security is tolerated and it frequently operates outside the rule of law.

Acquiescence and Consequences

Most informed observers quietly acquiesced to these changes at all levels of government, due to the existence of what was portrayed as an ongoing state of emergency associated with global terror. Certainly, there is another view in opposition to the highly charged ideological polices that emanated from Washington and extended to the hinterlands. It suggests that transnational terrorism is not as great a threat as is officially assumed.[127] In this view, a policy of consummate diplomacy with Islamic countries, combined with a carefully crafted campaign to degrade al Qaeda and related groups, might have been more effective than the "global war on terror," in which Iraq and Afghanistan were considered as major fronts by the Bush administration. But such a policy was not considered. After U.S. troops left Iraq, the chickens came home to roost, with wide disorder and war breaking out in the Middle East, beginning in Syria, and spreading to parts of Iraq, Turkey, and other states in the region. Iraq remained a focal point with widespread social disorder, suicide bombings, and the ascendance of radical Sunni insurgents including the Islamic State of Iraq and Syria, also known as ISIS.

In 2014, President Obama came under attack from the radical right in America and some U.S. allies for being "soft" in his response to the use of chemical weapons in Syria, as well as to the Russian annexation of Crimea. He could certainly have maintained a defense that the United States had no reason to recommence hostilities in the Middle East, considering the toll of blood and treasure already exacted by America's Counterterror Wars, as well as the impossibility of military intervention in Russia's near sphere of influence. Instead, he chose to respond in a graduation speech at West Point that America is tough on terrorism, and indeed has a new strategy. That strategy soon translated into another bombing campaign in Iraq against the Islamic State of Iraq and Syria, which was committing atrocities and advancing on major cities. Perhaps President Obama, who had campaigned on a pledge to end the war in Iraq, felt compelled to act as a riposte to the right-wing fringe in America.

Governor Rick Perry of Texas, who had just pleaded not guilty to two felony charges of "abuse of power," called for increasing air strikes against the Islamic State fighters before the group—as he thought—could commit acts of terror in the United States. "They need to be eliminated," he said, "and they need to be eliminated now." He proposed increasing drone surveillance and police presence along the U.S. southern border. Although he admitted there was "no clear evidence" that terrorists had entered the United States from Mexico, he nevertheless called for more stringent legislation against illegal immigration. He said, "I think there is the obvious, great concern that—because of the condition of the border from the standpoint of it not being secure and us not knowing who is penetrating across— that individuals from ISIS [the Islamic State fighters] or other terrorist states could be" entering the country.[128] One Southern senator, Johnny Isakson of Georgia, said, "There's only one thing, and one thing only, that ISIS understands, and that's force. We've got to kill 'em and exterminate 'em, so they're gone and destroyed."[129]

This refrain was echoed in other forums and by far more centrist politicians. No one seemed to understand that the Islamic State fighters were a direct result of the U.S. invasion and occupation of Iraq. No one seemed to appreciate the concept of "blowback"[130] or recognize the cycle of terror-counterterror-terror, a dynamic playing out in real time. If we were so afraid that the Islamic State group might send agents to the United States on suicide missions, the best thing to do would be to break the cycle and not give them a reason to seek revenge. After all, the United States invaded and occupied Iraq for no discernable reason, destroying its political, economic, and physical infrastructure, and proved incapable of restoring order. After creating the chaotic conditions for the rise of the Islamic State, and failing to install a stable, democratic government as it had promised, the United States put its tail between its legs and brought the troops home. But this is one of the inflection points where security becomes irrational, and this kind of belligerent behavior is an unwelcome complement of a democracy whose fundamental values have been compromised by a powerful and largely unaccountable security state-within-the-state.

CHAPTER III

IRRATIONAL SECURITY

The growth of internal security in modern liberal democracies is typically a response to the perception of a threat. And because it is a perception, it is not necessarily an accurate assessment of that which threatens us. This was true of Communism during the McCarthyism period, and it is true of "terrorism" today. We have no clear idea of the so-called terrorist threat.

Is it from Islamic State soldiers fighting in Iraq and Syria? Might they come to North America or Western Europe? Or will they convert citizens in the United States, the United Kingdom, and France to their cause and program them to commit atrocities? Or is the Islamist threat from persons who have become randomly and suddenly "radicalized" while browsing the Internet?

Or perhaps the threat is not related to Islamist militancy at all and is something entirely different. Does the threat stem from misguided interpretations of the Second Amendment, which gives angry, deranged, and even psychotic persons access to semi-automatic weapons that they turn against the police, children at school, national celebrations, and people dancing at a nightclub? One thing is for sure: The costs of countering the ill-defined terrorist threat are extremely high—to our society, to the troops, to the treasury, and to the historical progression of liberalism.

But clarity is apparently impossible to achieve, possibly because there is no adequate or even agreed definition of terrorism.[131] Moreover, terrorism may involve and cannot be distinguished from many other crimes including murder, kidnapping, arson, and, increasingly, active shooter events. Even if we say that terrorism is always a "political" act, we still cannot distinguish it from crime. The assassination of President John F. Kennedy was a violent political crime, but few would call it "terrorism."

Because of this ambiguity, the threat of terrorism is continuously manipulated by political elites, unelected intelligence officials, and disaffected groups in many countries of the world.[132] This problem interfaces both with the electoral prospects of officials, encouraging them to be "tough on terrorism," and with agencies such as the Federal Bureau of Investigation in the United States and MI5 in the United Kingdom, whose missions include counterterrorism as a central tenet. Politicians often use terrorist events to initiate or consolidate political gains, and intelligence officials continuously hype the threat of terrorism to bolster their legitimacy—to increase their budgets, authority, and power within the government.

Moreover, as tempting as it might be, for example, we cannot simply label the Islamic State as a "terrorist" group—even though it beheads, crucifies, and immolates prisoners in Iraq and Syria, puts the videos on YouTube, and calls for jihad against the West—all in the name of the Prophet. If the Islamic State is defeated, history will judge it to be a terrorist group or a failed insurgency; if it is victorious, it will be judged a revolutionary force and may become the legitimate government over some portion of the Middle East, a government with which the United State might eventually seek diplomatic relations. From the dawn of history, invading and insurgent armies bent on conquest have committed atrocities in the name of God, including the Christian Crusaders against Muslims from 1095 through 1291, and the U.S. coalition that invaded Iraq and Afghanistan in the first decade of the 21st century.

Although presidents, prime ministers, and the heads of intelligence units sounded the alarms, recruits from Europe and the United States who traveled to the Middle East to join the ranks of the Islamic State have yet to return in significant numbers to commit murder at home. It appears more likely that "lone wolves" or "wolf packs," as some are called, may become self-radicalized. Nevertheless, in anticipation of returnees bent on violence, the United Kingdom, Australia, and other countries passed strong terrorism laws, degrading the integrity of the open society that has taken hundreds of years to develop. The installation of counterterror infrastructure and the buildup of internal security police often lead to irrational outcomes, in part because the definition of terrorism changes with time and circumstance.[133]

All states experience terror. It is associated predominately with war and sophisticated weapons, but also with violent groups and individuals. It is too often self-inflicted by leaders against their own populations. Indeed, the word "terrorism" is so ideologically charged that in many instances it cannot be distinguished from other forms of political violence. It comes down to this: If you believe in the cause of the violent actors, then they are insurgents and may have a legitimate claim to the reins of power. If you disagree, then the violent adherents are terrorists. Moreover, in some cases, persons labeled as terrorists win the insurgency and become heads of state: Meacham Begin in Israel, Ahmed Ben Bella in Algeria, and Nelson Mandela in South Africa, for example.

And so the concept of terrorism dwells in the twilight of subjectivity, politically or ideologically driven, and perhaps resembles what Justice Potter Stewart had to say about "hard-core pornography." He wrote, "I shall not today attempt further to define the kinds of material I understand to be embraced within that short-hand description; and perhaps I could never succeed in intelligibly doing so. But I know it when I see it, and the motion picture involved in this case is not that."[134] The analog is of course that most violent crime is not terrorism; although we cannot distinguish one from the other, we know that when a suicide bomber enters a market in Baghdad or a nightclub in Orlando and randomly kills 50 people, that's terrorism.

A Masterpiece of Obfuscation

Too many leaders manipulate fear of terror as a political tool. This psycho-political mechanism creates both opportunities and grave liabilities for any elected leader who would go before the public and say that terrorism is a thing of the past, that it is time to stand down the Security Industrial Complex, to reprogram the hundreds of billions spent annually on internal security and the Counterterror Wars.

But the opposite scenario is far more likely and, indeed, was used effectively when George W. Bush and his closest advisors campaigned against the threat of terror as a means of justifying foreign invasions, and to achieve reelection throughout 2003. As one analyst explains, "Many Americans—and the majority of Bush supporters—continued to believe that Iraq was involved in the 9/11 hijackings and was prepared to use stockpiles of weapons of mass destruction against the United States despite incontrovertible evidence to the contrary."[135] They believed this because the president and his closest advisors said it on many occasions. Ostensibly, the United States and the United Kingdom invaded Iraq on March 19,

2003, because Iraq harbored terrorists, possessed weapons of mass destruction, and might act against the United States or its foreign interests. President Bush said, "The evidence indicates that Iraq is reconstructing its nuclear weapons programs."[136] Vice President Cheney said, "There is no doubt [that Saddam Hussein] is amassing [weapons of mass destruction] to use against our friends, against our allies, and against us."[137] Secretary of State Colin Powell said, "We know that Saddam Hussein is determined to keep his weapons of mass destruction, is determined to make more."[138] And Defense Secretary Donald Rumsfeld said, "We know where they are. They are in the area around Tikrit and Baghdad."[139]

The American public has rarely, if ever, been treated to such an egregious case of outright prevarication, cherry-picking of intelligence, and broad dissemination of disinformation to support a reelection campaign and a decision to go to war. Secretary Powell produced a masterpiece of obfuscation in his now infamous address to the United Nations Security Council on September 5, 2003, creating a smokescreen that led directly to the fog of war in Iraq.[140] The president and his top aides used questionable and falsely amplified intelligence to win the acquiescence of Congress and the American electorate.

They did so to invoke fear of catastrophic terrorism, to justify invasion of an unpopular and suspect country in hopes of gaining electoral advantage at home. To be clear: This is something that is not supposed to happen in a democracy. It nevertheless demonstrates that governments of liberal states are poised and ready to strike based on the perception or utility of the fear of terrorism. In the 21st century, domestic politics unquestionably does not stop at the water's edge.

No connection between the government of Saddam Hussein and external terrorist groups ever emerged, and no cache of weapons of mass destruction was found. A few chemical munitions in various states of decomposition were discovered during the 2003–11 occupation and were routinely destroyed by American forces, but they were orphan munitions predating the first Gulf War in 1990. Between 1991 and 2007, many hundreds of weapons inspectors were sent to Iraq by the International Atomic Energy Agency, the Organization for the Prohibition of Chemical Weapons, and various UN special commissions. These organizations destroyed not only the weapons but also the Iraqi infrastructure of mass destruction.

All of this is carefully documented and was part of the public record prior to the decision to invade Iraq in 2003. It is true the Iraqi regime presented records with references to a variety of weapons, but they could not be located. In a briefing to the UN Security Council two weeks before the United States invaded Iraq, chief weapons inspector Hans Blix contested part of the "evidence" provided by Powell and summed up, "How much, if any, is left of Iraq's weapons of mass destruction and related proscribed items and programmes? So far [the inspection team] has not found any such weapons, only a small number of empty chemical munitions, which should have been declared and destroyed."[141] The invasion of Iraq was an external manifestation of irrational internal security masquerading as counterterrorism, driven by electoral politics and by a terror-counterterror-terror dynamic.

This sequence played out at home and on the international stage. The United States commenced "Operation Iraqi Freedom," the official name for the 2003 invasion. Within a few months, angry young men from many nations toting guns converged on Iraq to harass U.S. forces and conduct a variety of attacks, often including suicide bombings or assaults with improvised explosive devises. As U.S. forces learned to detect tripwires or jam cell-phone detonators, the insurgents adopted incrementally more sophisticated tactics. In the larger picture, as the dynamic evolved and U.S. forces began to withdraw from Iraq, soldiers allied with the so-called Islamic

State converged on the Iraqi towns of Fallujah and Tikrit in the summer of 2014. President Obama at first authorized 300 military advisors to reenter Iraq. Soon thereafter, he called for lethal drone and F/A-18 strikes with laser-guided 500-pound bombs to take out selective artillery batteries and even some U.S. weapons that the Islamic militants had captured. The media referred to the Islamic State group as "al Qaeda on steroids." In a desperate attempt to stop the "terrorists," the bombing campaign was expanded to Syria. It was not clear whether the U.S. military effort inadvertently aided the brutal regime of President Bashar al-Assad. And so it goes.

These events had enormous impact on Iraq, over time killing an estimated 143,000 to 175,000 civilians[142], destroying cultural artifacts, demolishing civil society, setting sects and religions against one another, breaking apart established borders, creating widespread malnutrition of Iraqi children, and generally destroying the hopes and dreams of a whole generation. But all this remained distant and ephemeral to most Americans, many of whom thought the death toll in Iraq was fewer than 5,000 persons and could not immediately locate Iraq or Syria on a map.[143]

Where Has All the Terror Gone?

Without doubt, the United States suffered the worst non-state terrorist attack on record, but overall, it experiences less terrorism than much of the rest of the world. This is reflected clearly in data from the Global Terrorism Database, which is headquartered at the University of Maryland and affiliated with the U.S. Department of Homeland Security. It defines terrorism broadly as "the threatened or actual use of illegal force and violence by a non-state actor to attain a political, economic, religious, or social goal through fear, coercion, or intimidation."[144] (Notice that this definition does not exclude armed robbery, although most such crimes are not counted.) The Global Terrorism Database uses an open-source

TOTAL TERRORITS ATTACHS IN THE U.S. 1970-2013*

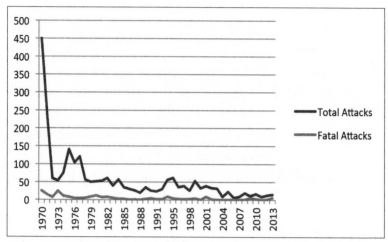

* GTD Global Terrorism Database, accessed at http://www.start.umd.edu/gtd/ on June 16, 2015. See also, LaFree, Gary, Laura Dugan and Erin Miller, "Integrated United States Security Database (IUSSD): Terrorism Data on the United States Homeland, 1970 to 2011," Final Report to the Resilient Systems Division, DHS Science and Technology Directorate. College Park, MD: START, 2012. Available at http://www.start.umd.edu/sites/default/files/files/publications/START_IUSSDDataTerroristAttacksUS_1970-2011.pdf, accessed on June 20, 2014.

methodology, capturing events that fit its definition worldwide. According to this source, in the 12-year period between 2001 and 2013 there were approximately 53,488 terrorist attacks worldwide, of which 236 took place in the United States. By this metric, the United States, with about 4.5 percent of the world's population, would expect to have had about 2,400 attacks, or roughly 10 times as many as it actually had.

Perhaps more important, **FIGURE III.1** shows that the number of terrorist attacks in the United States fell precipitously after the 1960s. The slope of the graph plummets after 1970 and continues to decrease through 2013. The figure also indicates that the number of attacks involving fatalities was actually quite low (the bottom line on the figure), an average of less than six such attacks each year, and far fewer after the 1980s. By 2005, terrorism was all but nonexistent in the United States.

GLOBAL TERRORIST ATTACKS 1970-2011*

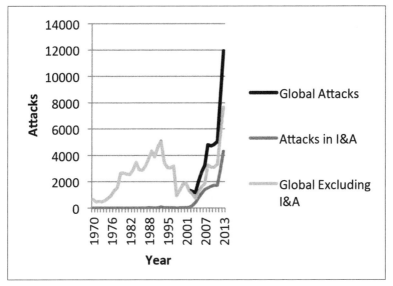

* GTD Global Terrorism Database, accessed at http://www.start.umd.edu/gtd/ on June 16, 2015.

This four-decade-long depiction compares quite favorably with the larger global data set from which it is drawn. **FIGURE III.2** presents a strikingly different image. The top line represents the total number of recorded terrorist incidents worldwide. In sharp contrast to the U.S. data, the data in Figure III.2 indicate that terrorism increased steadily from 650 attacks in 1970 to 5,100 in 1992, and then fell again to 1,200 in 2004.

But notice what happens after 2004. The number of global terrorist events skyrockets to 12,000, reflecting the occupations of Iran and Afghanistan, and possibly a definitional anomaly as well. How are attacks counted in a war zone or in a region subject to foreign invasion and occupation for more than a decade? The graph also reflects the ascendance of the Islamic State group after 2012, principally in Iran and Syria. Again, we run into the murky political ideology of labeling a state, an armed insurgency, or a militant group "terrorist." We do not know exactly what the word means in this context or how the counting is conducted, but it seems very likely that attacks on the U.S. Army, and later on the Iraqi Army or Kurdish military forces by Islamic State fighters, would be counted as "terrorist" incidents. President Obama and many other public officials routinely refer to the Islamic State as a "terrorist organization." If we look at the bottom (third) line, then, on the lower-right portion of the graph, we can see that Iraq and Afghanistan account for about one-third of all "terrorist" incidents listed in the global database. So it must be that war-related violence in these countries is often counted as terrorism—although not violence that was officially sanctioned by the governments of Iraq and the United States.

By 2004, the Counterterror Wars were well under way, and U.S. and allied troops battled significant insurgencies in both countries, as reflected in the graph. If we believe these data, then the Iraq and Afghanistan portion of Figure III.2 can be read as further evidence of the terror-counterterror-terror dynamic. These numbers suggest that the U.S. military effort to crush terrorism in Iraq and Afghanistan backfired, apparently causing significantly more violence to occur. This seems reasonable in light of the well-documented migration of militant Islamic fighters from many different nations to Iraq and Syria. One UN report said that the number of foreign fighters in these states had risen from a few thousand a decade earlier to more than 25,000 from 100 countries by 2015.[145] After the U.S. troops left Iraq in December of 2011, various extremist Islamist groups continued to commit atrocities, posting gruesome photos and videos of their victims on the Internet.

While recorded "terrorist" events increased in Iraq and Afghanistan after 2004, **FIGURE III.3** shows that the number of terrorist attacks declined steeply in the United States. One plausible explanation is that U.S. counterterror efforts have been extremely effective and have contained terrorism in the United States, even if

FIGURE III.3:
TOTAL TERRORIST ATTACKS IN THE U.S. 2001-2013*

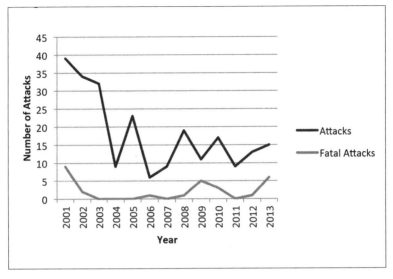

* GTD Global Terrorism Database, accessed at http://www.start.umd.edu/gtd/ on June 16, 2015.

they have stimulated it in the Middle East, South Asia, and North Africa. Such an assumption would certainly be heartening for the United States. But it is more likely that the steady decrease in terrorist events at home in the 10 years following 9/11 is part of the larger four-decade-long trend depicted in Figure III.1. After 2001, there were fewer than 20 attacks a year on average, only 6 attacks in 2006, and 9 in 2011, and no fatal attacks in 5 of the 13 years, 2001–13. It is instructive to contrast these numbers with the number of traffic accidents in the United States during the same period, which is estimated to have been on the order of 10.6 million per year.[146]

Of the 208 attacks in the figure, only 90 can be attributed to organized groups. The top two groups, the Earth Liberation Front and the Animal Liberation Front, accounted for 84 attacks, 50 and 34 respectively. Moreover, about 54 percent of the events in Figure III.3 involved attacks on facilities, not on people, and were "due to an increased reliance on arson, much of it associated with environmental and animal rights violent extremist groups."[147]

Clearly, the problem of terrorism in the United States is a diminished one, if we go by the numbers. But the situation in Iraq is entirely different. If we put Iraq at the center of the picture, which is a national and cultural nightmare for tens of millions of people, and turn to the suicide bomber database at the University of Chicago, the differences between the United States and Iraq are striking. From 1982 to 2013, there were 1,552 suicide attacks in Iraq causing 16,746 deaths and wounding 42,793 persons.[148] As staggering as these figures are, they are made even more poignant considering the population of Iraq is about 36 million, roughly 10 percent of that of the United States. When we scale up to U.S. population levels, that is, multiply these numbers by a factor of 10, the equivalent number of suicide attacks in the United States would have claimed something on the order of 167,000 dead, with about 428,000 wounded over three decades.[149]

To assess the magnitude of terrorism in the United States, it may be helpful to compare the data in Figure III.3 to another metric: the number of mass shootings in recent years. The Mass Shooter Index defines a mass shooting as gun violence in which four or more persons are shot and/or killed. In 2013, there were 363 such incidents; in 2014, there were 277 mass shootings; and in 2015 that number was 331.[150] This comes to approximately six mass-shooting incidents each week. When Americans hear about gun violence in the streets, they can hardly be surprised. It is a cost-benefit analysis that pits thousands of wounded and dead against a gun culture in which citizens claim a Second Amendment right to "keep and bear arms." Gun-related deaths reached 33,636 in 2013, or about 10.6 for every 100,000 persons.[151] But like the terrorism statistics, the numbers on gun violence are infinitesimal when considered in the context of the larger population. On any given day, the likelihood of being a victim of a mass shooter event (when four or more persons are shot) is something on the order of 1 in 80,400,000; and the probability of being a victim of a terrorist attack approaches zero.

So what is the takeaway from these various data? Clearly the United States has a *de minimis* terrorism problem compared to the scale of Iraq or Syria and the global norm, even considering the high level of sustained gun violence across America. Even when we consider the appalling loss of life and injury due to 9/11, it is far less by the numbers than what happened in Iraq and other places. Moreover, compared with the rest of the world—both today and over the past several decades—the United States has a very moderate terrorism problem. But it does have a problem.

Terrorism poses great challenges to the United States, and to all other modern liberal democracies. The first is clearer now that we have experienced mass-casualty terrorism: It is the apparition of the nuclear-armed terrorist. This *spiritus mundi* has troubled our sight for decades and will haunt us for the rest of our lives. We must continuously take steps to prevent it. The far greater menace, however, is the threat to liberty posed by the institutionalization of a permanent state of emergency. It is exemplified by the power and authority we have bestowed on the Security Industrial Complex, the hard core of a massive and secret internal security state-within-the-state at the dawn of the digital age in the 21st century.

Irrational Security in the Military Domain

The relationship between the Military and Security Industrial Complexes is more than mere analogy. The two share vital overlaps in multiple dimensions: politically, ideologically, economically, and even operationally. Indeed, we can say that the two systems—military security and internal security—were joined at the hip in the prosecution of the "global war on terror." The military was dispatched to Iraq and Afghanistan for more than a dozen years to prevent terrorist attacks on the United States and its far-flung interests. Special Operations forces are deployed globally in counterterror missions ostensibly to keep Americans safe at home and abroad. The intelligence agencies undertake dragnet internal security operations to contain terror in the United States as well as lethal drone strikes abroad.

Indeed, the distinction between military and internal security operations is increasingly ambiguous and often blurry. The Air Force and the Central Intelligence Agency both hunt militants, assassinating them with drone strikes. They share intelligence. The police use weapons supplied by the military for local SWAT deployments, and big-city police departments have stood up sophisticated intelligence units with strong links to national intelligence agencies, both domestic and foreign. The military embraced policing tactics in Iraq and Afghanistan, like Operation Pericles. Pericles involved detection work and house-to-house searches in 13 villages in the Diyala River valley in east Iraq.[152] The military participated in the response to Hurricane Katrina, preventing residents from returning to the Ninth Ward in New Orleans at gunpoint, and so on and so forth.

There is something in the nature of security—both military security and "homeland" security—that plays on human fears and the desire for power and invokes an irrational and completely disproportionate response. We can see from the data presented in Chapter II that the headlong investment and buildup of the Security Industrial Complex is a profoundly irrational overreaction to the events of 9/11. But it is also true that American leaders have found political traction in continuously reminding the people about the horror of 9/11, and in reassuring them that no expense will be spared and no opportunity lost to prevent a recurrence. If the people in modern liberal democracies believe that the threat of terrorism is real, they will support internal security and counterterror operations of almost any cost. And to the extent that their leaders present misinformation as facts, they are likely to be misled.

This situation is directly analogous to the military buildup that began after the Second World War, continued throughout the Cold War, and expanded into the 21st century of continuous Counterterror Wars and military operations. So it is not too great a supposition to think that in addition to irrational internal security, there must also be instances of irrational military operations and procurements. Perhaps the best example is drawn from the most decisive and costly military capability ever acquired: the advent of nuclear weapons and the development, maintenance, and storage of nuclear arsenals and related radioactive materials and infrastructure.

From the end of World War II to the end of the Cold War, the United States and the Soviet Union together produced many tens of thousands of nuclear weapons. This number is fantastically out of touch with reality. Experts today agree (and must certainly have known at the time) that a thousand, perhaps only a few hundred, survivable nuclear weapons are sufficient to retaliate against and completely destroy any nation on earth. But for reasons that are best understood in clinical or psychological terms, the two superpowers engaged in an all-out nuclear arms race that was unnecessary, dangerous, and expensive in the extreme. It was an exercise of the absurd.

At the time, it was clear that nothing good could come of building tens of thousands of nuclear weapons, especially because deterrence had been achieved almost from the beginning. Even the acronym MAD, which stands for "mutual assured destruction," shouts out a nauseating irrationality. Yet policymakers relentlessly engaged in Cold War fear mongering, and the American taxpayer continued to foot the bill of more than $5.8 trillion in the United

States alone over the life of the program in which it manufactured some 70,000 nuclear weapons.[153] All the while, the academic and think-tank communities debated deterrence theory, publishing thousands of articles and books, most of which were simply exercises in abstract argumentation. But careers were made in both policymaking and academic circles, and most experts turned a blind eye to the fact that the nuclear enterprise was propelled by psychological, political, bureaucratic, and market forces, but not by military necessity and certainly not with recourse to logic.

Indeed, there is no evidence to support a claim that the policy of mutually assured destruction was in any way affected by building additional nuclear weapons after each side had established a robust second-strike capability. Nevertheless, the policy continued even after both sides installed a strategic triad—with weapons on hair-trigger alert, continuously deployed in the air, at sea, and on land—which likely occurred by 1962, the year of the Cuban Missile Crisis. At that time, the United States reached 25,540 nuclear weapons and the Soviets 3,346, for a total of 28,886 in their combined stockpiles. That number climbed to an apex of 64,449 weapons deployed in 1986.[154]

By the end of the Cold War, it had become obvious that the nuclear arms race was economically and politically unsustainable, useless as a military asset and a driver of horizontal proliferation. The past quarter-century marked a partial return to sanity, coupled with many bilateral negotiations, in which the nuclear arsenals of the United States and Russia were vastly reduced to a combined total of 3,950 deployed warheads, 2,150 and 1,800 respectively— still a dangerously high number.[155] Moreover, in a 50-year period, nuclear force planners failed to come to an adequate understanding of the devastating global firestorm that even small numbers of nuclear explosions would inflict.[156] There is, of course, a very large hangover from the nuclear binge, including weapons in at least seven additional states: China, France, India, Israel, Pakistan, North Korea, and the United Kingdom. In addition to deployed warheads, there are stockpiled warheads and retired warheads, bringing the total inventory to approximately 17,200.[157] Moreover, there are thousands of tons of fissile material (principally highly enriched uranium and plutonium) located in many countries of the world in various states of irradiation, storage, and security. This dangerous circumstance is beyond the scope of the present discussion but is addressed in the next chapter.

The best thinking about nuclear weapons was articulated in a series of articles in *The Wall Street Journal* written between January 2007 and March 2013 and co-authored by the so-called "Four Horsemen": former chairman of the Senate Armed Services Committee Sam Nunn, former Defense Secretary William Perry, and former Secretaries of State George Schultz and Henry Kissinger. These past Cold Warriors argued that nuclear weapons have no role in war fighting, and that the dangers they pose are so extreme the only solution is to achieve "a world free of nuclear weapons."[158] Senator Nunn in particular devoted the rest of his working life to reducing the nuclear threat through an organization that he formed and chaired jointly with billionaire Ted Turner, the Nuclear Threat Initiative, based in Washington, D.C.

Nevertheless, many aspects of nuclear irrationality continue unabated, with a plan to modernize U.S. nuclear forces and related delivery vehicles over a 30-year period at a projected cost of $1 trillion. And this came from President Obama, who had campaigned for a "nuclear-free world." Senator Nunn expressed the views of many who had hoped for a different outcome. He said, "A lot of it is hard to explain. The president's vision was a significant change in direction. But the process has preserved the status quo."[159]

The production of tens of thousands of unnecessary, dangerous, and extravagantly expensive nuclear weapons over a half-century, as well as six decades of military budgets averaging more than $500 billion annually (see Figure II.6), can accurately be described as a kind of irrationality—a buildup of security, not to defend against realistic threats and opposing forces, but as an end in and of itself. Since the Korean War, the United States has maintained its military in a state of readiness, sufficient to confront every plausible military adversary. This form of militarism—which engages in preemptive and preventable wars and occupations—constitutes an increasingly neurotic response to the modern world. So too does the reckless expansion of the Security Industrial Complex and the antidemocratic powers at its disposal, carried out in the name of preventing another 9/11.

Not unlike the military buildup, irrational threat perceptions have driven counterterrorism policy, certainly since the events of 9/11, and possibly since the simultaneous bombings by al Qaeda in 1998 of the U.S. embassies in Kenya and Tanzania. This may be especially true of the United States, which sustained the most devastating non-state terrorist attack in history. The response was monumental, but it was also misdirected and disproportionate—creating and then amplifying a surveillance security state-within-the-state. The external manifestations of irrational internal security were the invasions and occupations of Iraq and Afghanistan. The former had nothing to do with the events of 9/11, and neither state possessed the ability to threaten the United States in any significant way.

The internal manifestation is an ongoing pathological response to terrorism. Even in the face of decreasing incidents of terror in the United States, U.S. security officials, especially those ambitious for high office, continue to hype the threat of terrorism. To commemorate the 14th anniversary of 9/11, for example, the House Committee on Homeland Security planned a "field hearing" in New York City. The wording of the opening statement by

Chairman Michael McCaul is instructive. He referred to a "generational struggle against Islamist terror" and warned that the "viral spread of violent extremism has allowed our enemies to spread globally and has brought the war back to our doorsteps." He alleged that "in the past eighteen months ISIS [the Islamic State group] alone has inspired or directed nearly sixty plots or attacks against Western countries, including America," in what he characterized as an "age of peer to peer terrorism and cyber jihad." He compared the ideology of Islamic terror to Communism and fascism and concluded: "We must also take the fight to the enemy before they can attack us at home, and we can do this by eliminating terrorist sanctuaries overseas."[160]

Clearly, McCall aimed to drum up support for the issues and operations of his committee and the Department of Homeland Security, and for further military adventures abroad. His reference to "the viral spread of terror" is just out of touch with the statistics on terrorist attacks over the past 40 years in the United States. Moreover, his unsubstantiated claim of 60 plots by the Islamic State group against the West must be taken with a grain of salt at best. Similar claims about terrorist plots that had been disrupted—made by President George W. Bush, General Michael Hayden, and President Obama—were either retracted or could not be documented.

But even this did not deter real-estate mogul and presidential candidate Donald Trump. He advocated killing the families of terrorists, ostensibly because while suicide bombers are ready to die, they still care about their families.[161] But Trump went even further in an interview with Fox News. He said that as president he would support a formal declaration of war against terrorism:

> This is a war against people who are vicious, violent people that we have no idea who they are, where they come from. We are allowing

tens of thousands of them into our country now so on top of wars on foreign land wait 'til you see what happens in the future. It's probably not going to be pretty . . . the world is at war.[162]

Quite clearly, emotional appeals to legitimize domestic surveillance and increase internal security and counterterrorism assets and militarism abroad are misplaced. A strong case can be made that the United States should direct its counterterror activity against a few international terrorist groups like al Qaeda, leaving other countries to deal with their own internal security problems. This point was forcefully driven home as the number of U.S. fatalities attributable to insurgency rose precipitously in Iraq. Indeed, we cannot avoid the conclusion that the United States and its coalition partners created the nexus for regional disorder, a magnet for foreign fighters, and a training ground for would-be insurgents by toppling the government in Iraq and prematurely disbanding the Iraqi Army and other security structures.[163] The civil war in Syria and the emergence of the Islamic State would seem to be direct consequences of irrational U.S. security policies, specifically including the Counterterror Wars in the Middle East.

What would rational internal security look like? It is actually fairly straightforward. We cannot surveil and secure everything. It is not possible to harden every public building, every movie theater, every school, and all public gathering places. Nor is it desirable. But there are facilities that should be made secure: These include banks, military facilities, nuclear reactors, chemical plants, and biology laboratories that handle pathogens and infectious diseases, especially BSL-3 and BSL-4 biocontainment labs. They are natural targets for criminals, psychopaths, and other malefactors who would damage critical infrastructure. This is certainly not an easy task. It is nevertheless achievable.

It turns out that many CBRN facilities—which stands for chemical, biological, radiological, and nuclear—are less secure than they should be. And the standard for security must be very high because some could be used to make highly dangerous items such as high explosives, infectious diseases, and "dirty" or radiological bombs. These facilities must be subject to safety and security procedures that pervade the culture of the facility, no matter where it is located.[164] And this would entail a rational application of internal security, because extremely dangerous facilities dealing with pathogens, fissile materials, volatile chemicals, and the like should be secure and their personnel need to be vetted on a continuous basis. And what is the guiding principle? Target internal security predominately to those few places and people where critical infrastructure and dangerous materials need to be protected— and not to the society in general.

Certainly we must still address the dreaded nuclear terrorist. And yes, we live in a world where science and technology have spread the secrets of destruction far and wide. Even before the first Gulf War in 1990, Saddam Hussein of Iraq had constructed nuclear, chemical, and biological facilities, in an effort to create weapons of mass destruction. Teams of inspectors from the Organization for the Prohibition of Chemical Weapons and the United Nations converged on Iraq for a seven-year period following the war. They destroyed tens of thousands of chemical munitions, including mustard and binary nerve agents. They also discovered that Iraq was attempting to develop a nuclear arsenal and that a nuclear explosive device might have been ready for testing in 12 to 18 months if the United States and its coalition partners had not intervened after Iraq invaded Kuwait in 1990. These and other relevant circumstances compel us to examine the possibility that terrorists might acquire weapons of mass destruction.

CHAPTER IV

CATASTROPHIC TERROR

On April 5, 2009, President Obama placed nuclear terrorism at the top of his foreign-policy agenda. In a speech delivered in Prague, he called for "a world without nuclear weapons" and designated nuclear terrorism as "the most immediate and extreme threat to global security." He went on to propose a global nuclear summit in which the leaders of concerned nations would come together "to secure all vulnerable nuclear material around the world within four years." To that end, Washington hosted the first of four biennial Nuclear Security Summits in 2010. Sustained, high-level attention to the problem of nuclear terrorism raises a simple question: What does terror look like, and how should we think about it?

The most important distinction is between *catastrophic* terror (large-scale crimes against humanity) and more limited *episodic* terror (violent crimes against society). While we have many examples of episodic terror, and these are analyzed in the next chapter, the only example that even approaches catastrophic terror in the United States—excluding the Civil War and the extermination of Native American populations—is the al Qaeda coordinated strikes of September 11, 2001, in which some 3,000 persons lost their lives. There can be no doubt that the perpetrators of 9/11 would have exploded nuclear devices over New York and Washington if they had gained access to those weapons. But given the gravity of such an action, what is catastrophic terror and who is likely to do it?

Catastrophic State Terrorism

Nations commit all kinds of terror, which cannot be excluded from this discussion, as though somehow terror gains legitimacy when it is sponsored or carried out by states. It does not. Indeed, state terror takes several distinct forms. Iran and Pakistan, for example, are often designated as sponsors and funders of terrorism. The U.S. State Department indicates "Iran continued its terrorist-related activity in 2014, including support for Palestinian terrorist groups in Gaza, Lebanese Hizballah, and various groups in Iraq and throughout the Middle East."[165] Many experts assert as well that Pakistan's military intelligence agency—the Inter-Services Intelligence, or ISI—has long trained and funded violent Islamist organizations including Harakat ul-Mujahideen, Jaish-e-Mohammed, and Lashkar-e-Taiba (LeT).[166] LeT alone is credited with the 2001 bombing of the Houses of Parliament in New Delhi in which 12 people were killed, the 2006 bomb attack on the Mumbai subway system (180 killed, 800 wounded), and the 2008 coordinated attacks across Mumbai (170 killed, 300 wounded).

In another kind of state terror, the United States and the United Kingdom operate drones in increasing numbers, often killing innocent civilians, and even targeting their own citizens in other countries. In a 2016 summary of drone strikes, the Director of National Intelligence indicated that over the previous seven years, the United States carried out 473 lethal drone strikes outside areas of hostility, but still within Afghanistan, Iraq, and Syria, killing between 2,327 and 2,581 combatants, and between 64 and 116 non-combatants.[167] These numbers are considerably lower than estimates of credible non-governmental organizations such as the Long War Journal, New America, and the Bureau of Investigative Journalism—which put the number of non-civilians killed by drone strikes at between 200 and 1,000.[168] And they say nothing about drone strikes in other nations such as Yemen and Libya. Other sources indicate still higher levels of civilian deaths: In Pakistan, a nation with which the United States is not at war, another source indicated that "More than 175 children are among at least 2,347 people reported killed in U.S. [drone] attacks since 2004. There are credible reports of at least 392 civilians among the dead."[169] State-sponsored remote assassinations began under President George W. Bush, accelerated to become a major tool under Obama, and are likely to be a fixture of intelligence and military operations for the foreseeable future.

A third kind of terror occurs internal to the state, turning security forces against rival ethnic populations, as in the cases of Idi Amin in Uganda and Saddam Hussein in Iraq. Amin presided over an eight-year reign of terror in which Ugandans of Asian heritage were expelled from that country. It featured "widespread killing, torture, and dispossession of multitudes and left the country pauperized."[170] Similarly, Hussein conducted the Al-Anfal campaign against the Kurdish population in Iraq. His cousin General Ali Hassan al-Majid (also known as "Chemical Ali") carried out a genocidal operation using chemical weapons. Various human-rights organizations put the number of dead at between 50,000 and 100,000. Kurdish authorities, however, suggest a much higher toll—182,000.[171] This is terrorism on a catastrophic scale.

And finally, states commit large-scale terrorism in war against internal populations as well as foreign enemies. This last category can often be classified as catastrophic terrorism. Here the nuclear bombings of Hiroshima (150,000 fatalities) and Nagasaki (100,000), the fire bombings of Dresden (30,000) and Tokyo (100,000), the Armenian genocide (800,000 to 1.5 million), and the Holocaust (6 million) readily come to mind. They are not the only ones. All involve numbers of fatalities on at least an order of magnitude greater than 9/11.

The Phantom of Nuclear Terror

Nuclear terrorism is often cited as the most likely candidate for catastrophic terrorism that is *not* committed by a state. In this case, what we have to imagine is a sub-state organization, not a country or an individual, but an aspirational group capable of constructing or stealing, and then arming and delivering, a weapon of mass destruction—a catastrophic nuclear device. But this is an extraordinarily difficult goal with a low to no probability of success. Nuclear terrorism is, of course, "the ultimate preventable tragedy," as has been pointed out time and again.[172]

We can surely conjure catastrophic, even existential incidents involving our supposed nuclear terrorist. The detonation of a nuclear weapon, however, is far more likely to come from a failure of deterrence and be executed by a state. There is even a remote possibility of an accidental nuclear attack. Terrorists will be deterred not on moral grounds or because they fear death or retaliation, but because nuclear weapons are hard to make and the processes of fabricating them cannot be concealed. There are two essential elements. The first is to design and construct a device that can produce a sustained fission reaction, essentially by slamming together two subcritical masses of fissile material, typically plutonium (PU) or highly enriched uranium (HEU), instantly transforming matter into energy. It is not an easy task. All the steps must be precise and taken in the right order. The second and harder part is to obtain sufficient quantities of fissile material, even though five to ten kilograms are certainly enough.

Making the device itself is no trivial pursuit. On August 6, 1945, the United States detonated a gun-type fission bomb code-named "Little Boy" over the Japanese city of Hiroshima. It was constructed using a sawn-off howitzer to crash two subcritical pieces of HEU together and had an explosive yield of 13 to 18 kilotons of TNT. Three days later, the United States dropped a second weapon, code-named "Fat Man," on Nagasaki. It was an implosion-type device with a PU core and a yield of 20 to 22 kilotons of TNT. In such a device, very precisely timed charges on the surface of a sphere explode in unison, compressing one or more subcritical plutonium pits, causing the nuclear explosion. Today's most powerful nuclear weapons are tiny in size by comparison but have approximately a thousand times the explosive yield as the bombs dropped on Hiroshima and Nagasaki. Those two weapons were developed under the Manhattan Project, which cost $25 billion–$30 billion (in constant 2016 dollars) and employed more than 130,000 people.[173] The United States proposes, even today, to upgrade its nuclear arsenal at an estimated cost of up to $1 trillion over the next 30 years.[174] And this despite the fact that some of the modifications call for lower yield weapons, raising the specter of their actual use in tactical warfare situations.[175] This program of modernization also indicates that the United States has no intention of divesting itself of nuclear weapons, as it is required to do under the terms of the Nuclear Nonproliferation Treaty.

In the late 1950s, however, when the United States, the Soviet Union, and the United Kingdom alone possessed nuclear arsenals, scientists and government officials debated if a fourth, fifth, or nth country could design a workable weapon—hence the "Nth Country Experiment." To answer this question, two newly graduated Ph.D. physicists, Bob Selden and Dave Dobson, were recruited as postdocs at the Lawrence Radiation Laboratory in California to determine if they could design a weapon without using classified information. The father of the hydrogen bomb, Edward Teller, interviewed both men to make sure they had little knowledge of the subject at hand. Between 1964 and 1967, they were nevertheless able to produce in Selden's words ". . . a short document that described precisely, in engineering terms, what we proposed to build and what materials were involved. The whole works, in great detail, so that this thing could have been made by Joe's Machine Shop downtown."[176] The Nth Country Experiment proved that any nation with sufficient political will could design a workable implosion-type nuclear weapon. By 1976, it was possible for a junior at Princeton University to accomplish a similar feat using only publicly available information to satisfy a requirement for a term paper.[177] After all, it had been more than three decades since the technology was invented.

Obtaining the fissile material, it turns out, is the more difficult part of building a nuclear weapon. Some 27 countries possess enough highly enriched uranium and/or plutonium to fuel a nuclear arsenal. Advanced industrial states like Canada, Germany, Italy, Japan, and South Korea, among others, come immediately to mind. All could produce a nuclear weapon in a matter of months, but have chosen not to do so, remaining in compliance with the Nuclear Nonproliferation Treaty. But while not impossible, it has proved extremely difficult for less developed states to fabricate fissile material for a nuclear weapons program, and especially to do so without detection.

Indeed, inspectors from the International Atomic Energy Agency uncovered the North Korean effort to build a nuclear bomb in 1993. They discovered that irradiated PU had been diverted from a nuclear reactor to a plutonium separation facility at the Yongbyon Nuclear Scientific Research Center. The facility was designed to clean up plutonium from spent fuel assemblies, which is an unfortunate byproduct of nuclear energy production, making it into fissile material that could be used in a nuclear bomb. So the first underground test of a North Korean nuclear device had long been expected, and had been the subject of negotiations for 13 years when it finally occurred in 2006. It was impossible to hide the preparations for the test as well as the test itself.

Pakistan and India both possessed the ability to produce an explosive nuclear device years before each conducted five nearly simultaneous tests in 1998—setting off a nuclear arms race in South Asia. It was more than an open secret. In 1985 the U.S. Senate passed the Pressler Amendment; it required the president to certify each year that Pakistan did not have a nuclear weapons program before foreign aid (including conventional arms) could be provided to that nation. Despite overwhelming evidence to the contrary, Presidents Ronald Reagan and George H.W. Bush made the certification. They did so largely because the Central Intelligence Agency was supplying billions of dollars in arms to Islamic militant groups, many based across the border in Afghanistan, including to Osama bin Laden.[178] The covert CIA program, Operation Cyclone, is credited with turning the tide of the Afghan war against the Soviets by supplying Stinger missiles, man-portable heat-seeking weapons that can destroy military aircraft in flight. This kind of missile, which can be carried and fired by a single individual, is reported to have destroyed countless Russian military aircraft and at least 30 civilian aircraft since 1976.[179]

India had previously conducted a nuclear test in 1974, code-named "Smiling Buddha." Although the United States and other countries detected the test, India maintained it was a "peaceful nuclear explosion." It caught the U.S. intelligence community and the Nixon administration off-guard because they were preoccupied with Vietnam and China and were not expecting or looking for an Indian nuclear weapons program.[180] In the intervening 40 years, the accuracy, reach, and resolution of national technical means and the scope of surveillance assets have improved exponentially so that such an oversight would be impossible today.

The Iranian nuclear program is another case in point. Iran came under intense pressure from the international community when it first began to enrich uranium to levels that might give it a breakout capability to build a weapon. In 2003, the International Atomic Energy Agency demanded that Iran suspend all uranium enrichment and reprocessing-related activities. Three years later, the UN Security Council unanimously adopted Resolution 1737, imposing sanctions on Iran for failing to suspend its enrichment-related activities. In 2008, the Security Council passed yet another measure, Resolution 1803, further expanding the sanctions against Iran.

But Iran failed to comply and in 2010 the gloves came off. The National Security Agency, working in concert with its Israeli counterparts, wrote the code for the Stuxnet digital weapon.[181] It is thought to be the first computer virus capable of destroying physical equipment, while masking the fact that it was doing so.[182] An employee with a thumb drive introduced the Stuxnet worm to Iran's vast underground nuclear-enrichment facility at Natanz. As engineers in the control room monitored what appeared to be normal operations, hundreds, perhaps thousands, of centrifuges that were being used to enrich uranium spun out of control and were damaged or destroyed. The world was determined that Iran should not build a nuclear arsenal. In June of 2015, the P5+1 negotiators (the five permanent members of the UN Security Council plus Germany) reached a historic deal in which the nuclear sanctions were lifted, and Iran agreed in exchange to limit its nuclear program and provide access to international inspectors.[183]

We can just note in passing that while the Stuxnet incident was a National Security Agency program, it coincided with the creation of the United States Cyber Command in 2010. In 2016, President Obama proposed a $14 billion budget for cybersecurity, of which $5.5 billion was slated for the military.[169] The Stuxnet attack also corresponds roughly with the rise of drone warfare and with a growing global deployment of and dependence on U.S. Special Operations forces. These events dovetail with the rapid development of digitally driven, surveillance-dependent remote sensing and attack weapons. It would appear that the battle space is once again being transformed, that acts of war have become more casual and politically neutral. War as we knew it in Saddam Hussein's 1991 "mother of all battles" can surely be relegated to the past.

In a very different case, South Africa built and then dismantled six nuclear weapons, but this did not go undetected. In 1977, South Africa made preparations for a "cold" test of a nuclear weapon, that is, a test in which the fissile core is not present in the weapon. But before it could be carried out, the Soviet Union discovered the site and passed the information to the United States. The U.S. Air Force was able to confirm test preparations using a long-range supersonic reconnaissance aircraft. And so the pressure of many countries was eventually focused on South Africa. In 1979, a U.S. Vela satellite recorded a double flash over the Indian Ocean, suggesting a nuclear test, but it was never confirmed. In the run-up to the end of apartheid, South Africa dismantled and destroyed its nuclear arsenal, the only state ever to do so. And in 1991, South Africa acceded to the Nuclear Nonproliferation Treaty—sealing an end to its nuclear weapons ambitions.

These states, together with the five permanent members of the UN Security Council—China, France, Russia, the United Kingdom, and the United States—account for the nine states that possess nuclear weapons. Israel, alone, follows a policy of opacity, that is, neither confirming nor denying its possession of nuclear weapons. The quest for a nuclear arsenal is, nevertheless, as old as the state itself. Israel probably built its first nuclear weapon in 1966 and is thought to possess between 100 and 200 nuclear warheads. Israel is generally considered to be a responsible country with the capacity to safeguard its nuclear arsenal. In any case, it is very difficult to open a discussion because the government of Israel never signed the Nuclear Nonproliferation Treaty and has never declared its nuclear arsenal.

There are many journalists and proliferation experts who wring their hands over the possibility of nuclear terrorism. Some say it is not a question of if, but when, the dreaded event will come to pass. They have been pulling on this bleak string for decades. But no sub-state group or terrorist organization possesses the resources to design and acquire the fissile materials necessary to build a nuclear weapon. If they tried to do so, they would be discovered, as were the states discussed above. Moreover, it is inconceivable that any country, even a rogue state, would make a nuclear weapon or fissile material available to a terrorist organization. It would be exposed and punished for its complicity; it might even sustain a nuclear attack in retaliation if the weapon was used.

Nuclear weapons, often referred to as the "crown jewels" of nations, are closely guarded and controlled by the governments and militaries that hold them. The process of moving a nuclear weapon from one side of a storage depot to the other in the United States, for example, involves several levels of approval and compliance with detailed handling protocols and security procedures. Moreover, nuclear weapons have to be activated and require secret codes before they can be armed, launched, and detonated. Mistakes certainly do occur. In 2007, for instance, a B-52 bomber was flown over the central United States with six nuclear-armed cruise missiles mistakenly attached to the wing.[185] Heads rolled and stronger policies were put in place. But this story still resonates a decade later, most likely because it is one of a kind.

Many weapons, including those possessed by China, India, and Pakistan, are widely reported to be de-alerted, meaning that the warheads are stored separately and not mated with delivery vehicles. This is also the case for the vast majority of nuclear weapons in the United States, although prominent scientists including twenty Nobel Laureates continue to urge that all nuclear weapons be de-alerted to prevent accidental nuclear war.[186] Moreover, nuclear weapons cannot be deployed without formal approval at the highest level of government. They are typically defended by encryption, sophisticated electronic measures, and by military personnel with special training and equipment, which includes overwhelming firepower to resist incursion. No nuclear weapon has ever been stolen or sold. Because nations guard information about nuclear weapons so closely, it is impossible to know with confidence the exact state of readiness of any nuclear arsenal. Bottom line: The likelihood that a terrorist organization could steal a nuclear weapon from a nation and actually deploy it approaches zero.

There are, nevertheless, numerous reports of accidents involving nuclear weapons, some lost at sea or in other circumstances where they could not be retrieved. This happened largely because the United States and the Soviet Union conducted a policy during the Cold War of keeping nuclear-armed aircraft aloft at all times. In this way, they hoped to deter a nuclear attack, and failing that, to retaliate even if all land-based nuclear assets had been destroyed in a first strike.[187] In some cases of lost weapons, the nuclear core was retrieved with no evidence of contamination. But between 1945 and 1989, as many as 50 nuclear weapons went missing at sea, including one incident in which a Soviet submarine sank to the bottom with its complement of 30 nuclear weapons. Few if any have been recovered.[188]

On February 5, 1958, a B-47 bomber dumped a Mark 15 thermonuclear weapon into the waters off of Savannah, Georgia, after colliding with another Air Force plane. Although search and recovery missions were immediately launched, the bomb slid down into the silt off nearby Tybee Island. The weapon was never found. There is some speculation as to whether it was actually fitted with a fissile core.[189] In another case, the U.S. Navy attempted to transfer a nuclear weapon from one ship to another in the Pacific when a large wave caused the weapon to slip into the water at a depth of about 3,000 meters. It was never found.[190] These cases are certainly of interest, but there is no reason to think that a sub-state organization like al Qaeda, Lashkar-e-Taiba, or Hezbollah would be able to find the missing weapons when the nation-states that lost them were unable to do so.

Far more legitimate concern has focused on the nuclear-production and fissile-materials storage facilities of the former Soviet Union. After the fall of the USSR, nuclear weapons were consolidated from Belarus, Kazakhstan, and Ukraine into Russia, but it soon became apparent that the Soviet system for materials protection, control, and accounting was deeply flawed. Perhaps it was a consequence of the Soviet command economy in which central planners rather than market forces set production levels. If a manager of an automobile factory was told to produce 40,000 tires, for example, he was expected to make or exceed that number. If the factory produced only 35,000 tires, the manager would likely have been demoted or punished. But if he exceeded his quota, and the factory produced 45,000 tires, it was an acceptable outcome. The same principle operated in the nuclear field. The managers of uranium enrichment and plutonium separation facilities likewise knew that they would be rewarded for exceeding their targets and punished for missing them. At the end of the Cold War, fissile material production facilities in the former

Soviet Union were in disarray, lacking adequate physical security, inventory controls, and accounting procedures.

Over the course of the next quarter-century, the United States and Russia took many steps to help former Soviet republics dismantle and store nuclear weapons and to safeguard facilities in which fissile material was stored or handled. The Nunn-Lugar Cooperative Threat Reduction Program was the single most important initiative. Its many accomplishments included securing thousands of kilograms of weapons-usable nuclear materials, assisting in the transportation of 92 trainloads of nuclear weapons to dismantlement facilities, retraining former Soviet nuclear scientists, maintaining security systems at 23 storage sites for nuclear weapons in Russia, conducting dozens of courses on nuclear security for officials of the Russian Ministry of Defense, and broadly exchanging best practices in nuclear security.[191] The list goes on and on. The concern driving these efforts was that fissile materials or nuclear weapons might fall into the hands of criminals. Nunn-Lugar was incrementally expanded to engage nations around the world in broad programs of cooperative threat reduction and security—aimed at safeguarding nuclear materials and other weapons of mass destruction, specifically including potential biological weapons.[192]

But what about fissile material? How much of it exists, where is it stored, and will it ever decay? The plain fact is the nuclear age left us with a monumental hangover of fissile material in many countries of the world, a vast quantity, which for all practical purposes will be here forever. The half-life of plutonium-239—the primary fissile isotope used in nuclear warheads—is 24,110 years, which means that half of the existing stocks will have decayed in that time period. But that is nothing next to uranium-235, which has a half-life of 703.8 million years. It is, in fact, immortal.

Even though countries go to great lengths to conceal basic nuclear facts, very good estimates of the worldwide inventory of fissile materials have been available for years. One highly respected source, the Institute for Science and International Security, estimates the global inventory of highly enriched uranium and plutonium to have reached 4,005 metric tons at the end of 2014. Of that, approximately 1,892 metric tons is suitable for use in a nuclear weapon.[193] Since it takes between 5 and 10 kilograms of fissile material to make a bomb, existing stocks would be sufficient to fuel between 378,400 and 756,800 nuclear weapons.

And so it is a very big problem, one that is compounded by the fact that this fissile material is spread among 27 nations, including the 9 states that currently possess nuclear arsenals, and 18 additional countries that exert varying degrees of control over their stocks of fissile material. But it is also a problem that has been the focus of sustained global nonproliferation efforts, perhaps beginning with President Eisenhower's "Atoms for Peace" speech in 1953 and the subsequent creation of the International Atomic Energy Agency, extending right up to and including the Nuclear Security Summits of 2010 (Washington), 2012 (Seoul), 2014 (The Hague), and 2016 (Washington). On these occasions, world leaders came together to design and impose greater nuclear-security measures on a global basis. But they did not start from scratch. They built, instead, on the foundation of an extensive global nonproliferation regime, which has grown incrementally for more than six decades.

While all reasonable people must be concerned about the security of fissile materials and nuclear weapons, a far more likely scenario might involve the theft, loss, or diversion of *radiological* materials that cannot be used in nuclear weapons. It might be a commercial device, perhaps one used in nuclear medicine, food irradiation, or mineral analysis. In several cases, thieves who did not know what they were taking have stolen radioactive devices. But while the theft of commercial radioactive sources is certainly cause for concern, it pales in comparison to the possible theft of fissile material or an actual weapon. Some commercial radiological devices could be converted into so-called "dirty bombs," by dispersing radioactive material with high explosives. Exploding such a bomb might kill dozens of persons immediately, depending on location-specific factors and the kind of conventional explosive used in the device. Persons exposed to the radiation might develop cancer years in the future, and the area in which a dirty bomb exploded might be contaminated for a very long time, depending on the quantity and nature of the radioactive source involved. But we would not think of it as catastrophic terrorism because it would likely only involve a few dozens of persons—extensive cleanup costs and psychological trauma to the contrary notwithstanding.

And there is, of course, legitimate concern that terrorists might attempt to sabotage a nuclear power plant or research reactor. This could have occurred if the 9/11 hijackers had opted to fly one of the planes into a nuclear power plant. Or it could occur during a lapse in nuclear-security culture, inside a reactor, if a disgruntled employee attempts to sabotage the facility. It is also possible that an armed group outside a reactor would undertake a suicide mission to enter and destroy the reactor core. But this scenario, while not impossible, has been evaluated ad infinitum, and the assault would have to overcome robust security measures. Even though a nuclear meltdown would be horrific, as in the cases of the Chernobyl Nuclear Power Plant in 1986 and the Fukushima Daiichi Nuclear Power Station in 2011, loss of life would not approach the levels associated with catastrophic terrorism.

Despite all the considerations described above, political leaders, the media, and unelected intelligence officials continue to summon the specter of catastrophic terrorism, no matter how slight the probability of an actual event may be. This fear mongering, invoking an unjustified and irrational fear of terrorism, does not excuse the invasiveness, the monetary costs, or the threat to liberty posed by the Security Industrial Complex. This complex is constructed to peer into the lives of ordinary people, not to defend nuclear weapons and power plants. It is a scattershot approach that seeks to gather as much information as possible on a multitude of people in order to detect persons who might engage in terrorism. It is not an approach that can secure weapons of mass destruction, much less associated materials and technologies. That would require completely different methods, and, fortunately, the world has been working at it for more than six decades. Over this time, we have gradually constructed a broad-based global nonproliferation regime.

The Global Nonproliferation Regime

An alternative and superior approach to building a Security Industrial Complex is to place weapons, materials, and technologies of mass destruction beyond the reach of sub-state actors and potential terrorists. Indeed, it is an ongoing activity that dates at least to 1925, when revulsion against the use of chemical weapons in World War I led to the adoption of the Geneva Protocol, which prohibited the use of chemical weapons in warfare. Since that time, the international community has effected literally scores of treaties, conventions, initiatives, resolutions, agreements, partnerships, codes of conduct, export controls, and other arrangements—all designed to stanch the spread of CBRN materials, technologies, and weapons. These efforts have accelerated over time. They constitute a global nonproliferation regime, which, unlike the Security Industrial Complex, has long been recognized as the best way to address the threat of catastrophic terrorism.

In the modern era, almost all states are parties to three major treaties: the Treaty on the Non-Proliferation of Nuclear Weapons (1968), the Biological Weapons Convention (1975), and the Chemical Weapons Convention (1997). Many states are also members of other broad-based control efforts such as the Missile Technology Control Regime (1987), the Wassenaar Arrangement (1996), and the Arms Trade Treaty (2014). Some of these treaties have implementing bodies such as the Organization for the Prohibition of Chemical Weapons (OPCW) and the International Atomic Energy Agency (IAEA). As we have seen, the IAEA is instrumental in monitoring the use of nuclear energy and enforcement of the Nuclear Nonproliferation Treaty. And the OPCW is so successful that it has nearly eliminated Cold War stocks of chemical weapons, and in 2013 won the Nobel Peace Prize for its efforts. In addition, government programs like Cooperative Threat Reduction in the United States and the European Stability Fund are designed to control dangerous technologies, materials, and facilities.

Formal and informal groups of states maintain lists of controlled substances and technologies such as the Australia Group, which works to ensure that chemical exports do not contribute to the development of chemical or biological weapons. There is also the Zangger Committee and the Nuclear Suppliers Group, both of which exert controls over trade in nuclear-related items. States also coordinate law-enforcement efforts, especially border controls aimed at nuclear smuggling with local, national, and regional police including Europol and Interpol. Governments undertake multilateral efforts with the intent to control dangerous materials and technologies, including four Nuclear Security Summits (2010, 2012, 2014, and 2016) and the ongoing G-7 Global Partnership Against the Spread of Weapons and Materials of Mass Destruction (GP). The GP, which is a G-7 working group, has contributed over $20 billion in nonproliferation funding initiatives over the past 10 years.

International governmental organizations such as the UN Office of Disarmament Affairs and the UN International Crime and Justice Research Institute coordinate elements of the overall nonproliferation regime on a global basis. Multiple international legal instruments and UN resolutions contribute to breaking the link between weapons of mass destruction and terrorism. The most important is UN Security Council Resolution 1540 (2003), which legally binds all state parties to prevent weapons and materials of mass destruction from falling into the hands of non-state actors. And the EU continues to support a network of CBRN security centers focused on controlling weapons and materials of mass destruction.

Many international non-government organizations work against proliferation, such as the Center for International Trade and Security at the University of Georgia, the Stockholm International Peace Research Institute in Sweden, and the Japan Institute of International Affairs. Finally, the U.S. departments of Defense, State, and Energy, among others, have sophisticated strategies for countering weapons of mass destruction. Taken together, these entities and their corresponding international and national legal architectures have formed a bulwark against the spread of weapons, materials, and technologies of mass destruction.

FIGURE III.5 (below) provides a skeletal depiction of the interlocking set of treaties, resolutions, agreements, and organizations that form the backbone of the international nonproliferation regime. It is also a timeline of both the coming into force of the various legal/treaty instruments, as well as the dispersion of weapons technology. The global regime to prevent proliferation is far from perfect. It is criticized because it cannot control all proscribed items, ensuring that they move though global trade to legitimate end users, and do not fall into the hands of criminals. In many developing areas of the world, borders are porous, and all kinds of illegal international commerce is transacted.

Moreover, the regime has not stopped the spread of nuclear technology and weapons to India, Israel, North Korea, and

THE GLOBAL NONPROLIFERATION REGIME
(WEAPONS AQUISITION 1944-2015)

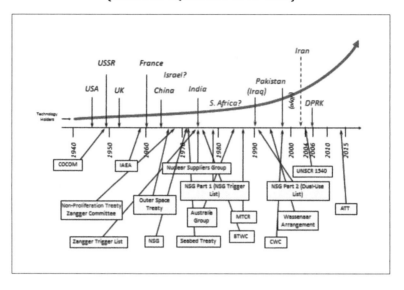

Pakistan. But these states, excluding North Korea, never joined the Nuclear Nonproliferation Treaty, and their acquisition of nuclear technology and weapons is directly attributable to what I have elsewhere called the "paradox of proliferation."[194] The paradox is that the global spread of scientific knowledge and industrial capacity encompasses both the promise of development and the threat of annihilation. Nuclear, chemical, biological, digital, genetic, and other technologies that lead to wealth and a higher standard of living also provide the building blocks for the most pernicious weapons. It is, however, in the nature of paradoxes to operate at high levels of abstraction. Just because many countries of the world could develop nuclear, biological, chemical, genetic, or other massively malevolent weapons does not mean they have the political motive or will to do so. It is a testimony to this fact that even though chemical weapons were widely used during the

First World War, they remained banned and vanquished throughout the Second World War. It must be acknowledged, however, that the conglomerate I.G. Farben and other German companies manufactured the poison gas Zyklon B, a cyanide-based pesticide, which was used by the Nazi regime during the Holocaust to murder approximately a million people, primarily at Auschwitz, but at other concentration camps as well.

Nuclear weapons have spread far more slowly than many pundits and politicians predicted. In a press conference in 1963, President John F. Kennedy famously warned, "I am haunted by the feeling that by 1970, unless we are successful, there may be ten nuclear powers instead of four, and by 1975, fifteen or twenty."[195] Fifty years later, only five additional states possess nuclear weapons, although many more are capable of fabricating them, and states including South Africa, Argentina, and Brazil have either unilaterally dismantled their weapons or have voluntarily terminated their weapons programs. Of all the former Soviet Socialist Republics, only Russia retains a nuclear arsenal. Moreover, all states have committed to the complete elimination and future prohibition of both chemical and biological weapons, the transgressions of Syria's degenerate Assad regime in 2013–16 to the contrary notwithstanding. This is, in essence, testimony to the success of the nonproliferation regime. Such is the category of catastrophic or existential terrorism.

But the plain fact is that most internal security and counterterror efforts are not aimed at controlling materials, technologies, and weapons of mass destruction, or even catastrophic terror. This would be a more logical and rational approach than what has occurred. It would mean securing those operations that involve highly dangerous materials and technologies such as nuclear power reactors, BSL-3 and BSL-4 biocontainment laboratories, and certain chemical production, storage, and transpiration facilities.

Instead, the intelligence agencies and the political leadership act as though all terrorist events are equal. The prevailing attitude is that every instance of terror must be addressed preemptively and contained before the fact of its occurrence. It is clearly an impossible task and will remain so until we are able to predict the future with certainly.

The effort to address all terror has nevertheless led to economy-wide irrational surveillance that seeks to sweep up all digital information. And it is happening even when it is crystal clear that metadata surveillance programs do not predict terrorist activities and have not prevented terrorist events. They have only compromised the privacy of persons in formerly liberal democracies and placed information into the hands of largely unaccountable secret government organizations, where it is subject to abuse by officials whose activities are shielded from public view.

CHAPTER V

///////////////////////

EPISODIC TERROR

Avoiding catastrophic terror must of course be the number one goal of internal security. Even a single instance could produce profound changes in the society, the economy, and the governance of a nation. Securing dangerous facilities is a manageable task that does not entail loss of liberty associated with economy-wide surveillance of the populous. It is only necessary to designate and secure all facilities where dangerous chemical, biological, radiological, or nuclear (CBRN) materials are produced, stored, or in transit. These must be subject to the most strict and unrelenting security protocols. And it is a feasible job. Indeed, security for CBRN facilities is already in place, although occasional mistakes are made.

In 2015, for instance, the Department of Defense unwittingly sent live anthrax spoors to 52 labs in 18 states, Washington, D.C., and three foreign countries—Australia, Canada, and South Korea.[181] The spores had been irradiated and were presumed to be dead. But a few survived in each sample and weeks later began to propagate. The incident received a great deal of attention, likely because it is the exception that proves the rule. There have been, in fact, only one or two incidents of CBRN terror attempted by non-state organizations. And they were not successful.

But there is another category, that of limited or *episodic terror,* which is often coextensive with violent crime—especially bombings, arson, kidnapping, and murder, which are most appropriately dealt with by local police in a court of law. Indeed, most bombings in the United States prior to the events of 9/11 were treated as crime, not terrorism. But that was prior to the vast expansion and ascendance of the surveillance security state. It was a common phenomenon, with 45,573 actual and attempted bombings in the United States from 1973 through 1999, resulting in 840 fatalities and 6,779 injuries.[197] These incidents were not thought to be terrorism or designated as such by the Federal Bureau of Investigation.

With the onset of Secure Democracy, however, terrorism is conceived of in very different terms. All "terror" plots must be broken up in advance, or else it is an intelligence failure. The intelligence agencies and allied companies are, accordingly, even attempting to develop predictive biometric tools. The Intelligence Advanced Research Projects Agency, or IARPA, is now attempting to develop biometric technologies that sort through millions of stored images in real time. The idea is to identify terrorists before they are able to explode a bomb or become active shooters. In this view, the Security Industrial Complex is only as successful as it is proactive, locating the terror cell or identifying the perpetrator(s) in advance of the event. But we know this is not possible because of the episodic character of most terrorist actions.

It is therefore important to disaggregate the kinds of events that are construed as terrorism today. **TABLE V.1** is a typology of limited *episodic terror* (as opposed to *catastrophic terror*), which presents various different classes of terrorism and corresponding cases. The table is not intended to be comprehensive, and some incidents will fit more than one class of events:

TABLE V.1:

CLASSES OF LIMITED EPISODIC TERROR

1. Viable terrorist plots that are prevented
   - 2011 Spokane, WA parade bomber

2. Bombs that fail to explode
   - 2002 shoe bomber
   - 2009 underwear bomber
   - 2010 Times Square bomber

3. "Lone wolf" single-point security failures
   - 1978–93 Unabomber
   - 2009 Fort Hood shooter
   - 2012 Sandy Hook shooter

4. Two- or three-person ("wolf pack") attacks that succeed
   - 2002 Beltway sniper attacks
   - 2013 Boston Marathon bombers
   - 2015 San Bernardino shootings

5. Attacks perpetrated by organized groups
   - 1992–present Earth Liberation Front (50 attacks)
   - 1976–present Animal Liberation Front (34 attacks)
   - 1982–present Army of God (dozens of attacks)

6. Counterfactual conspiracies
   - 2001 West Coast Airliner Plot
   - 2014 Khorasan Group Plot
   - 2011 plot to kill the Saudi Ambassador to the United States

7. "Conspiracies" inspired by government
   - 2006 Sears Tower plot
   - 2010 Mosque infiltration in Irvine, CA (Craig Monteilh)
   - 2009 Newburgh Four

These examples of limited *episodic terror* are presented to demonstrate the concept of proportionality in relationship to *catastrophic terror* events. We should note at the outset that the concept of proportionality is lost on the guardians of internal security, and especially in the United States, where the Security Industrial Complex is constantly on hair-trigger alert. They attempt to detect the next episodic terror event in advance, or to stimulate one in the field, and overreact when one does occur. Here internal security becomes pathological or succumbs to irrationality because all potential terrorism is treated as though it resides on a catastrophic or existential plane. For that reason, every instance of terror must be prevented at all costs; and the costs are enormous, both in terms of the budgets needed and the diminution of human freedom associated with Secure Democracy.

Seven distinct kinds of episodic terror events are shown in Table V.1, but they share a common element; they operate on a relatively small scale that does not begin to approach the numbers associated with murder, armed robbery, and a variety of other serious crimes. There were, for example, 14,224 murders in the United States in 2008, 13,164 in 2010, and 12,765 in 2012.[198] These figures dwarf the numbers of fatalities attributed to episodic terror and shown in figures III.1 and III.3. Episodic terror is not unlike murder or arson; and nations, while not tolerating terrorism, have always had to deal with it—just as they have had to deal with other forms of violent crime. It makes sense then to disaggregate the various kinds of terror, and to present a few cases to demonstrate their similarities and differences. In this way we can clearly see the disconnect between the minute number of terrorist events and the magnitude of the response.

One class of episodic terror events is *viable terrorist plots that are prevented* because they are discovered at the last minute. These are very rare, but on January 17, 2011, three parade workers spotted a pipe bomb along the Martin Luther King Jr. parade route in Spokane, Washington. They noticed a Swiss Army backpack with wires visibly protruding from it. A spokesperson of the Federal Bureau of Investigation said that if the bomb had been remotely detonated, as planned, it would have sprayed parade marchers with shrapnel. It also contained an anticoagulant rat poison, which was intended to prevent wounds from clotting. The bomb was defused, and one Kevin William Harpham was charged with multiple crimes, convicted in a court of law, and sentenced to 32 years in prison. Several press reports alleged that the attempt was racially motivated and that Harpham had ties to a white supremacist group, the National Alliance, but the group denied any association.[199] That same year, there were over 300 other hate crimes in the United States, most of which were not labeled as terrorism.[200]

A somewhat different kind of episodic event involves terrorists who attempt to detonate *bombs that fail to explode*: The 2001 shoe bomber, the 2009 underwear bomber, and the 2010 Times Square bomber are recent examples. In the first, Richard Reid attempted to blow up a flight while over the Atlantic with a bomb concealed in his shoe. He was apparently unable to ignite the explosive and was subdued by the crew and passengers. Reid, an unrepentant, self-proclaimed al Qaeda operative, told Judge William G. Young of the Federal District Court, "I am at war with your country. I further admit my allegiance to Sheik Osama bin Laden, to Islam and to the religion of Allah."[201] He was sentenced to three consecutive life sentences in federal prison.

On December 25, 2009, Umar Farouk Abdulmatallab attempted to explode a bomb concealed in his underwear on a flight from Amsterdam to Detroit. The bomb failed to detonate and his underwear caught fire. Abdulmutallab was reportedly inspired by the fiery sermons of Anwar Al-Awlaki, an American citizen who was targeted and killed in Yemen by an attack drone operated by the Central Intelligence Agency. Abdulmutallab unexpectedly pleaded guilty and was sentenced to life in prison on February 16, 2012.[202]

In a final case of this type, Faisal Shahzad attempted to detonate a car bomb in Times Square in New York City on May 1, 2010. Two street vendors noticed smoke coming from the car and called the police, who disarmed the device. Shahzad, a naturalized citizen of the United States, was arrested as he attempted to board a plane bound for Dubai. He is believed to have traveled into Pakistan's remote Federally Administered Tribal Areas for training in explosives in 2009. He stated he was motivated by the large number of drone strikes the United States had launched against Pakistan.[203] Can we assume that Harpham, Reid, and Abdulmatallab acted alone, incubating their ideas, choosing their attack venues, assembling their explosive devices, and committing their crimes? Probably not, although Harpham may have acted alone.

Another class of episodic terrorist events is the *"lone wolf" single-point security failure*—the school shooter and the long-range sniper. This kind of episodic terror poses considerable challenges because it involves a security failure that is almost impossible to detect until after the fact. A fictitious example would be one in which a Secret Service agent turned a gun on a president or another protected person without warning or any previous indication. There is no defense against this kind of attack short of profiling hundreds of thousands of individuals and developing software that can identify likely perpetrators before they act. This too is a very tall order, intrusive, expensive, and probably not possible.

Examples of the *"lone wolf"* phenomenon abound: the Sandy Hook school shooter, the Unabomber, and the Fort Hood assassin among many others. On December 12, 2012, Adam Lanza drove to the Sandy Hook Elementary School in Newtown, Connecticut, and opened fire, killing six staff members and 20 children at the school. Before heading for the school he also apparently killed his mother, who worked there, and after the school shootings he took his own life.[204] He was clearly a criminally insane psychopath capable of inflicting terror and devastation on a limited scale.

In a different and far more sophisticated example of lone-wolf activity, Ted Kaczynski, also known as the Unabomber, sent letter bombs to persons often located at universities or airlines involved in different aspects of technology and business. He killed 3 persons and wounded 23 others over 15 years between 1978 and 1993. Kaczynski was admitted to Harvard University at age 16, earned a Ph.D. in mathematics at the University of Michigan, and was hired as an assistant professor at Berkeley at the age of 25. Subsequently, he became a survivalist and recluse, assembling his letter bombs from a cabin in Lincoln, Montana. A relative who recognized his ranting finally identified him, after *The New York Times* and *The Washington Post* published an excerpt from his 35,000-word manifesto, "Industrial Science and Its Future."[205]

A final lone-wolf example of an episodic terror event occurred on November 5, 2009, when U.S. Army major and psychiatrist Nidal Malik Hasan fatally shot 13 people and wounded more than 30 at the Fort Hood military base in Texas, to which he was assigned. U.S. Senator Joe Lieberman, General Barry McCaffrey, and others labeled the event a terrorist attack, although the Department of Defense classified it as an act of workplace violence. Hassan appears to have had no motive and may have been suffering from a stress disorder.[206] Alternatively, he may have been influenced by religion or by radical ideology when surfing the Internet. According to the prosecutor at his trial, he "searched the Internet for information about the Taliban and shouted 'Allahu akbar' or 'God is great' in Arabic before opening fire."[207] But no direct connection to a co-conspirator or terrorist group surfaced. He was found guilty of 13 counts of premeditated murder and 32 counts of attempted premeditated murder and sentenced to death on August 28, 2013.[208] The incidence of lone-wolf attacks appeared to accelerate in the mid-2010s, with several such events occurring in 2016. These prompted two veteran reporters at *The New York Times* to question whether the perpetrators were in fact "terrorists" or simply "deranged" persons. "The age of the Islamic State," they wrote, "in which the tools of terrorism appear increasingly crude and haphazard, has led to a reimagining of the common notion of who is and who is not a terrorist."[209]

A fourth class of limited episodic terror involves *two- or three-person attacks that succeed*. Two events, separated by eleven years, come immediately to mind: the 2002 Beltway sniper attacks and the 2013 Boston Marathon bombing. Over the course of three weeks in October 2002, John Allen Muhammed and Lee Boyd Malvo terrorized the Washington metropolitan area by shooting 13 persons at long range, killing 10 and seriously wounding 3. Prior to the Beltway sniper attacks, the two conducted a crime spree spanning seven states, killing six people and wounding six others, reminiscent of several scenes from an Elmore Leonard crime novel. The killings catalyzed one of the largest manhunts in history. Muhammed "began leaving threats: 'Your children are not safe, anywhere, at any time.' Parents panicked; schools closed."[210]

At the trial, the prosecution characterized the attacks as part of an Islamic jihad against the United States. Others have dismissed this motive, saying it was based on rants and writings Muhammed made after his arrest. These outbursts featured individuals such as Osama bin Laden, Saddam Hussein, and characters from a science fiction movie, *The Matrix*. Another hypothesis is that Muhammed was unhinged, killing his estranged wife in order to gain custody of their children. By making hers just one death in a random series of murders, the motive would be less obvious. Muhammed was sentenced to death and executed on November 10, 2009. Malvo was sentenced to six consecutive life sentences without the possibility of parole. It is true that many people felt terrorized by Muhammed and Malvo, that some parents kept their children at home, and that local, state, and federal police conducted a massive manhunt. But these events pale in comparison to the police response in Boston.

Another example of the *two- or three-person attacks that succeed* category is the 2013 bombing at the Boston Marathon. Chechen brothers Dzhokhar and Tamerlan Tsarnaev set off bombs at the marathon's finish line, killing three persons and injuring some 264 others. Tamerlan was shot several times in an exchange of gunfire with the police and was subsequently run over by his brother, who was attempting to escape in a stolen car. He was pronounced dead at the scene.[211] In short order, the police locked down the Boston metropolitan area, confining more than a million people to their homes. Four days after the bombing, thousands of police and other government agents converged on the neighboring municipality of Watertown. Dzhokhar Tsarnaev was holed up in a boat in a suburban backyard. The authorities conducted door-to-door searches, occupying several homes in the process. When the police discovered Tsarnaev—who was wounded and unarmed—they began discharging their guns in a disorderly fashion, strafing houses and other structures in the area with automatic-weapons fire.[212] This shocking police activity, which was entirely unnecessary to apprehend a single unarmed man, seemed to have been acceptable to most people at the time.

Political authorities, the police, local and national intelligence agencies, the Department of Homeland Security, state and local counterterrorism, and SWAT units—in sum a local manifestation of the Security Industrial Complex—delivered a disproportionate and arguably pathological response. One of America's oldest and largest cities was on "lockdown." What would John Adams or Thomas Jefferson have thought as "SWAT teams moved block-by-block, knocking on doors and asking people if they had seen anything suspicious"?[213] They would have been hard-pressed to recognize the Republic they had helped to fashion.

The media pelted Boston and the world with one news report after another regarding every aspect of the bombings; it was prurient, the manhunt and the trial for months on end. The media coverage became almost intolerable to ordinary citizens. While the loss of life and pain and suffering inflicted on the victims in Boston is deplorable, its scale was small compared to the hundreds of bombings in Iraq, the Bali bombings, the London and Madrid subway bombings, the missile attack on Malaysia Airlines Flight 17 over Ukraine, and the Dubrovka theater and Beslan school massacres, among others. Moreover, it garnered significantly more media attention than most of these events. We can also compare the Boston bombing to other events that received little attention in the national and international media, for example, the 523 juvenile gang killings that took place in the United States in 2011[214] and the 32,367 traffic fatalities that same year.[215] But then there is no ideological component to the crime of murder or to carnage on the highways compared to the security breach of a successful terrorist attack on the homeland.

A final example of *two- or three-person ("wolf pack") attacks that succeed* occurred in December 2015 in San Bernardino, California, where a husband-and-wife team engaged in an active shooter event. Using semiautomatic weapons and donning tactical gear, Syed Rizwan Farook and Tashfeen Malik attacked the holiday party of the county health department where Farook worked as a health inspector. They fired some 150 bullets, leaving 14 dead and 21 wounded. The crime immediately attracted round-the-clock media coverage, no doubt amplified because it followed closely on attacks in Paris, staged by adherents to the Islamic State, in which

118 persons were killed. There was intense speculation by authorities and in the media as to the motive or "inspiration" for the San Bernardino attack. Approximately 300 law-enforcement officers from local, county, state, and federal agencies initially responded to the shootings.[216]

The couple had assembled a small arsenal in their home but appeared to neighbors to be typical suburbanites. Immediately preceding the attack, they dropped their 6-month-old child at a grandmother's house. Because the attack took place at the Inland Regional Center, where Farook worked, it initially appeared to be an act of workplace violence. But possibly because the perpetrators were Muslims, the authorities looked for a connection to radical Islamist militant organizations. The woman was a Pakistani national who grew up in Saudi Arabia and had attended the Al-Huda Institute in Multan, a women-only, fundamentalist Muslim school where she studied pharmacology.

About a week following the attack, Facebook revealed that Malik had posted a pledge of support for the Islamic State group. This was big news. The Federal Bureau of Investigation declared it could no longer rule out "terrorism" as the motive and would pursue the investigation on that basis, even though no direct connection to any terrorist organization had yet emerged. The new theory was that the couple might have been "inspired" or "self-radicalized" by militant Islamist ideology, possibly over the Internet.

But of course, the attack *was* terrorism from the outset, even if the authorities initially failed to use that term. Anytime anyone randomly murders people in a public place, that's terrorism. It would have been terrorism even if the perpetrators were insane and did not understand the implications of their actions, just as it would be terror if they were "inspired" by radical Islamic propaganda or had been trained and directed as part of a cell. But when the Federal Bureau of Investigation announced that the incident would be treated as "an act of terror," it stimulated the media feeding frenzy. If we make a distinction between "terrorism" on one side and "active shooter" incidents that are not terrorism on the other, there are significant consequences. And this is exactly what the authorities did.

Because it was labeled an act of "terrorism," the event was immediately politicized. Republican Party presidential candidates used it to stake out "tough on terrorism" positions. Candidate Ted Cruz took the opportunity to attack President Barack Obama and the Democratic presidential front-runner, Hillary Clinton. He said, "America is at war [with] . . . radical Islamic terrorism. We have a president who is unwilling to utter its name. The men and women on this stage, every one of us, is better prepared to keep this nation safe than is Barack Obama or Hillary Clinton." Another presidential hopeful, Chris Christie, engaged in fear mongering. He said, ". . . if a center for the developmentally disabled in San Bernardino, California, is now a target for terrorists, that means everywhere in America is a target for these terrorists." During this Republican presidential debate, the words "terror," "terrorism," and "terrorist" were used 75 times.[217]

The Federal Bureau of Investigation also attempted to gain political advantage in the week following the San Bernardino attack. Over the past two years, its director, James Comey, had argued that advanced encryption on smart phones and software applications was making the Internet "go dark," essentially putting text messages and emails beyond the reach of law-enforcement and intelligence agencies. He argued for a "back door" to all communications, a way for government to open them—ostensibly to prevent terrorist attacks. But the Obama administration rejected that position, siding with encryption experts, Internet companies, and privacy advocates. In the wake of the San Bernardino attack, and in the media haze surrounding it, Comey renewed his efforts, telling the Senate Judiciary Committee that shooters in Garland, Texas, had "exchanged 109 messages with an overseas terrorist" the morning of that attack, although he declined to comment on the San Bernardino events.[218]

Clearly, unethical politicians attempted to use the San Bernardino attacks to gain political advantage. They asserted their opponents were "soft on terrorism" or had somehow invited the attacks because they failed to design an effective military strategy to attack and defeat foreign terrorist organizations. As a result, opposition politicians and elected officials called for a tougher foreign policy, for example, incursions by Special Forces, intensified bombing campaigns in Iraq and Syria, and an investment of $3 billion to expand the drone program.[219] Throughout 2015 and 2016, a series of mass shootings in Europe and the United States again elevated terror and counterterrorism to the front burner of European and American politics. While the likelihood of a person being the victim of a terrorist attack remained minute, politicians and the intelligence agencies under the thrall of Secure Democracy continued to instill irrational fear into the hearts and minds of ordinary citizens.

The attacks in Paris in January (*Charlie Hebdo*) and November (coordinated bombings and mass shootings) as well as in San Bernardino and then Orlando shed additional light on the terror-counterterror-terror dynamic. Is it possible that these attacks were a result, perhaps an unintended consequence, of French and American counterterrorism activities launched against the Islamic State group in the Middle East? Did the Islamic State plot or encourage terrorist actions in response to intensified military bombardments from the West? Islamic State leaders discovered that cutting off the heads of journalists and other forms of barbarity would terrify people throughout the world. They manipulated the press to carry their message. While al Qaeda sought to spread terror through high-profile attacks and mass casualties, the Islamic State found that terror could be generated locally, on a small scale, and then amplified over social media and disseminated globally. Would the West have to obliterate the Islamic State completely, and if that proved to be difficult, would the Islamic State intensify efforts to recruit fighters from the West or designate more targets for its adherents? It would appear to be a drawn-out cycle of terror and counterterror, with increasing violence on all sides. And important to our discussion, the cycle would likely result in yet more resources dedicated to counterterrorism in the name of internal security—with Secure Democracy continuing to expand at the expense of liberty in the 21st century.

A fifth kind of episodic terrorism involves *attacks perpetrated by organized groups.* Al Qaeda and the Islamic State come immediately to mind, no doubt because of the scale of 9/11 and broad media coverage of extreme brutality carried out by the Islamic State. By far the greatest numbers of terrorist events, however, fall into the category of white hate crime, of which the Ku Klux Klan is the most notorious perpetrator.

The Klan was founded after the American Civil War in 1866. Chapters sprang up in every Southern state and soon spread to the north and west. In 1871, the U.S. Congress passed the Third Force Act, also known as the Ku Klux Klan Act, making hate crimes federal offenses. But it was not until 1918 that a spike in Klan activity engaged the Bureau of Investigation, as the FBI was then called. In that year, the bureau opened investigations of the Klan and other white supremacist groups. In more recent times, the Ku Klux Klan and fellow-traveler white supremacist groups became increasingly active during the civil-rights movement in the 1960s, prompting the FBI to launch the White Hate Groups Cointelpro.

It is not possible to determine the number of white supremacist terror attacks over the past century and a half, but it must be in the tens of thousands. Under the Hate Crime Statistics Act, the federal government compiles statistics on hate crimes. In the most recent accounting, "law enforcement agencies reported 5,479 hate crime incidents involving 6,418 offenses to our Uniform Crime Reporting Program in 2014. And these crimes—which often have a devastating impact on the communities where they occur—left 6,727 victims in their wake."[220] The Southern Poverty Law Center estimates that there are today between 5,000 and 8,000 Klan members, split among various different affiliated organizations.[221] But hate crimes are typically not reported as terrorist events by law enforcement or the media. This underscores the ambiguity of the word "terrorism" because these crimes have frequently involved beatings, lynching, shootings, and other forms of violence and murder; and they are carried out by secret organizations.

Apart from the white supremacist groups, the Earth Liberation Front (ELF) and the Animal Liberation Front (ALF) account for the vast majority of terrorist attacks perpetrated by organized groups in the United States. The Animal Liberation Front is an international movement without leaders that takes illegal actions in pursuit of animal rights. Much like the Earth Liberation Front, it focuses on vandalism or arson, inflicting economic damage while refraining from violence against animals and humans. According to a Department of Homeland Security–funded research group at the University of Maryland, "Between 1995 and 2010, there were a total of 239 arsons and bombings committed by animal rights or environmental rights extremists."[222] In describing the prevalence of eco-terrorism, former FBI Director Robert Mueller "cited the pursuit of environmental and animal rights-related criminal perpetrators as among the agency's 'highest domestic terrorism priorities.'"[223]

The Earth Liberation Front is often intermingled with the Animal Liberation Front. Both ELF and ALF have no discernable hierarchal structure and comprise autonomous groups and individuals acting on their own. For this reason, it is extremely difficult to anticipate or infiltrate their activities. The ALF website describes a typical action in which a person discovers an animal-trapping operation and removes and destroys the traps so that animals will not be hurt. In this scenario, any individual can initiate an ALF or ELF action, and because there is no chain of command, the action can rarely be traced back to the group.

The Earth Liberation Front has nevertheless claimed responsibility for serious crimes, including burning down Bureau of Land Management horse corrals and attacking the U.S. Forest Industries headquarters in Oregon in the late 1990s. The Animal Liberation Front also claims credit for those attacks. A group known as "The Family" has been associated with ELF and ALF and is thought to have engaged in Operation Backfire, which caused $26 million in damage at a ski resort in Vail, Colorado.[224] In 2001, ELF released a techniques manual, as well as a list of possible targets.[225] According to its website, ALF "carries out illegal actions against industries who profit from animal exploitation."[226] The group has frequently vandalized vehicles, especially sports utility vehicles and Hummers.

A final example of *attacks perpetrated by organized groups*— those of the "Army of God"—clearly overlaps with other kinds of episodic terrorism, including the *lone wolf* and *wolf pack* classifications. On November 27, 2015, for example, lone shooter and Christian militant, Robert Lewis Dear, Jr. attacked a Planned Parenthood Clinic in Colorado Springs. He killed three people, including a police officer, and wounded nine others.[227] A photograph of him is prominently displayed on the Army of God website with the caption, "Honoring heroes who stood up for the unborn."[228] His crime has not been widely interpreted as an act of terrorism, perhaps due to the political struggle surrounding the issue of abortion. In a bizarre twist, Senator Ted Cruz of Texas—who was campaigning for the Republication presidential nomination—suggested that Dear might be "a transgendered leftist activist."[229] It is likely that Cruz, a staunch opponent of abortion, sought to minimize this heinous and terroristic crime for political reasons. Indeed, it would appear that many in law enforcement and the media have accepted the idea that the subjective term "terrorism" should only be coupled with the government's "war on terrorism." But as I have stated elsewhere, all terrorism is a criminal act and most serious crimes involve elements of terror.

The Army of God has perpetrated anti-abortion violence since at least 1982, including kidnappings, arson, and murder. In that year, three men who identified themselves as "the Army of God" kidnapped Hector Zevallos, a doctor who performed abortions, and his wife. They were held for eight days but were released without apparent physical harm.[230] Since then, various individuals and factions, identified as adherents or members of the Army of God, have engaged in violent activity against reproductive health facilities, specifically targeting Planned Parenthood and other organizations that facilitate women's access to abortion. According to a review in *Perspectives on Terrorism,* members of the organization have "taken numerous lives, destroyed health care facilities, and threatened the safety and freedom of both those accessing and those providing reproductive healthcare."[231] The National Abortion Federation, which publishes detailed statistics of attacks on women's health facilities, characterizes the Army of God as "an underground network of domestic terrorists who believe that the use of violence is appropriate and acceptable as a means to end abortion."[232] Indeed, the Army of God has published a manual that provides step-by-step instructions on how to manufacture C-4, a powerful plastic explosive.[233]

Counterfactual and Government-Inspired Terror

Another distinct type of episodic terror listed in Table V.1 is *counterfactual conspiracies.* This includes terrorist events that did *not* occur because counterterror agents or the military took actions to thwart them. It is argued that if the United States and coalition forces had not destroyed many of the leaders and rank and file of al Qaeda at Tora Bora—including subsequent targeting by Special Forces and drone strikes against known terrorists in Afghanistan, Iraq, Pakistan, Syria, and Yemen—the list of terrorist events might look far more robust than it looks today.

Following 9/11, law enforcement adopted a new approach to certain aspects of crime fighting. Instead of waiting for terrorism-related crimes to occur, and then tracking down the perpetrators, the emphasis turned to discovering the conspiracy or intention to commit the crime before it occurred—what might be called proactive or preventive crime fighting. This of course entails close surveillance of persons and groups who might be more likely than most to commit a crime. The idea is to infiltrate the suspected conspiracy, and then foil the plot before it can be brought to fruition. While this technique is used in breaking up criminal syndicates and has been employed in the past by intelligence agencies, it has only in recent years been widely accepted as a counterterror instrument.

While this perspective cannot be dismissed, it is inherently problematic because it involves predicting the future. It is as though internal security successes are generated in an alternative reality, one that must be kept secret to protect sources and methods and ongoing sensitive operations. It cannot, accordingly, be held up to public scrutiny. These "successes" nevertheless carry considerable weight because they may in fact have averted actual attacks, although there are few, if any, instances where this can be shown with certainty. Moreover, counterfactual conspiracies are used to garner political support for the Security Industrial Complex. They lend legitimacy to counterterror policies, and to the intelligence officials and politicians associated with them. Even though the events in question do not come to fruition, it is nevertheless argued that stopping them is a critical element in defeating terrorism. But when they are divulged to the public, the context can be so political that it is difficult to assess the validity of the claim.

On February 9, 2006, for example, the White House released a list of 10 foiled terrorist plots, several of which it said would have occurred in the United States. One of the listed conspiracies, the "West Coast Airliner Plot," was allegedly planned by Khalid Shaikh Mohammed, the architect of the 9/11 catastrophe, who was tortured and waterboarded 183 times by the Central Intelligence Agency[234] and then imprisoned indefinitely at the U.S. detention facility at Guantánamo Bay in Cuba.[235] In a speech to the National Guard in Washington, President George W. Bush described the foiled plot:

> We now know that in October 2001, Khalid Shaykh Muhammad—
> the mastermind of the September the 11th attacks—had already
> set in motion a plan to have terrorist operatives hijack an airplane
> using shoe bombs to breach the cockpit door, and fly the plane into
> the tallest building on the West Coast. We believe the intended
> target was Liberty [sic] Tower in Los Angeles, California.[236]

Of course, the president meant the Library Tower in Los Angeles. Whether or not a "shoe bomb" could be used in this manner without depressurizing the cabin or otherwise disabling an aircraft is uncertain and a question for the experts. But even more interesting was the explanation given in a teleconference press briefing the same day by Frances Townsend, assistant to the president for homeland security and counterterrorism. She was asked repeatedly about the timing of the release of such sensitive information, coming as it did five years after the plot had been disrupted, and fast on the heels of media criticism of the National Security Agency for spying on Americans. She refused to answer whether or not information gleaned by the agency had in any way been "instrumental" in breaking up the West Coast Airliner Plot.

Even though the president had very publicly announced the alleged conspiracy, Townsend was unable to provide any substantive details. Her press briefing was obtuse and obscure. She said, "I thought I'd start with a general statement and then go to the West Coast plot. . . . We are facing a global terrorist network and that requires a global alliance to combat it." But when she was asked about the actual conspiracy, she did not provide specifics. Was there a connection to the would-be shoe bomber Richard Reid? Townsend answered, "It was clearly the same technique that they were intending to use, the shoe bomb. More than that, we don't have the intelligence to tell us whether the cells—that is, Richard Reid and this cell—knew each other or had contact with one another. We just don't know that." She observed that the plotters had sworn *biat*, an oath, to Osama bin Laden in Afghanistan in 2001 or possibly 2002, when U.S. troops were there. But Townsend did not know where the four plotters were arrested and was not permitted to release their names. Moreover, she said they did not have intelligence as to the specific flight or the airport the plotters intended to use or even if the Library Tower was definitely the intended target. It was, Townsend said, ". . . an analytic judgment by the intelligence community . . ." because they thought the intended target was the tallest building on the West Coast.[237]

Very little was clarified by the president's statement, the release of the list of 10 alleged plots, or the subsequent press briefing that day. Several reporters appeared to make a connection between the release of the information and recent disclosures that the National Security Agency had conducted warrantless surveillance on Americans. Indeed, it looked like the president and his advisors sought to deflect attention from the internal surveillance activities that were exposed in a series of articles beginning in December 2005.[238] The president even made a visit to the National Security Agency to defend the surveillance programs two weeks before announcing the West Coast Airliner Plot.[239] Using a secret executive order in 2001, President Bush had granted unprecedented authority to the intelligence agencies to conduct warrantless surveillance of millions of Americans.[240] According to the Electronic Frontier Foundation, a technician and "whistleblower" from AT&T provided the foundation with documentary evidence that the company had "installed a fiberoptic splitter at its facility . . . in San Francisco that makes copies of all emails, web browsing, and other Internet traffic to and from AT&T customers and provides those copies to the NSA."[241] It would seem that the government wanted to demonstrate the necessity of the illegal surveillance and the president was ready to play ball. As one former National Security Agency official put it:

> The advent of the September 11 attacks brought a complete change in the approach of the NSA toward doing its job. [The] Foreign Intelligence Surveillance Act ceased to be an operative concern, and the individual liberties preserved in the U.S. Constitution were no longer a consideration. It was at that time that the NSA began to implement the group of intelligence activities now known as the President's Surveillance Program.[242]

Another clear instance of *counterfactual conspiracy* was brought to light by President Obama, who spoke to the American people concerning the decision to expand his bombing campaign against the Islamic State fighters in Iraq to Syria. The president explained he had assembled a broad coalition in support of the air strikes, including America's allies and several states in the Persian Gulf region. But in making his announcement, he added:

Last night, we also took strikes to disrupt plotting against the
United States and our allies by seasoned al Qaeda operatives in
Syria who are known as the Khorasan Group. And once again, it
must be clear to anyone who would plot against America and try
to do Americans harm that we will not tolerate safe havens for
terrorists who threaten our people.[243]

The Khorasan Group was unknown to most intelligence analysts,
academics, reporters, and of course the American public. It was
variously characterized as both an "imminent threat" and "aspir-
ing" by commentators and intelligence officials. Director of National
Intelligence James Clapper said, "[I]n terms of threat to the homeland, Khorasan may pose as much of a danger as the Islamic
State."[244] This is an interesting statement because to that point, there
was no evidence of Islamic State activity in the United States, even
though many politicians and intelligence officials spoke about it in
ringing tones. Another "senior American official," who remained
anonymous because he was speaking unofficially, "described the
Khorasan plotting as 'aspirational' and said that there did not yet
seem to be a concrete plan in the works."[245]

Several reports suggested that the group consisted of one to
two dozen fighters, led by the infamous terrorist Muhsin al-Fadhli,
a onetime close associate of Osama bin Laden with a $7 million
bounty on his head. Al Qaeda leader Ayman al-Zawahiri reportedly sent the Khorasan fighters to Syria from Pakistan. They were
different from the Islamic State fighters, who wanted to take territory and establish a caliphate. Their mission, it was said, was to
train and equip radicalized American and European citizens to
commit acts of terror when they returned to their countries of
origin.[246] Is this fact or fantasy? There was some speculation that
the name Khorasan—which is a reference to an historic region of
Muslim conquest that lies generally in the territory of modern-day

Afghanistan, Pakistan, Iran, and Turkmenistan—was assigned to the group by intelligence officials.

It was not immediately clear if the U.S. military assault had killed al-Fadhli or not. Nor was it clear that the plot, possibly against airliners, would take place in Europe or if it was to take place in the United States. No conclusive evidence emerged in the public domain that the group was developing a plot to attack the West. It is, in fact, quite likely that the U.S. targeting of the group was based on two unrelated factors: First, actionable intelligence apparently existed that could pinpoint the location of the group's leaders for attack; and second, political authorities in the United States perceived a threat that could be sold to the American people and would help to justify broadening an unpopular war to include targets in Syria, with all the dislocation and death that entailed. Such is the role of *counterfactual conspiracy* and the power of the secret government in Secure Democracy.

Yet another genre of episodic terrorist events involves *"conspiracies" inspired by the government*, alleged plots that are "uncovered" and prevented by counterterror informants. There is a very fine line between government infiltration of a conspiracy and what looks very much like entrapment, although entrapment is almost never an effective legal defense in "national security" cases. Nevertheless, entrapment would occur if a person who was not capable of carrying out a plot, and was engaged, assisted, and otherwise motivated to participate in a conspiracy organized by a government informant or another agent. This was almost certainly what happened in an alleged plot to blow up the Sears Tower in Chicago as well as several FBI offices in 2006. According to press reports, the seven "perpetrators" thought they were meeting with a representative of al Qaeda, but the representative was actually a government agent, working for the South Florida Joint Terrorism Task Force. The men were videotaped pledging allegiance to

Osama bin Laden, but it was an FBI informant posing as an al Qaeda operative who administered the oath.[247]

Attorney General Alberto R. Gonzales announced the discovery of the plot. He initially called it a "terror cell inside the United States, hailing 'our commitment to preventing terrorism through energetic law enforcement efforts aimed at detecting and thwarting terrorist acts.'" But according to court records, "what Gonzales described as a 'deadly plot' was virtually the pipe dream of a few men with almost no ability to pull it off on their own."[248] According to the local U.S. Attorney R. Alexander Acosta, in this case the FBI "successfully performed its mission to prevent terrorism by identifying, disrupting and prosecuting these individuals before they posed an immediate threat to our nation."[249] Deputy FBI Director John Pistole took a different line. "This group," he said, "was more aspirational than operational." Later, Gonzales "stressed that there was no immediate threat in either Chicago or Miami because the group did not have explosives or other materials it was seeking."[250] The FBI director said, "Today's threat is just as likely to come from our own streets as it is from people who are sent from overseas."[251] If the director had taken the time to consult the record, he would have discovered that almost all terrorism in the United States is homegrown. No revelation there. Perhaps a significant part of what is commonly called "terrorism" in the United States is just as likely to be manufactured by law-enforcement and counterterrorism authorities, at least in the Sears Tower plot as well as in other *"conspiracies" inspired by the government.*

A comprehensive study conducted by Human Rights Watch in 2014 found that many human-rights abuses occur in federal prosecutions of terrorism cases in the United States. It reviewed the role of informants, concluding that the government too often inspires terrorism conspiracies. The report said the government appears to have taken a "preventive" approach, attempting to find individuals who might commit an act of terrorism at some future date.[252] In their words:

> [N]early 50 percent of the more than 500 federal counterterrorism convictions [between 2002 and 2011] resulted from informant-based cases; almost 30 percent of those cases were sting operations in which the informant played an active role in the underlying plot. In the case of the "Newburgh Four," for example, a judge said the government "came up with the crime, provided the means, and removed all relevant obstacles," and had, in the process, made a terrorist out of a man "whose buffoonery is positively Shakespearean in scope."[253]

In 2009, federal prosecutors charged four black Muslim men living in Newburgh, New York, with plotting to bomb a Jewish community center and a synagogue in Riverdale, New York, and to fire a Stinger surface-to-air missile at planes parked at the Stewart Air National Guard Base in Newburgh. The FBI informant tried to recruit members of a local Muslim mosque, Masjid al-Ikhlas, but only one of the men was known at the mosque and he had only visited two or three times. All were petty criminals who were unemployed and did not possess the resources or knowledge to conceive or carry out the plot. Two had histories of mental disability.[254] The FBI informant promised one of the men, James Cromitie, $250,000 to participate in the plot, and promised another funds to help pay for a liver transplant for his brother. None of the defendants had serious offenses on their criminal records. At the trial, the defense argued that they could not have accomplished the plot without the provocation and material assistance of the informant.[255]

Over an 11-month period, FBI informant Shahed Hussain recruited the "plotters," selected the targets, planned the operation, organized logistics, provided cars and funds, and arranged for the

FBI to deliver inert bombs and a deactivated Stinger surface-to-air missile to a storage facility in Connecticut.[256] In this way, the men would have to cross state lines to collect the government-provided weapons, making it a federal crime. Because a Stinger missile is an anti-aircraft missile that can be classified as a weapon of mass destruction, upon conviction, a mandatory sentence of 25 years in federal prison would be imposed. And it was.[257]

The plan hatched by the FBI informant was to set off the bombs and then hightail it to the Stewart Air National Guard Base to fire the missile, presumably at planes on the ground, although the plan was not well defined. Cromitie, who was supposed to "arm" the bombs, had no idea how to do it and no clue that the bombs were dummies supplied by the government. And there was no articulated plan as to how to fire the missile at the base. The Stinger missile is a complex system and requires training and experience if it is to be effective. Moreover, it is a heat-seeking missile, which means that it cannot detect and acquire its target unless its target is hot, which would require that the planes have their engines running—most likely in the air, not on the ground. So there is no possibility that the weapon could have been fired at a parked airplane, even if government technicians had not previously disabled it.

The Newburgh Four case is a particularly egregious instance of terrorist *"conspiracies" inspired by the government.* When the plotters arrived at the scene of the crime, plainclothes police and federal agents from multiple departments swarmed the location—in all, more than 100 law-enforcement personal, some carrying automatic weapons, others descending from helicopters. The government positioned a large flatbed truck as a roadblock at one end of the street and an armored vehicle at the other. The officers smashed the windows of the car and dragged the men to the street. It was a show for the media, but it was also destined to become the subject of an HBO documentary, *The Newburgh Sting*, based on "more than 100 hours of FBI undercover video, photos, and aerial surveillance."[258]

The government nevertheless orchestrated a media blitz praising the Federal Bureau of Investigation for apprehending the terrorists and preventing another attack in New York. The media and political elites bought into the feeding frenzy. All the elements were in place: Muslims attacking Jews, "bombs" and a "weapon of mass destruction" confiscated by the police, a location not far from the site of the 9/11 atrocity, the drama of a high-profile law-enforcement intervention. Mayor Michael R. Bloomberg said in a statement, "This latest attempt to attack our freedoms shows that the homeland security threats against New York City are sadly all too real. . . ."[259] But they were not. New York Senator Charles E. Schumer chimed in, "This incident shows that we must always be vigilant against terrorism—foreign or domestic." The pontifications of politicians to the contrary notwithstanding, it was plainly a setup engineered by the Federal Bureau of Investigation that could not possibly have occurred without recruiting, encouragement, funding, instigation, and logistical support—all supplied by the government. Nevertheless, the courts have rejected appeals, saying the FBI's tactics do not meet the legal definition of entrapment. In 2013, the federal appeals court upheld the conviction on a vote of two to one.

It is evident from this sampling of cases that episodic terrorism comprises a number of different kinds of events. Some originate abroad or are international in character, but most are homegrown, at least in the United States. Many involve single actors, and others, larger-scale conspiracies. If we return for a moment to the data in Figure III.1 and III.3, it is clear that the number of terrorist attacks in the United States has declined steadily since the 1960s. Overall, the vast majority of the episodic terror falls in two categories.

The first is *attacks perpetrated by domestic groups* like the Earth Liberation Front, the Animal Liberation Front, the Ku Klux Klan, and various other hate groups. Apart from the hate groups, most of these "liberation" factions have focused their attacks on property and not on people, often involving the crime of arson.

The history of hate groups is different. The Ku Klux Klan, the Aryan Nation, and other white hate groups do perpetrate violence against individuals. It is an old American story involving racism, arising from the struggle over slavery and the Civil War. The Federal Bureau of Investigation targeted these groups with the White Hate Groups Cointelpro beginning in the early 1960s. But Congress terminated the program when it came to public attention after 1975. They did so because the Federal Bureau of Investigation violated basic liberal democratic principles of due process, the right to face one's accuser, and so on. It was found that the groups could be prosecuted in a court of law, and many individuals belonging to such organizations have gone to jail for their crimes—and rightly so.

The second most populous class of episodic terror is the *"lone wolf" single-point security failure.* These crimes are extremely difficult to interdict because the perpetrator is almost always silent about his or her intentions, has ready access to semiautomatic firearms (at least in the United States), and rarely has a criminal record indicating a potential for murder. Moreover, almost all lone-wolf attackers commit suicide or are killed by law enforcement during or right after the commission of their crimes. Motives can only be surmised and are often inscrutable.

Easy access to semiautomatic weapons has made the carnage from such attacks all the more devastating. This problem is closely linked to the Second Amendment of the U.S. Constitution, which many interpret to mean that ordinary citizens have a right to "keep and bear arms" of increasing range, accuracy, and firepower. It has in fact created a need for police to arm themselves with incrementally more powerful weapons, because criminals have access to a wide variety of precision scopes and semiautomatic guns that are available at local stores across the United States. In fact, guns have killed well over 2,000 police officers in the line of duty since 9/11.[260]

But the Second Amendment is not an important aspect of modern liberal democracy. It does not protect or defend the rights of citizens; to the contrary, it results in tens of thousands of unnecessary deaths every year. One might even be tempted to conclude the opposite: that the Second Amendment presents a challenge to liberal democracy because it enables "lone wolf" terror, mobilizes counterterror agents, necessitates heavily armed police, and perpetrates a level of violence and murder not found in any other democracy of the world.[261]

But a day of reckoning is apparently not at hand. In the immediate aftermath of the lone-wolf attack in Orlando, in which 100 people were killed or wounded by a single man wielding a semiautomatic pistol and an assault rifle, the U.S. Senate failed to pass four gun-safety measures. One of them would have banned persons on the government's terrorist watch list from buying guns. Liberal members of the House of Representatives staged an unprecedented "sit-in" demonstration in the House legislative chamber, but so far that is the extent of the Congressional response to the massacres in San Bernardino and Orlando.

If one strips away the political rhetoric of the "war on terror" and other ideological components, events involving episodic terror appear to be largely unrelated. In the United States, at least, there are few distinct patterns, apart from the racist linkage between the Ku Klux Klan, neo-Nazis, and other violent white supremacists. But this fact was overlooked in the wake of 9/11.

In an address to a joint session of Congress just two weeks following the 9/11 attacks, Israeli politician Benjamin Netanyahu chose to portray the fight against terrorism in unabashedly apocalyptic and even xenophobic terms. He asserted: "What is at stake today is nothing less than the survival of our civilization." He compared the threat of "Islamist militancy" to the threat of Communism and took pains to play upon the fears of the Congress and of the American people. "Some of you," he said, "may find it hard to believe that Islamic militants truly cling to the mad fantasy of destroying America. Make no mistake about it. They do." He personalized his message. "Each one of us today," he said, "understands that we are all targets, that our cities are vulnerable, and that our values are hated with an unmatched fanaticism that seeks to destroy our societies and our way of life."

Apparently he hoped to project Israel's fear of foreign fighters/terrorists onto the American people. But the situations are clearly not analogous. Unlike Israel, the United States is not surrounded by hostile militants and neighboring states bent on its destruction. And its citizens need not be concerned with terrorism in their daily lives. But Netanyahu was not content to stop there. In a statement that paired Islamic militancy with catastrophic terrorism, he raised his rhetoric to conjure up the ultimate calamity. "But does anyone doubt," he asserted, "that given the chance, they will throw atom bombs at America and its allies? And perhaps long before that, chemical and biological weapons?"

Now, it was quite true at the time, just as it is true today, that no "Islamist terrorists" are going to "throw atom bombs" at the United States or any other country. It is a ridiculous idea. Perhaps Netanyahu conflated catastrophic terror with episodic terror. Possibly he confused emerging nuclear states with sub-state terrorist groups. Or perhaps the fact that Israel is surrounded by hostile Muslim majority states, and had been in perpetual conflict with Hamas and Hezbollah, clouded his vision. He nevertheless contributed his part to the pathology of counterterrorism, a fanaticism that somehow became the received wisdom within government, especially the secret government, propagating an irrational fear that is used to justify, augment, and build up internal security agencies and budgets within the context of Secure Democracy.

Given this rhetorical rampage, is there any indication that episodic terrorist events in the United States can be connected to one another or is there a discernable a pattern related to Islamist militancy? Hardly. As one careful study of "Islamic terror" concludes, "On both analytical and empirical grounds, there is not a significant basis for anticipating that Muslim Americans are increasingly motivated or capable of successfully engaging in lethal terrorist attacks in the United States."[262] Of the 18 plots and attacks attributed to Muslim Americans from 2001 to 2010, only two were successful: the Fort Hood shooting (discussed above) and the 2009 drive-by shooting of two soldiers by Carlos Bledsoe outside the U.S. Army recruiting office in Little Rock, Arkansas. Both incidents appear to have been lone-wolf attacks in which the perpetrator acted alone and was apprehended. Perhaps more important, law-enforcement agents and informants were involved, sometimes as an enabling force, in 12 of the 18 Muslim-related incidents.[263] This fact would lead a reasonable observer to place at least several of the 12 incidents in the category of episodic terrorism described above as *conspiracies inspired by the government*. Another study found that of the 74 deaths attributed to terrorism in the 14 years following 9/11, 26 could be attributed to "deadly jihadist attacks" (including 13 by the Foot Hood shooter) and 48 to "deadly right wing attacks."[264] If we exclude the Foot Hood incident, which the Department of Defense classified as an act of workplace violence, deadly jihadist attacks accounted for less than one each year since 9/11.

Just as the Security Industrial Complex corresponds to the Military Industrial Complex, the pathological responses of each to certain kinds of stimuli are consonant as well. The reaction to the cases cited above would appear to be extreme—both for the real cases and the counterfactual ones. Even though a great deal of what is called "terrorism" looks a lot like ordinary criminal or insane behavior, all incidents classified as terrorism (apart from racist terror) appear to elicit an extraordinary overreaction on the part of counterterror authorities. Even in clear cases of limited episodic terror, authorities appear to react to the fear or perception that terrorists will somehow inflict catastrophic damage on the United States (as demonstrated by law-enforcement overreaction to the Boston Marathon bombing case), or that they may do so in another modern liberal polity. We might call this the "Netanyahu Syndrome," a condition that presents all acts of violence as connected and apocalyptic. Since the events of 9/11, this perception has ignited a fear of existential terror, both in government and in civil society. It is as though al Qaeda and the Islamic State are armed with weapons of mass destruction. But of course, they are not.

The remedy to this intolerable state of affairs was, of course, to create a counterterror infrastructure so powerful and ubiquitous that it could detect and prevent each and every act of terrorism. But this is clearly not possible and it is certainly not desirable— even in the digital age where surveillance is ubiquitous. The unprecedented buildup of intelligence assets in the United States can be explained as an irrational manifestation of the subversion of democracy. The net effect was to stimulate the growth of an outsize and disproportionate Security Industrial Complex that is plainly hostile to the open society in which it is embedded. And this occurred even though the data indicate that the number of terrorist events in the United States steadily declined in the half century following the 1960s.

It is here that the deep descent into Secure Democracy becomes apparent. In the several decades prior to the events of

9/11, a much smaller and less capable internal security apparatus in government focused on social protest, civil disorder, race riots, and on bombings perpetrated by the Weather Underground and other violent groups and individuals. The level of violent political activity was much higher than in any subsequent period. Nevertheless, the development of an internal security state-within-the-state could be arrested by legitimate, constitutionally appropriate powers of government, namely the United States Senate Select Committee to Study Governmental Operations With Respect to Intelligence Activities.

Today, counterterror officials presume to tell their oversight committee, the Senate Intelligence Committee of the U.S. Congress, what it can and cannot publish. They advise the president to attack the forces of the Islamic State, arguing that if the group succeeds in Iraq or Syria, as they think it might, its soldiers would soon mount attacks on the United States. And this despite the fact that U.S. actions in Iraq propelled the rise of the leader of the Islamic State, Abu Bakr al-Baghdadi, the self-proclaimed caliph of the Muslim world.[265] Erroneous intelligence funneled through the George W. Bush administration asserted that Saddam Hussein possessed weapons of mass destruction and was in league with al Qaeda. Then–Secretary of State Colin Powell used this fabrication to justify the invasion of Iraq in 2003.

Clearly the deliberations, actions, and disinformation of the intelligence community bracket the conflict in Iraq, from the run-up to the 2003 invasion to the bombing campaign against the Islamic State in 2014–17. It was not possible for Saddam Hussein to target the United States in 2003, but under the auspices of Secure Democracy, facts can be conveniently invented or discarded. Likewise, it is highly unlikely that without U.S. military intervention in Iraq, the Islamic State group would have come to exist as a fighting force in the Levant. It may be that militants associated with the Islamic State will eventually attack America or Western Europe. But if they do, it will be an attack of our own making. The terror-counterterror-terror dynamic is a central characteristic of degraded democracy. It tells us that governments and terrorist organizations can become locked in a cycle of action and reaction, where the motive for future attacks on the United States may well be retribution or revenge for lethal U.S. drone and F/A-18 strikes in Iraq in 2014–2017.

If we consider the overall picture, the response to terrorism was not rational or proportionate, even to the horrific attacks of 9/11. The United States reacted by occupying Iraq and Afghanistan at a cost estimated variously at $4 trillion–$6 trillion[266] and 6,280 U.S. military casualties with more than 52,000 wounded in action[267]; building a reconnaissance-strike drone capability; arming local U.S. law enforcement with military-grade weapons; torturing suspected terrorists; implementing society-wide surveillance; and generally expanding and empowering a Security Industrial Complex that creates chaos abroad and constitutes a threat to liberty at home in 21st-century America. A far better course would have been to target the central elements of and adherents to al Qaeda, especially its leaders, training facilities, known soldiers, banks, businesses, financial transactions, communications, propaganda, sympathizers, and supporters. A global, nebulous, and costly "war" motivated by the fear of "terrorism" provided no solutions at all.

Instead, as we have seen, the George W. Bush and subsequent administrations attempted to buttress *irrational security*, frightening the electorate into acquiescence by constructing sham intelligence reports, disinformation, and outright lies. Certainly, this is not the first time that leaders of great states have engaged in what can only be described as extreme and neurotic behavior, dragging their constituencies and nations into dangerous and ultimately insupportable commitments.

CHAPTER VI

//////////////////

TORTURE AND DETENTION

In the first decade of the 2000s, the Central Intelligence Agency rounded up hundreds of suspected terrorists from many countries of the world, subjecting them to illegal imprisonment and torture at undisclosed facilities outside the United States. The activity was so highly classified that only a handful of elected officials were aware of it, and even they were not fully informed of the extent and brutality of the incarceration. But such secrets are difficult to keep. In 2004, the International Committee of the Red Cross presented reports to the U.S. government documenting torture of detainees imprisoned at the U.S. Naval Station at Guantánamo Bay, Cuba. From the outset, and increasingly as details seeped into the public domain, the agency attempted to downplay, deny, and destroy evidence of the worst aspects of its conduct.

Between May 2002 and November 2005, CIA headquarters exchanged polite yet detailed memoranda with agents in the field who were in charge of torture at undisclosed locations. The subject was the disposition of 92 videotapes of the "enhanced interrogations" of notorious al Qaeda operatives—Abu Zubaydah, Khalid

Sheikh Muhammed, and Abu Faraj al-Libbi. CIA headquarters, or "HQS," evinced considerable concern that videotapes documenting torture might somehow become public. As early as September 2002, top agency officials discussed the matter:

> . . . the continued retention of these tapes, which is not/not [*sic*] required by law represents a serious security risk for [redacted] officers participating in [redacted] operations . . . [and a] danger to all Americans should the tapes be compromised. . . . [T]here also exists a clear danger that the officers pictured on the tapes could be subject to retribution from Al-Qa'ida elements. Accordingly, the participants [in a meeting at CIA headquarters] determined that the best alternative to eliminate those security and additional risks is to destroy the tapes. . . .[268]

As the exchanges between headquarters and the field continued, the production of additional tapes assumed greater importance. CIA leadership articulated a new procedure to control videotapes of the torture/interrogation sessions. "Starting immediately," they wrote, "it is now HQS policy that [redacted] record one day's worth of sessions on one videotape for operational considerations, utilize the tape within that same day . . . and record the next day's sessions on the same tape. Thus, in effect, the single tape in use [redacted] will contain only one day's worth of interrogation sessions."

By November of 2005, the agency had constructed an elaborate rationale to support destruction of the tapes. At CIA headquarters, "the Inspector General had advised that . . . [the] video tapes were no longer required for his investigation," and the CIA Office of the General Counsel reported that the "cable traffic accurately documented [redacted] activities recorded on video tape."[269] Accordingly, the director of the CIA National Clandestine Service, Jose A.

Rodriguez, ordered their destruction, and "all ninety-two [redacted] video tapes were destroyed on 09 November [2005]."[270]

But the reasons given for the destruction of the video tapes—that they posed a danger to CIA officers and "all Americans," that they were adequately documented in cables, and so on—were entirely self-serving. Another declassified memorandum was more direct and revealing:

> As Jose [Rodriguez] said, the heat from destroying [the videotapes] is nothing compared to what it would be if the tapes ever got into public domain—he said that out of context, they would make us look terrible; it would be "devastating" to us.[271]

And so it would have been.

But mortification of the Central Intelligence Agency is not the crucial point. The U.S. government subjected prisoners to cruel and unusual punishments. Justice Department lawyers John Yoo and Jay S. Bybee, Vice President Dick Cheney, and a few others in the George W. Bush administration sought to justify such actions. And they are not contrite, even today. Addington, Bush, Cheney, Tenet, Yoo, and others who authorized the torture continue to defend it. Their thoroughly discredited legal memoranda, testimony, and subsequent public statements do not change the fundamental illegality and profoundly antidemocratic quality of the "harsh interrogations"—the torture—in which agents of the United States government engaged. No doubt, the actions and rationalizations of the torturers have alienated friends and weakened the democratic narrative in the Middle East and even into Asia and Europe. But this may not be the most important outcome. After all, people are tortured by more authoritarian regimes and ad hoc military forces the world over every day.

The more critical questions engage the effects of torture on liberal democracies that conduct or condone it. Two related issues come to the fore. The first focuses on the centrifugal forces that torture unleashes within democracy, specifically including disabling the balance of powers and the oversight capacity of the legislative branch. The torture of suspected terrorists pitted the Central Intelligence Agency against its oversight committee, the Senate Committee on Intelligence of the U.S. Congress. The agency attempted to obstruct and delay the Senate investigation, and, in the end, campaigned to block the release of the committee's findings. Moreover, its spokesmen denied taking actions to suppress the Senate investigation and never admitted that the allegations of torture were true, employing the euphemism "harsh" or "enhanced" interrogation in its stead.

The second issue has to do with the consequences of disabling the writ of *habeas corpus*, which is fundamental to rule of law and due process everywhere. Justice Hugo Black called it "the loftiest power with which the Constitution has endowed" the courts.[272] *Habeas corpus* is "[a] writ issuing out of a court of justice, or awarded by a judge . . . requiring the body of a person restrained of liberty to be brought before the judge or into court, that the lawfulness of the restraint may be investigated and determined." The first English-language reference to the term occurred in 1465: "*Now ther ys com down an habeas corpus for hym*," meaning that the prisoner had to be taken before a court.[273] Torture is impossible in a liberal democracy when *habeas corpus* is fully functional because it is always and everywhere illegal. No court of law would have the power to impose such a sentence.

By conducting torture in the absence of any visible juridical process, employees of the Central Intelligence Agency distorted the foundations and conceptual underpinnings of the legal system and of democracy itself. In effect, they destabilized the balance of powers, transferring oversight responsibility from the legislative and judicial branches to a small but extreme coterie in the executive branch. They usurped authority under the rubric of a national emergency and in connection with the Authorization for Use of Military Force (AUMF) against terrorism.[274] The Central Intelligence Agency took matters into its own hands, relying on the trumped-up authority of a few ideologues in the Department of Justice and the White House. In so doing, they abandoned due process and other fundamental principles universally embraced by the Founders of the American Republic and the Western tradition of liberal democracy. No one has been brought to justice for the crimes against humanity they committed.

The Struggle over Torture

Callous disregard for due process and basic human rights is a strong indicator that Secure Democracy has invaded or supplanted the liberal state. As secrecy becomes more pervasive, internal security agents of all kinds gain greater latitude in the activities they undertake, and the justification of their actions, no matter how grotesque, becomes increasingly administrative, arbitrary, and divorced from rule of law. As reports about torture trickled into the public domain, the Central Intelligence Agency conducted a number of internal investigations and declassified several documents. These heavily redacted papers provided only a partial and inadequate picture of the torture operations. At the same time, Congress and the George W. Bush administration invented a new category of persons, "illegal enemy combatants," to justify continued detention of persons who had been tortured by the Central Intelligence Agency and the military services.

These programs were initiated during the tenure of then–CIA Director George Tenet, who 10 years later orchestrated a cabal to suppress the findings of a Senate Intelligence Committee investigation of the agency's programs. Torture chambers were located at "black" sites—military bases and other secret locations around the world, in Asia, Europe, and the southern Americas—so that they would not be subject to the laws of the United States and its Constitution. It was a complete betrayal of the democratic ideal.

Deputy Assistant Attorney General John Yoo helped to construct the rationale for torture. He enshrined presidential power in secret memoranda, attacking the Constitution in close consort with his boss, former Assistant Attorney General Jay S. Bybee.[275] They framed legal arguments advising the Central Intelligence Agency, the Justice and Defense Departments, and the White House that the use of torture was defensible under applicable statutes, international law, and an expansive interpretation of presidential authority.[276] Yoo concluded that the Constitution does not extend to enemy combatants held abroad. He argued that the application of U.S. statutes forbidding torture "to the interrogation of enemy combatants . . . would conflict with the Constitution's grant of the Commander in Chief power solely to the President."[277] Yoo, a vigorous opponent of the Fourth Amendment, also claimed that the president's Article II powers permitted warrantless searches.[278] These and other discredited legal opinions are notable for their complete disregard for the long-established democratic principle that torture cannot be tolerated. The UN Committee Against Torture characterized the Yoo and Bybee memoranda as "deeply flawed legal arguments used to advise that interrogation techniques, which amounted to torture, could be authorized and used lawfully."[279]

But because the process was shrouded in secrecy, they were able to approve cruel and unusual punishment by the Central Intelligence Agency, torture that abrogated the Geneva Conventions and the UN Convention Against Torture. It was, on its face, clearly contrary to the underlying concept and spirit with which the Founders animated the American Republic.

In March of 2009, the Senate Committee on Intelligence voted 14–1 to open an investigation of the detention and interrogation programs of the Central Intelligence Agency. Over the next four years, the committee staff compiled a comprehensive 6,300-page report documenting the torture programs. During 2013 and 2014, this report became the focus of a power struggle between the Senate and the Central Intelligence Agency. In many respects, this Congressional investigation might have been analogous to the Church Committee, which investigated the misconduct and illegal activities of the intelligence agencies in the middle 1970s, even though the Church Committee had a more expansive mandate. But there is an even more profound difference. The Church Committee was able to obtain secret documents and to compel the cooperation of the intelligence agencies. It ultimately published some of the most sensitive classified documents, largely without redaction, exposing the existence of a domestic intelligence state-within-the-state.

In the second decade of the 21st century, however, under conditions of Secure Democracy, it is no longer clear that the power of the Congress of the United States, which represents the power of the people, is sufficient to compel full cooperation from the Central Intelligence Agency, which set onerous conditions for Congressional review and oversight.

The agency permitted its oversight committee access to relevant documents only at its secret facilities in northern Virginia, although copies of documents could easily have been conveyed to a secret compartmented information facility (or SCIF) located in the Capitol complex. Moreover, the agency attempted to withhold documents related to its own internal investigation, deemed the "Panetta Review," which presaged the conclusions of the Senate report. It withdrew access to electronic documents previously provided to committee investigators. In an audacious challenge to the legislative branch, the agency hacked into the committee's secret computer networks, attempting to discover which Senate staff had gained access to the Panetta documents. And in an act of intimidation, CIA officers attempted to initiate a criminal investigation of the committee's staff, threatening them "with legal jeopardy just as final revisions to the report [were] being made so that parts of it [could] be declassified and released to the American People."[280] And what of the agency officers who illegally hacked into the Senate computers? A panel investigating their activities decided not to recommend disciplinary action.[281] In Secure Democracy, it would appear that intelligence officers can attack fundamental political institutions with impunity.

Senator Tom Udall of New Mexico commented that "[t]he CIA's unauthorized search of the committee's computers tells me that the CIA not only hasn't learned from its mistakes, but continues to perpetuate them." Unabashed, CIA Director John Brennan assumed a combative and arrogant stance with the Senate oversight committee. He hoped to frustrate the investigation, challenge its findings, and prevent the release of even a portion of the report.[282] Moreover, Brennan convened a meeting of former officials who had overseen the torture program, including George J. Tenet, the agency's director at the time, and Cofer Black, then head of its Counterterror Center and administrator of the torture program.[283] Under Tenet's leadership, the group conspired to block release of the Senate report, and failing that, to restrict as much material as possible.[284] As one authoritative source put it, President Obama ". . . has allowed the C.I.A. to oversee the redaction process of this [the Senate] report, and is now apparently allowing Mr. Tenet to run a publicity campaign against it."[285] Evidently, the Central Intelligence Agency was determined to interpret and write its own history of the torture programs.

Speaking from the floor of the Senate, Intelligence Committee chair Dianne Feinstein accused the agency of obfuscation, deleting documents, tampering with Senate computers without authorization, breaking federal laws, and taking action in violation of the Constitution. She specifically noted that when John Brennan hand-delivered the CIA's response to the Committee's report, it was labeled "deliberative, processed, privileged document." She said, "Congress does not recognize these claims of privilege when it comes to documents provided to Congress for our oversight duties." In an address that was punctuated with flashes of anger, Feinstein pointed out discrepancies between the agency's internal Panetta report and its response to the committee. She concluded:

> Based on what Director Brennan has informed us, I have grave concerns that the CIA's search [of Senate computers] may well have violated the separation of powers principle embodied in the United States Constitution, including the speech [or] debate clause. It may have undermined the constitutional framework essential to effective congressional oversight of intelligence activities or any other government function. [286]

In response, John Brennan contradicted the senator, disseminating what can only be interpreted as an outright lie or, at best, disinformation: "We are not in any way, shape, or form trying to thwart this report's progression [or] release," he told an MSNBC anchor at a Council on Foreign Relations event later that day. He continued, "As far as the allegations of, you know, CIA hacking into, you know, Senate computers, nothing could be further from the truth. I mean, we wouldn't do that. I mean, that's—that's just beyond the—you know, the scope of reason in terms of what we would do."[287] Clearly, Brennan was playing it fast and loose with the facts. Perhaps his training and indoctrination rendered him incapable of distinguishing the truth from political expediency.

A preliminary report by the CIA's inspector general concluded that "[f]ive Agency employees, two attorneys, and three information technology (IT) staff members improperly accessed" the committee's computers looking for evidence of criminal wrongdoing.[288] The CIA's Office of the Inspector General confirmed these findings, affirming that CIA officers sought to bring criminal charges against Senate staff.[289] Senator Saxby Chambliss, vice chair of the Senate Intelligence Committee and a staunch supporter of the agency, commented, "I am extremely disappointed in the actions of the agents of the CIA who carried out this breach of the committee's computers."[290]

Four months after Senator Feinstein's speech, Brennan slunk back to the Senate Intelligence Committee to "apologize." He admitted that the agency had improperly "penetrated" the computer network set up by the Senate to investigate the agency's torture programs and had attempted to intimidate Senate staff with threats of prosecution.[291] But how is such misconduct interpreted in the context of Secure Democracy? Was Brennan fired for his intransigence and deliberate obfuscation of the truth about torture? No. He was able to block the release of more than 90 percent of the Senate report, redacting information from what was released and providing a rebuttal of the report at the same time.

The Obama White House mounted a spirited defense. The spokesman said of Brennan, "He is somebody who has a very difficult job, who does that job exceptionally well." When asked if this episode created a credibility issue for Brennan, the White House spokesman replied, "Not at all."[292] Such is the power wielded in Washington by the unelected leaders of the surveillance security state.

In December of 2014, nearly six months after Senator Feinstein castigated Brennan and his agency for illegally hacking the Senate's computers, the Senate Intelligence Committee released a 500-page summary, with redactions, of the 6,300-page Senate torture report amid political confusion and controversy. The summary is monumental, uncompromising, and unequivocal. While it presents 20 major findings and conclusions, its central import can be summarized as follows. First, the CIA's "enhanced interrogation techniques" program was not an effective intelligence-gathering operation and did not elicit cooperation from the detainees. Second, the program was far more brutal than the CIA reported. Third, the CIA misrepresented the program to political authorities including the Congress, the White House, and the Department of Justice, as well as to the media and the public. Fourth, the CIA actively avoided oversight. And finally, the CIA mismanaged the operation of the program, employing contractors who used torture techniques that had not been approved.[293]

Confusion about the report was compounded at the eleventh hour when Secretary of State John Kerry called Senator Feinstein, warning that release of the report might further inflame militants in the Middle East, perhaps endangering Americans and American interests in that region.[294] While Kerry agreed the report should eventually be published, he argued for delay, citing the complexities of foreign policy.[295] It is inconceivable that Kerry acted without the consent of the president. Moreover, he must have realized that a recent Republican Party sweep in the midterm Congressional elections would result in an indefinite delay and might even bury the report. But here we see another manifestation of the tendency of internal security to overwhelm liberal democracy. Even the president of the United States had to hedge his bets. It is true that President Obama banned the torture program by executive order at the beginning of his first term. And he agreed that the report should be released. But he also permitted Brennan to do everything in his power to prevent that release. And when these tactics failed, President Obama took a line in full support of the Central Intelligence Agency.

This was cast in news reports as part of the close personal relationship between the president and the CIA director, who had previously served as the White House counterterrorism chief, and before that as chief of staff of the agency under George Tenet. Brennan met with President Obama a few hours before the release of the torture report, ostensibly to give the president an intelligence briefing, but also no doubt to coordinate the White House and CIA responses.[296] Although the president took pains to distance himself from the political fray, his position was quite clear. "John Brennan is a decorated professional and a patriot," intoned the White House press secretary. "And he is somebody that the president relies on, on a daily basis, to keep this country safe."[297]

The White House is, of course, highly attuned to public opinion. Perhaps the views of Americans influenced the process. In a *Washington Post*/ABC poll conducted in 2014 following the release of portions of the Senate report, respondents were asked: "Do you personally think the CIA treatment of suspected terrorists amounted to torture, or not?" Forty-nine percent responded "yes" and 38 percent said "no." In the same poll, 53 percent thought "the CIA treatment of suspected terrorists" produced "important information" and 31 percent said it did not. When asked if the "CIA treatment of suspected terrorists was justified," 59 percent responded that it was justified and 31 percent said no. And finally, when asked if "torture of suspected terrorists" could be justified in the future, 57 percent of respondents thought it could "often" (17 percent) or "sometimes" (40 percent) be justified, while 39 percent said it could "rarely" (19 percent) or "never" (20 percent) be justified.[298]

For his part, Brennan continued his official opposition to the Senate report, contradicting its central findings in a rare media event, conducted from inside the Central Intelligence Agency's headquarters at Langley, Virginia. In his public response to the Senate report, Brennan gave an emotional and patriotic review of the events of 9/11. In his opening words:

> It was 8:46 a.m. on the morning of September 11th, 2001, when
> the North Tower of the World Trade Center in New York City
> was struck by an aircraft commandeered by al-Qa'ida terrorists.
> Seventeen minutes later, the clear blue skies over Manhattan
> were pierced yet again. . . . In the short span of seventy-seven
> minutes, four terrorist attacks would forever change the history
> of our country.[299]

He went on to extoll the critical role of the Central Intelligence Agency in responding to al Qaeda, noting that a young CIA officer was the first U.S. casualty in Afghanistan. At the same time, he agreed that the president had properly terminated the torture program (although he did not use the term "torture" in a speech on that subject that exceeded 2,500 words). And he admitted mistakes in his agency's administration of the program.

But he also played on partisan divides in Washington, obscuring the question as to whether or not the program produced useful intelligence (he said both yes and no). And perhaps most important, he took issue with the report, saying that his agency did not mislead Congress, the executive, or the public—directly contradicting the published assertions of Senators Feinstein, Rockefeller, Wyden, Udall, Heinrich, and King.[300] All in all, the speech was a masterful defense of unethical and illegal activity that, while tolerated by a majority of Americans, damaged the United States in the court of world opinion.[301] All common indicators of a bold and functioning Secure Democracy.

But it was former Vice President Dick Cheney who attempted an outright justification of the program, mounting a spirited if perverse defense of torture. He said, "I would do it again in a minute." Regarding the report's description of forced "rectal feeding" and "rectal rehydration" of detainees, he said, "I believe it was done for medical reasons."[302] Apparently Cheney sought to rehabilitate his image by supporting torture. He was not alone. In a rare media appearance, in which he engaged in rationalization and denial, former President George W. Bush told CNN, "We're fortunate to have men and women who work hard at the CIA serving on our behalf. These are patriots. And whatever the report says, if it diminishes their contributions to our country, it is way off base."[303] Several former intelligence chiefs, including George Tenet and Michael Hayden, went so far as to launch a website castigating the Senate report.[304]

It is notable that so many detractors of the report were Republican Party politicians and their appointees. But this is somewhat explainable because the torture programs were conceived and executed on their watch. Perhaps more remarkable is the way in which the director of the Central Intelligence Agency skillfully promoted and exploited the partisan character of Washington politics in the 2010s. The growth and excessive power of the intelligence community are, however, not a partisan issue. Indeed, the Senate Intelligence Committee voted 11–3 to release the summary of the torture report.[305]

President Obama did what needed to be done to outlaw torture, ordering that the "CIA shall close as expeditiously as possible any detention facilities that it currently operates and shall not operate any such detention facility in the future."[306] But he also tolerated the machinations of the Central Intelligence Agency, specifically its attempts to intimidate the Senate and stifle debate about torture. More than any other president, he empowered the agency to conduct paramilitary operations abroad, and to launch a full-blown program to execute individuals he believed to be enemies of the United States, in at least eight countries of the world.

We can certainly imagine how the president relied on the CIA chief, especially with respect to the lethal drone program. Drone activity accelerated under the Obama administration, killing thousands of suspected terrorists, most of them designated by the agency. Many involved the death of innocent bystanders—so-called collateral damage. It may be that President Obama needed Brennan as a salve to his conscience. Certainly, John Brennan is not the first intelligence chief able to manipulate elected political elites to expand the authority and budgets of the Security Industrial Complex.

Unlike the president, the editors of *The New York Times* found the resolution of the "torture debate" so unsettling that they called for the prosecution of the "torturers and their bosses." The Senate report, they wrote, "erases any doubt" about the "depravity and illegality" of the torture programs. They cited "new revelations of sadistic tactics like 'rectal feeding'" and detailed that "scores of detainees were waterboarded, hung by their wrists, confined in coffins, sleep-deprived, threatened with death, or brutally beaten," including "one detainee who was chained to a concrete floor [and] died of 'suspected hypothermia.'" But as important, they named the perpetrators and proposed further investigation. In their language:

> [A]ny credible investigation should include former Vice President Dick Cheney; Mr. Cheney's chief of staff, David Addington; the former C.I.A. director George Tenet; and John Yoo and Jay Bybee, the Office of Legal Counsel lawyers who drafted what became known as the torture memos. There are many more names that could be considered, including Jose Rodriguez Jr., the C.I.A. official who ordered the destruction of the videotapes; the psychologists [Jim Mitchell and Bruce Jessen, who were paid over $80 million for their services[307]] who devised the torture regimen; and the C.I.A. employees who carried out that regimen.[308]

In the final analysis, the CIA conducted a program of brutal and unusual punishment in the absence of due process, disabled the "sacred writ" of *habeas corpus,* and was subsequently able to maintain a defiant stance against its oversight body, the Senate Committee Intelligence. The agency never admitted that its detention facilities and "enhanced interrogation techniques" were actually torture chambers in which crimes against humanity were committed.

Habeas Corpus in the Crosshairs[309]

The political struggle over torture between the Senate and the Central Intelligence Agency should never have taken place. Torture is illegal and prohibited by the Eighth Amendment of the U.S. Constitution: *"Excessive bail shall not be required, nor excessive fines imposed, nor cruel and unusual punishments inflicted."* This seems plain enough on its face, especially when examined in tandem with the Geneva Conventions, Common Article 3, which prohibits "torture" as well as "outrages upon personal dignity, in particular humiliating and degrading treatment,"[310] and the United Nations "Convention Against Torture and Other Cruel, Inhuman or Degrading Treatment or Punishment."[311] Moreover the War Crimes Act of 1996, which incorporates Common Article 3, makes torture committed by members of the U.S. Armed Forces or by U.S. nationals illegal and punishable by imprisonment, and "if death results to the victim, [the perpetrator] shall also be subject to the penalty of death."[312]

Beyond these explicit prohibitions, there is an even more fundamental consideration: Torture cannot take place in a modern liberal democracy when the writ of *habeas corpus* is fully effective. When the prisoner is brought before an impartial justice, charges and evidence must be produced to determine if he is illegally imprisoned or not. This in turn activates juridical processes, specifically due process. If the evidence is unconvincing, the prisoner must be released. And when there are grounds for imprisonment, law specifies the punishment. Clearly, the torture techniques employed by the Central Intelligence Agency, the Defense Intelligence Agency and the U.S. Armed Forces crossed a line, both in terms of illegal suspension of *habeas corpus* and because the torture techniques inflicted were also illegal.

And what were the torture techniques?

Former Director of Central Intelligence George Tenet approved a highly sanitized description of 10 "Enhanced Interrogation Techniques" shown in Box VI.1. These include attention grasp, walling technique, facial hold, facial or insult slap, cramped confinement, insects placed in confinement box, wall standing, stress positions, sleep deprivation, and the waterboard. But as detailed in the reports of the Senate Committee on Intelligence, a report by the CIA Office of Inspector General, and numerous other formerly classified documents, the "interrogations" incorporated many other violent acts intended to cause extreme pain and suffering, and to intimidate, humiliate, and break the detainees.

In a process known as "extraordinary rendition," U.S. agents and foreign governments captured suspected terrorists and handed them over to U.S. authorities. They were shackled, deprived of sight and sound (blindfolds, earmuffs, and hoods), and transferred to a "black site" with no interaction with their captors. Many were put on planes and traveled in this condition for thousands of miles. Upon arrival at the black site, they found themselves in an almost clinical situation: minimal coercion, medical assessment, psychological interview, head and face shaved, stripped and photographed while naked. Within a few hours of arrival at the black site, the transition to increasingly more brutal interrogation began with "conditioning" techniques, followed by "corrective" techniques and "coercive" techniques. Conditioning techniques include nudity, sleep deprivation, and dietary manipulation. Corrective techniques involve physical interaction with the detainee such as the insult slap, abdominal slap, facial hold, and attention grasp. Coercive interrogation techniques escalated to slamming the detainee against a wall with the use of a collar while shackled, dousing with cold water, stress positions, cramped confinement in a large or small coffin-like box (sometimes with insects), and the waterboard. In the waterboard technique, the prisoner is strapped to a board with his head lower than his feet, while his captors stretch a cloth over his nose and mouth and pour water on the cloth, to simulate drowning.

These techniques could be applied in combination and over long periods of time—weeks, months, and even years. Many unauthorized techniques were employed as well, such as threats with a handgun and power drill, smoke, pressure points, mock executions, sexual assault including sodomy with a broom handle, severe beatings, hanging by the wrists shackled to a beam, forced rectal feeding, and rectal rehydration. These and other torture techniques could be applied in combination. From the outset, CIA headquarters exerted very little control over what transpired in its torture chambers in the field. Moreover, the techniques were developed and executed mainly by CIA contractors who had little or no experience in interrogation of any kind. No written description can convey the full weight of what transpired in America's torture chambers. But there is a Channel 4 (U.K.) documentary that re-creates enhanced interrogation and torture at a black site. It is titled *Torture: The Guantanamo Guidebook* and can be found on YouTube.[313]

BOX VI.1

CIA ENHANCED INTERROGATION TECHNIQUES (EITS)

According to the interrogation guidelines issued in January 2003 by then–Director of Central Intelligence George Tenet, "enhanced interrogation techniques" were defined as techniques that "incorporate significant physical or psychological pressure beyond standard techniques."[314]

Ten enhanced interrogation techniques were authorized in 2003:[315]

- The *attention grasp* consists of grasping the detainee with both hands, with one hand on each side of the collar opening, in a controlled and quick motion. In the same motion as the grasp, the detainee is drawn toward the interrogator.
- During the *walling technique*, the detainee is pulled forward and then quickly and firmly pushed into a flexible false wall so that his shoulder blades hit the wall. His head and neck are supported with a rolled towel to prevent whiplash.
- The *facial hold* is used to hold the detainee's head immobile. The interrogator places an open palm on either side of the detainee's face, and the interrogator's fingertips are kept well away from the detainee's eyes.
- With the *facial or insult slap*, the fingers are slightly spread apart. The interrogator's hand makes contact with the area between the tip of the detainee's chin and the bottom of the corresponding earlobe.
- In *cramped confinement*, the detainee is placed in a confined space, typically a small or large box, which is usually dark. Confinement in the smaller space lasts no more than 2 hours, and in the larger space it can last up to 18 hours.
- *Insects* placed in a confinement box involve placing a harmless insect in the box with the detainee.

- During *wall standing*, the detainee may stand about four to five feet from the wall with his feet spread to approximately shoulder width. His arms are stretched out in front of him, and his fingers rest on the wall to support all his body weight. The detainee is not allowed to reposition his hands or feet.
- The application of *stress positions* may include having the detainee sit on the floor with his legs extended straight out in front of him with his arms raised above his head or kneeling on the floor while leaning back at a 45-degree angle.
- *Sleep deprivation* will not exceed 11 days at a time.
- The application of the *waterboard technique* involves binding the detainee to a bench with his feet elevated above his head. The detainee's head is immobilized, and an interrogator places a cloth over the detainee's mouth and nose while pouring water onto the cloth in a controlled manner. Airflow is restricted for 20 to 40 seconds, and the technique produces the sensation of drowning and suffocation.

There are always consequences when due process, and specifically *habeas corpus*, is abandoned. Officers at the Central Intelligence Agency, the Defense Intelligence Agency, and the military prisons all should have known better and put a stop to it. *Habeas corpus*—Latin for "thou (shalt) have the body (sc. in court)"[316]—is an ancient writ referenced in 13th-century English law and even earlier. The idea that a person should not be unjustly deprived of liberty is, of course, as old as written history. One early articulation is found in 1215, article 39 (1225 version) of the *Magna Carta*. It decrees: "No free man shall be seized or imprisoned . . . nor will we proceed with force against him, or send others to do so, except by the lawful judgment of his equals or by the law of the land."[317]

In the beginning, the writ probably only required that a person be present in court before a proceeding could be brought against him or on his behalf, and accordingly, might even be viewed as an extension of the power of the executive or king. By the middle of the 17th century, however, it had become a vehicle through which a detained person could challenge the legality of his or her detention. In 1629, the *Chambers* case addressed the issue.[318] The Star Chamber, an English court of law, imprisoned Richard Chambers for refusing to pay taxes and subsequently defaming the Crown.[319] The court operated in the royal Palace of Westminster in London from the late 15th to the middle 17th century. It was composed of privy councilors and common-law judges. Chambers's offense was a speech crime. He is reported to have said "the merchants of England were screwed up here in England more than in Turkey" and was imprisoned for that statement. He brought an action in the King's Bench, an English court of common law, for *habeas corpus* relief, arguing that under the law that created the Star Chamber, a person could not be incarcerated for what he said. The King's Bench denied his *habeas* petition and returned him to jail. It held that the Star Chamber existed before the enabling statute and was an old and venerable court.[320] Now this may have been an odd and unjust decision, but it is among the first cases establishing a prisoner's right to have his day in court for the purpose of contesting the legality of his incarceration.

The modern-day writ of *habeas corpus* is explicitly preserved in the U.S. Constitution as ballast against illegal imprisonment. Although the Constitution does not specifically create a right to *habeas corpus* relief, it does mandate that the "... *Writ of Habeas Corpus shall not be suspended, unless when in Cases of Rebellion or Invasion the public Safety may require it.*" In theory, suspension of the writ can only be accomplished by an act of Congress or by Congressional delegation of that power to the executive. At the beginning of the American Republic, Congress passed the First Judicial Act of 1789. Section 13 of that act vests the power of *habeas corpus* in the U.S. federal courts.

But this was not the view of Justice Department lawyers John Yoo and Jay S. Bybee, or Vice President Dick Cheney and his chief of staff, David Addington. They crafted and/or approved secret memoranda advising the Central Intelligence Agency and the Department of Defense that torture outside the territory of the United States was permissible. Judge A. Raymond Randolph of the D.C. Circuit Court of Appeals, a conservative jurist and author of two relevant majority opinions, formulated the essential question in a speech he made at the Heritage Foundation in Washington, D.C.: "Did the writ of *habeas corpus* reach alien enemies captured abroad during war and held beyond the sovereign territory of the United States?"[321]

Although Judge Randolph does not agree, the answer to his question is unequivocally yes. The U.S. Supreme Court reversed both of his opinions, concluding instead that the writ applies to prisoners held incommunicado at the U.S. Naval Station at Guantánamo Bay. There is, however, a very significant caveat. Even though the Supreme Court has explicitly ruled that *habeas corpus* must be extended to persons held at Guantánamo, prisoners are still there and have not been charged with crimes or tried. This would suggest that for whatever reasons, military and security agents are not abiding by the Court's decisions, an ominous instance in which rule of law is effectively disabled.

But perhaps more important, during the decade of the 2010s, while Secure Democracy insinuated itself into the core of the American state, the Supreme Court consistently opposed efforts by the president and the Congress to limit or suspend *habeas corpus*. This is a potentially countervailing trend to Secure Democracy, and so it is important to get to the bottom of it.

On April 27, 1861, President Abraham Lincoln unilaterally suspended the writ of *habeas corpus* in Maryland because he thought it necessary to detain suspected Confederate saboteurs and spies. He also used the "suspension clause" to round up members of the Maryland House of Representatives so that the Legislature could not meet. Chief Justice Roger B. Taney opposed the president's actions but was ignored in the context of a war emergency. On March 3, 1862, Congress belatedly passed the *Habeas Corpus Suspension Act*.[322] It indemnified the president for past actions and authorized him to suspend *habeas corpus* during the remainder of the Civil War. But because most of the clauses in the act relate to the Civil War, it was rendered inoperative in 1864 as the war drew to a close. Lincoln is the only U.S. president to suspend the writ until George W. Bush did so in 2006 with the help of Congress.

One adverse *habeas* case arose at the close of the Second World War. *Johnson vs. Eisentrager*[323] involved the imprisonment of 21 German nationals captured and tried in China for giving information about American troop deployments to Japanese authorities— after the surrender of Germany but before the surrender of Japan. They were convicted by an American military tribunal sitting in China, and then transported to Germany to serve their sentences in Landsberg Prison, then administered by Allied forces, including Americans. The prisoners filed a *habeas* action in the D.C. District Court, which was denied, but the Court of Appeals reversed the lower District Court, granting *habeas corpus*. When the case reached the Supreme Court, it was again reversed. The Court held that *habeas* relief was not available because U.S. courts had no jurisdiction over German war criminals held in a U.S. prison in Germany. The court said, "No such basis can be invoked here, for these prisoners at no relevant time were within any territory over which the United States is sovereign . . . [and] were all beyond the territorial jurisdiction of any court of the United States."[324]

This of course is the same argument implied in Judge Randolph's question. It is also the last time that the argument held sway. It is true that a majority in the *Eisentrager* case held that the scope of the writ was limited to the sovereign territory of the United States. But Justice Hugo Black gave a powerful dissent:

> *Habeas corpus*, as an instrument to protect against illegal imprisonment, is written into the Constitution. Its use by courts cannot in my judgment be constitutionally abridged by Executive or by Congress. I would hold that our courts can exercise it whenever any United States official illegally imprisons any person in any land we govern. Courts should not for any reason abdicate this, the loftiest power with which the Constitution has endowed them.[325]

Justice Black's view of the matter is well grounded in English law, in the debates surrounding the ratification of the U.S. Constitution and even in *Federalist* 84, in which Alexander Hamilton quotes renowned English jurist Sir William Blackstone. Hamilton wrote, "[T]he practice of arbitrary imprisonments, have been, in all ages, the favorite and most formidable instruments of tyranny. The observations of the judicious Blackstone are well worthy of recital:

> To bereave a man of life . . . or by violence to confiscate his estate,
> without accusation or trial, would be so gross and notorious an
> act of despotism as must at once convey the alarm of tyranny
> throughout the whole nation; but confinement of the person, by
> secretly hurrying him to jail, where his sufferings are unknown
> or forgotten, is a less public, a less striking, and therefore a more
> dangerous engine of arbitrary government.[326]

As the 20th century drew to a close, a rising fear of terrorism began to generate legislation that infringed the writ of *habeas corpus*. In 1996, for example, Congress passed the Antiterrorism and Effective Death Penalty Act. Among other things, it imposed a one-year statute of limitations on *habeas* petitions and created procedural hurdles at the state and local levels. The act was passed by a wide bipartisan margin in both houses. It was largely a reaction to the bombings of the World Trade Center in New York City in 1994 and of the Alfred P. Murrah Federal Building in Oklahoma City in 1995. This act marks the beginning of a concerted effort by Congress and the executive to weaken *habeas corpus* in the context of terrorism, emanating both from foreign and domestic sources.

Now it is clear that Congress should have passed legislation that unequivocally barred torture and extraordinary rendition. But in fact the opposite came to pass. Every time the Supreme Court found procedural or constitutional problems with laws bearing on persons illegally detained, the president proposed and the Congress passed countervailing legislation. The George W. Bush administration was determined to capture, interrogate, torture, and incarcerate indefinitely suspected "terrorists"—even in the absence of any semblance of due process. And Congress was its willing handmaiden.

Following the atrocities of 9/11, Congress immediately passed the 2001 Authorization for Use of Military Force.[327] This law gave the president the power to use all necessary and appropriate force against those who he determined had "planned, authorized, committed, or aided the terrorist attacks that occurred on September 11, 2001, or harbored such organizations or persons."[328]

On November 13, 2001, President George W. Bush signed a military order titled "Detention, Treatment, and Trial of Certain Non-Citizens in the War Against Terrorism." It mandated that only a military tribunal could try noncitizens. The secretary of defense was given authority to appoint military commissions. And in an opening salvo against *habeas corpus*, Section 7 stated:

> [T]he [detained] individual shall not be privileged to seek any remedy or maintain any proceeding, directly or indirectly, or to have any such remedy or proceeding sought on the individual's behalf, in (i) any court of the United States, or any State thereof, (ii) any court of any foreign nation, or (iii) any international tribunal.[329]

This order is characteristic of a fundamental difference in the way in which U.S. and European authorities have approached suspected terrorists and terrorism in general. In the United States, terrorism is largely construed as a threat to national security, requiring a military response. This perspective is certainly apparent in the ill-conceived invasion of Iraq in 2003. In Europe, terrorism is more typically seen as a crime.

Indeed, the major European powers have far more experience with terrorism and have dealt with it for centuries. They have experienced thousands of kidnappings, bombings, assassinations, and arson. And they have prosecuted and otherwise confronted numerous terrorist organizations including the Algerian Front de la Libération Nationale (FLN) and Action Directe in France; the Baader-Meinhof Gang and the "Revolutionary Cells" in Germany; and the Irish Republican Army in the United Kingdom. Officials in these states tend to view terrorism not as a threat to the nation but as a species of crime. In the United States, conversely, terrorism is always ideologically charged.

On October 16, 2002, Congress enacted a separate Authorization for Use of Military Force to pave the way for military action against Iraq.[330] But as the so-called "global war on terror" ground on, large numbers of prisoners began to be taken, especially in Iraq and Afghanistan. Some were enemy combatants captured on the battlefield or suspected terrorists. Others were not hostile and had committed no crime but found themselves in the wrong place at the wrong time. This created a conundrum for the Bush administration, in particular Secretary of Defense Donald Rumsfeld and his deputy Paul Wolfowitz—who had jurisdiction over the military internment centers. If the prisoners were brought to the United States, they could file a writ of *habeas corpus*. The U.S. government would have to explain why they were being held and tortured without a trial. They might even be released.

It was a public-affairs nightmare, but one with a ready, if unprincipled, solution. The administration would rely on the 1950 *Eisentrager* case. It argued that *habeas corpus* was not available to prisoners held outside U.S. sovereign territory because the U.S. courts lacked jurisdiction—places like Abu Ghraib and Camps Bucca, Cropper, Whitehorse, Samarra, and Qaim in Iraq, at the Parwan Detention and Bagram Theater Internment facilities in Afghanistan, at CIA black sites and, of course, at the U.S. Naval Station at Guantánamo Bay, Cuba.

But this approach did not stand for long. In *Rasul v. Bush,*[331] the first of four Guantánamo-related cases, the Supreme Court established that the U.S. court system does indeed have the authority to hear *habeas* petitions and decide whether or not foreign nationals detained at Guantánamo Bay are illegally imprisoned. The Court "held in *Rasul* that the prisoners could file their *habeas* petitions because for all practical purposes Guantanamo was part of the United States."[332] However, the Court decided the case on statutory grounds and not as a constitutional principle, leaving Congress and the executive free to resolve their differences with the Court by enacting further legislation. Writing for the majority, Justice Stevens stated:

> Petitioners contend that they are being held in federal custody in violation of the laws of the United States. No party questions the District Court's jurisdiction.... We therefore hold that §2241 [Judiciary and Judicial Procedure] confers on the District Court jurisdiction to hear petitioners' *habeas corpus* challenges to the legality of their detention at the Guantanamo Bay Naval Base.[333]

On the same day, June 28, 2004, the Court decided *Hamdi v. Rumsfeld*,[334] a second defeat for the executive. Yaser Esam Hamdi, an American citizen born in Louisiana, was captured in Afghanistan by American forces, taken to Guantánamo, and then transferred to a Navy prison in South Carolina. While the Court recognized the power of the government to detain enemy combatants, including U.S. citizens, it ruled that detainees who are U.S. citizens must have the rights of due process and the ability to challenge their "enemy combatant" status before an impartial authority. This, of course, included the right to file *habeas* petitions. Justice Sandra Day O'Connor wrote, "We hold that . . . due process demands that a citizen held in the United States as an enemy combatant be given a meaningful opportunity to contest the factual basis for that detention before a neutral decision maker."[335]

Essentially, the Court said that U.S. citizens held by the United States have the right to challenge their detention by filing for a writ of *habeas corpus*—no matter where they were captured or what they were doing. These two decisions caused great alarm in Congress and the Bush administration because, in addition to Hamdi, some of the prisoners held and tortured at Guantánamo were in fact U.S. citizens.

On December 30, 2005, in a direct response to the *Rasul* and *Hamdi* cases, Congress passed and the president signed the Detainee Treatment Act. It sets forth standards for treatment of persons in the custody of the Department of Defense and those held at Guantánamo Bay, Cuba. The act prohibits "cruel, inhuman, or degrading treatment or punishment" and requires military interrogations to be performed according to the U.S. Army field manual for "Human Intelligence Collector Operations."[336] It further directed the Defense Department to establish Combatant Status Review Tribunals to determine whether or not a person was an enemy combatant and therefore lawfully held.

However, the act also stripped the Federal District Courts of jurisdiction to hear *habeas* petitions from prisoners held at Guantánamo Bay. It states, "no court, justice, or judge shall have jurisdiction to . . . consider . . . an application for . . . habeas corpus filed by or on behalf of an alien detained . . . at Guantanamo."[337] Even though the Washington, D.C., Circuit Court of Appeals was granted authority to review decisions of the military tribunals, the act failed to provide operating procedures for the conduct of the tribunals. And in what amounted to a preemptive Nuremberg defense, immunity was granted to government agents and military personnel from civil and criminal action for using interrogation techniques (torture) that "were officially authorized and determined to be lawful at the time they were conducted."[338]

In 2006, the Supreme Court decided a third Guantánamo-related case, *Hamdan vs. Rumsfeld*.[339] Salim Ahmed Hamdan, a Yemeni citizen, had been Osama bin Laden's chauffeur and personal bodyguard and was trained in the use of military equipment. The Court conceded that the "Government's charge against

Hamdan [is] true . . . that Hamdan is a dangerous individual . . . [who] would cause great harm and even death to innocent civilians . . . if given the opportunity." Nevertheless, in the last sentence of the decision, Justice Stephen Breyer wrote, "But in undertaking to try Hamdan and subject him to criminal punishment, the Executive is bound to comply with the Rule of Law that prevails in this jurisdiction."[340] Handan was granted a writ of *habeas corpus*. In this case as before, the Court elected to address various statutory matters and not to decide the case on Constitutional grounds. In essence, the Court held that the Combatant Status Review Tribunals established by order of U.S. Deputy Secretary of Defense Paul Wolfowitz lacked power to proceed against prisoners because the structure and procedures of the tribunals violated both the Uniform Code of Military Justice and the Geneva Conventions.

In the wake of the *Hamdan* decision, Congress responded with the Military Commissions Act of 2006. That law divided prisoners into classes of "lawful" and "unlawful" enemy combatants. Those detainees who were classified as unlawful enemy combatants, or were awaiting hearings on their status, were prohibited from using *habeas corpus* to petition federal courts in challenges to their detention. As a result, all pending *habeas* cases at Federal District Courts were stayed. It would appear that when the Supreme Court took action to preserve or strengthen the writ of *habeas corpus*, Congress and the president enacted legislation or issued executive orders[341] to weaken it, and then in due course, the Court reasserted *habeas*. And the struggle was to continue.

Two years later in 2008, the Supreme Court took a commanding position, dramatically expanding the territorial reach of *habeas corpus* in *Boumediene v. Bush*.[342] Speaking for the Court, Justice Kennedy set forth the position of the parties:

> The Government contends that noncitizens designated as enemy combatants and detained in territory located outside our Nation's borders have no constitutional rights and no privilege of habeas corpus. Petitioners contend they do have cognizable constitutional rights and that Congress, in seeking to eliminate recourse to habeas corpus as a means to assert those rights, acted in violation of the Suspension Clause.[343]

The Court ruled that the Suspension Clause, as Article I, Section 9, Clause 2 of the Constitution is colloquially known, affirmatively guaranteed the right of *habeas* review to everyone, everywhere the United States holds jurisdiction. Indeed, *habeas* is a broad-based constitutional right, just as Justice Black argued in his eloquent dissent in *Eisentrager* case 65 years before. As Justice Stephen Breyer put it, in the *Boumediene* case, the Court "held that the constitutional words 'Writ of Habeas Corpus' did apply to Guantanamo's prisoners and that Congress had unconstitutionally suspended the writ."[344] Guantánamo detainees might finally have their day in court. But in a critical omission, the Court elected not to specify procedural requirements for the conduct of a *habeas* hearing. It simply set forth broad outlines of what is required by the Constitution. It said only that the judicial officer must have adequate authority to make a *habeas* determination, and to formulate and issue appropriate orders for relief, including if necessary an order directing the prisoner's release. As to the future, the Court said, "The extent of the showing required of the Government in these cases is a matter to be determined. We need not explore it further at this stage."[345]

In May 2009, Congress passed the Military Commissions Act after the Obama administration announced that it was considering restarting the military commission system. The new version of the act authorized the trial of "unprivileged enemy belligerents," a class of persons including those who "purposefully and materially supported hostilities against the United States or its coalition partners."[346] Detention authority under the act is broader than the trial authority of a military commission. It extends at least to traditional prisoners of war, and arguably to other categories of persons.[347] At a minimum, it reaches anyone subject to a military commission trial, including those who are part of forces associated with al Qaeda or the Taliban or those who purposefully and materially support such forces in hostilities against U.S. Coalition partners.[348]

Could persons illegally detained and tortured get their day in court? After all the legislative wrangling and landmark cases affirming the writ of *habeas corpus*, could they get a fair trial? Apparently not. According to the U.S. Army's appointed defense attorney for five of the 9/11 defendants, the military tribunal held in 2014 was little more than a "show trial." There was no possibility that the "high value detainees" would ever be released, even if found not guilty, despite the fact that some had been tortured and held incommunicado for more than 10 years at the U.S. military prison at Guantánamo Bay. Their attorneys alleged that the government installed recording devices disguised as smoke detectors in the rooms used to interview clients, and that FBI informants infiltrated the defense team.[349] "We have basically had a spy within our team for a number of months," said one defense attorney.[350] He described the torture documents that were released by the Central Intelligence Agency as incomplete and accused that agency of continuously trying to hide the truth about torture from the American public.[351]

This is the present status of *habeas corpus* as that writ applies to prisoners detained without trial by the U.S. government: The Federal District Court for the District of Columbia is empowered to try all *habeas* cases. But the higher court, the District of

Columbia Circuit Court of Appeals, has continuously instructed the lower court that the burden of proof the government has to meet is less and less. The standard is not proof "beyond a reasonable doubt" or even "probable cause." Hearsay evidence is admissible, as are unchallenged and secret government documents. The appellate court ensures this outcome by telling the lower court to reconsider its opinion, or it finds in favor of the government as a matter of law.

The decisions about whether to grant *habeas* relief fall to the District Court because that court has jurisdiction over the persons with authority to imprison suspected terrorists, specifically the president and his subordinates in the Department of Defense, the Central Intelligence Agency, the Federal Bureau of Investigation, and so on. Other federal district courts, which might hold the government to a higher standard, are not permitted to hear these *habeas* cases. We must therefore conclude that a small number of persons have subverted the protection of the Constitution, and arguably of the court system as well, to promote their vision of national security in the context of Secure Democracy.

CHAPTER VII

////////////////////////////

SURVEILLANCE
AND CONTROL

James Madison wrote in *Federalist* 51, ". . . the great difficulty lies in this: you must first enable the government to control the governed; and in the next place oblige it to control itself." Madison, of course, believed that division of powers, particularly within the legislative branch, would provide a necessary check on tyranny. But he could not have anticipated the rise of a Security Industrial Complex or the unaccountable powers that the digital revolution would bestow on secret government agencies. Nor could he foresee the rise of the imperial presidency.

Nevertheless, if we are to reclaim liberal democracy in the 21st century, Madison's admonition must apply directly to the internal security state—specifically including surveillance of the populace, interception of their papers and electronic communications, and the circumstances under which they may be detained or imprisoned.

Contending factions surely attempt to bend or conform the law to support their interested perspectives. Legal interpretations often vary from one administration, court, or generation to the next and are sometimes contradictory. Courts often defer to the executive in matters of national security. And in a war emergency, even the most basic rights and principles of jurisprudence can be suspended for some classes of individuals or abandoned for military expediency. In Secure Democracy, where extreme internal security measures are the "new normal" and institutionalized under the perception of a permanent emergency, rule of law is routinely set aside by agents of the surveillance-security state.

By virtue of the surveillance programs they have developed, government agencies can invade and misappropriate the electronic transmissions and intellectual property of unsuspecting "targets." They can compile remarkably detailed dossiers on any individual. Portions of the court system are permitted to operate in secrecy—a direct assault on liberal democracy—dispensing opinions and warrants in non-adversarial proceedings. Security agents conduct extraordinary rendition of persons they suspect of terrorism and other crimes, often based on digital information surreptitiously obtained. Many detainees are handed over to political authorities in countries where they are certain to meet with harsh treatment. The executive can promulgate secret executive orders that may be illegal or unconstitutional, maintain secret prisons with torture chambers, and suspend the writ of *habeas corpus* for suspected terrorists.

As the degree of government secrecy and coercion increases in liberal democracy, rule of law recedes to the background. Fundamental protections that undergird rights and freedoms are degraded. Illegal searches and theft of electronic data, often referred to as warrantless surveillance, are commonplace. No one will disagree that the technology is outpacing the legal system, and the ability of legislatures and courts to regulate both private and public sector surveillance in a meaningful way.

After all, law is conservative, in the sense that libraries conserve the intellectual progress of the past. But technology knows no limits. In 1965, the founder of Intel Corporation, Gordon Moore, published a brief paper in which he argued that the complexity and computing power of microchips would double roughly every two years but that the cost of production would remain relatively stable.[352] "Moore's Law," as it came to be known, is essentially a techno-economic prediction that the pace of development in digital technology proceeds in a geometrical progression. That is, if the computing power of a machine doubled every two years from 1965 to 2015, the new machine would be approximately 33.5 million times more powerful than a computer built in 1965. And a machine built in 2017 would have about 67 million times more computing power than the original 1965 model.

Moore's Law is not a physical law, but its accuracy captures the explosion of digital innovation over the past half century, together with the invention of myriad new devices in the 21st century. Contrast this trajectory with the snail's pace at which law proceeds. By the time the legal system can understand and regulate an emerging digital technology, the particular device or method of storing, transmitting, or manipulating data is often obsolete.

Transition to Secure Democracy

Coercion is essential to the administration of justice in liberal democracy, as in all forms of governance. Taxes cannot be collected if penalties do not attach to tax evasion. Contracts and property rights must be enforced to maintain order in society. The police must confront traffic violations, disorderly conduct, larceny, embezzlement, fraud, armed robbery, and murder and mayhem of all kinds. The renowned American political scientist Theodore

J. Lowi has characterized this attribute as "incomplete conquest," arguing that liberalism differs from other forms of governance because it embodies principles, institutions, and practices that create space for fundamental rights of persons.

As coercion and secrecy increase, however, rule of law becomes more attenuated. A greater degree of license and empowerment attaches to the agency of internal security. This creates transformative conditions for the onset of Secure Democracy and other forms of governance that are potentially far more authoritarian. This idea is depicted in **FIGURE VII.1**, Transition to Secure Democracy.

Activities listed in cell A can lawfully be conducted in the context of modern liberal democracy. History demonstrates, however, a clear propensity to scale up coercion against internal threats in a national emergency, typically a state of war, where the techniques listed in cell B are likely to be applied: Civil War suspension of *habeas corpus*, WWI Palmer Raids, WW2 internment of U.S. citizens of Japanese descent, Cold War FBI Cointelpros. These infringements announce the prospect of Secure Democracy, but not necessarily its arrival. In these cases, when the war emergency ended, so too did the more aggressive cell B–type internal security activities. But we had not yet entered the 21st century, characterized as it is by unending war and the fear of terrorism.

In the late-20th-century view, then, some combination of pluralism and interest-group liberalism governed or delimited the American response to terrorism at home and abroad. There were limits as well: no state-sponsored internal assassinations of protest leaders, no torture chambers for dissidents, no death squads for enemies of the regime, and certainly no assassinations carried out by remotely piloted aircraft. Moreover, the system appeared to have self-correcting features. As one academic noted in early 2001, "American counterterrorism policy is not just a response to the

FIGURE VII.1:

TRANSITION TO SECURE DEMOCRACY
(ATTENUATED RULE OF LAW)

	Mode of Counterterror Application	
	Internal	External
Passive c o e r c i o n	**A** Stockpile security Port/container security Transportation security Passive intelligence collection Surveillance under warrant Border/immigration controls Investigations/audits	**C** Travel document security Passive intelligence collection Antiterrorism Assistance (ATA) Surveillance (all kinds) Extradition Interrogation (limited) Intimidation
i n d e x **Aggressive**	**B** Targeting lists "Black bag jobs" Extraordinary Rendition Intrusive investigations Intimidation/threats Incarceration /detention Disruption of groups Economy-wide surveillance Internment of classes of people	**D** Infiltration/disruption of groups Incarceration Torture Assassination Preemptive strikes Predator/drone military strikes Invasion/occupation Indiscriminate murder War crimes

threat of terrorism, whether at home or abroad, but a reflection of the domestic political process."[353] True to a point, but in 2001, the demise of liberal democracy had only begun.

Under conditions of Secure Democracy, internal security operations of the United States and other formerly liberal countries have become far more aggressive. Increasing infringements tend to outlive their initial causes. Indeed, Moore's Law and the onslaught of digital technology have deeply enabled the coercive powers of government. The scale of intelligence operations has exploded, in tandem with technological advances, largely in response to the politics of fear promulgated by political elites and unelected leaders of the intelligence agencies.

Although it is ultimately an empirical matter, it is not clear that the body politic can retain a full range of civil liberties in light of the rise of a potent Security Industrial Complex, the digital revolution, and the radical transformation of democratic theory set forth above. Civil liberties have already been withheld from suspected terrorists and profiled groups. No doubt, these would come under renewed and harsh assault if another 9/11-type mass-casualty terrorist attack occurs. Liberty might also be further compromised in the wake of a series of smaller, episodic terrorist events such as multiple coordinated suicide bombings at shopping centers, attacks at sports stadia, or assassinations in legislative chambers.[354] The politics of fear was codified by the Bush administration and extended under Obama in executive orders, repressive legislation, and secret surveillance programs, and by generally building up the bureaucratic infrastructure of internal security.[355]

Figure VII.1 also suggests a far darker side of internal security in its external or global dimensions. Cells C and D describe the illiberal side of Secure Democracy, scaling up to atrocities that would clearly be illegal and intolerable if inwardly directed. If these counterterror measures were initiated against citizens within a state's jurisdiction, it would introduce authoritarian dimensions to the state in question. President George W. Bush—who exhibited a less than robust grasp of democracy—was fond of saying that terrorists attack us because they hate our freedom.[356] The same would be true of political elites and intelligence officials who authorized internal use of the range of counterterror methods suggested in cells C and D. The important question is whether the *internal* versus *external* division suggested in Figure VII.1 can be maintained, because it is this difference that genuinely distinguishes Secure Democracy from outright authoritarian tyranny. Cell D activities like remotely targeted assassination or torture conducted by one state in another country are clearly repugnant to liberalism. This analytical distinction suggests that Secure Democracy occupies an intermediary position between more liberal and more authoritarian governance.

There can be no doubt that Secure Democracy promulgates authoritarian practices in response to threats to domestic security based outside the sovereign territory of the state. The evidence comes from the black sites in which the Central Intelligence Agency and the military tortured persons in the absence of any legal process. In authoritarian regimes, there are few if any inhibitions. Political elites authorize or otherwise tolerate a broad range of coercive instruments—from surveillance and rendition to torture, assassination, and military occupation. The only limiting factor is the ability of the state to project power in the international or regional system. For this reason, the right (or "external") side of Figure VII.1 includes the most coercive counterterrorist methods and operations, all of which have been deployed in the not-too-distant past. Nevertheless, such methods appear, for the time being, to be externally focused in the context of Secure Democracy and its 21st-century manifestation.

But a state of permanent emergency could arise and perhaps has already arisen, even in the United States, as a pathological response to a single instance of high-casualty terrorism. Permanent emergency could also appear in reaction to threats posed by accelerating proliferation of technologies and materials that underlie chemical, biological, radiological, and nuclear (CBRN) weapons. One can imagine the emergence of a new form of the state beyond Secure Democracy, a kind of authoritarian democracy in the mid-21st century. It would be aided and abetted by public-sector intelligence bureaucracies tightly coupled with lucrative private-sector security interests. From a theoretical perspective, then, the interesting movement is taking place inside the formerly liberal polities, not the more authoritarian ones, and among cells B, C, and

D of Figure VII.1. The important question is the extent to which the liberal state adopts illiberal internal security measures. This is the crucial dimension on which Secure Democracy can be distinguished (at least for now) from its more authoritarian cousins.

The foregoing chapters have argued that liberal democracy as envisioned by Enlightenment thinkers and by America's Founding Fathers has been transmuted. It is a direct result of the empowerment of a global Security Industrial Complex, exemplified by the United States and stretching into the democracies of Western Europe and Asia, in much the same way that the U.S. Military Industrial Complex dominates and infuses itself into the military establishments of its counterparts in those same regions.

At the beginning of his second term in May of 2013, President Obama made a major speech on counterterrorism at National Defense University. He declared, "America is at a crossroads . . . we have to recognize that the scale of this threat closely resembles the types of attacks we faced before 9/11." He nevertheless endorsed a policy of winding down the "global war on terror," employing a more measured use of lethal drone attacks, closing the detention camp at Guantánamo Bay, and, importantly, "engaging Congress and the American people in efforts to refine and ultimately repeal the Authorization to Use Military Force" enacted following the attacks of 9/11. The speech is important because the president attempted to use just-war theory to explain a more limited approach to counterterrorism.[357] But the corrections that the president envisaged did not come to pass.

The following month, Obama nominated James B. Comey as director of the Federal Bureau of Investigation, replacing Robert S. Mueller III, who had built up the counterterror orientation and assets of the bureau. As deputy attorney general in the George W. Bush administration, Comey had challenged the legality of the NSA surveillance programs and opposed CIA torture. Given

President Obama's speech and Mr. Comey's prior inclinations, it was widely anticipated that he would rein in the counterterror obsession within his bureau. But a year after assuming the post as director, Comey acquiesced, "I didn't have anywhere near the appreciation I got after I came into this job just how virulent those [al Qaeda] affiliates had become. There are both many more than I appreciated, and they are stronger than I appreciated."[358] Comey assured the Senate Committee on Homeland Security, "Counterterrorism remains our top priority. The FBI works with our law enforcement and intelligence community partners to integrate intelligence and operations and to detect and disrupt terrorists and their organizations."[359]

President Obama came into office promising to close down the detention center at the U.S. Naval Station at Guantánamo Bay. Despite a spirited effort, Congress would not acquiesce, and the president was unable to do so. He clearly felt that his predecessor had gone too far in the areas of surveillance, detention, torture, and invasion. But in the main, and to the consternation of many of his supporters, Obama continued the counterterror and internal security policies put in place following 9/11. It is also clear that once in office, FBI Director Comey had a change of heart, almost a revelation that the problem of terrorism was much greater than he had previously assessed it to be. President Obama may have come to the same conclusion.

It may also be that when outsiders take up the mantel of protecting the internal security of the nation, their objectivity is compromised. They are inducted into a world in which the threat of terror is paramount. It is their reason for being. And believing this to be the case even when it is not, they act accordingly. This characteristic tends to permeate the culture of security organizations. And with the growth of the Security Industrial Complex, the culture of internal security is reinforced and amplified. This explains in part the willingness of CIA Director John Brennan to defy and confront the Senate Select Committee on Intelligence, his agency's oversight committee. When coupled with secrecy and the mandate to defeat terror, internal security culture helps to explain the insular and autonomous aspects of intelligence operations.

If significant terrorist attacks again take place in the United States, or if a broad-based terrorist organization surfaces, operating under a cohesive ideology, a wide range of counterterror techniques would likely be deployed. Europe has generated the most important cases to date, the Madrid and London subway bombings in 2004 and 2005 and the 2015 *Charlie Hebdo* massacre and the coordinated attacks that killed 130 in Paris, among others. Many were carried out by EU citizens but inspired by radical Salafist and jihadi ideology.[360] Because the major European powers have large and alienated Islamic populations, Europe will likely present more test cases for the limits of liberal tolerance pushed outward by the security requirements of the state.[361] But in this respect, Europe is not alone, as the San Bernardino and Orlando attackers both pledged allegiance to the Islamic State, although no direct connection to the group was found in either case.

Terrorism poses its most serious challenge to the liberal democratic tradition globally, precisely because fear of terrorism invokes draconian responses from political authorities and intelligence units.[362] In the United States, the precedents are already clearly drawn, and particularly the advent of widespread government surveillance of the society, and indeed the world, which political elites consider necessary to detect and prevent terrorist attacks.

Economy-Wide Warrantless Surveillance

Is privacy a thing of the past? As the digital age unfolded at the turn of the 21st century, it seemed so to the CEO of Sun Microsystems, who called consumer privacy "a red herring." As he put it, "You have zero privacy anyway. Get over it."[363] Despite the blunt quality of this statement, it may provide a lens into the meaning of privacy and its antonym, surveillance. As we have seen, the information-technology industry not only generates records on everyone and everything, but also has long been both complicit and compelled in government spying. Perhaps as important, people (often teenagers and young adults) throw caution to the wind, posting intimate details of their lives on social-media outlets, where it can be misused and rarely if ever recalled. If many people do not care about privacy, then perhaps privacy is a compelling but not the most important issue. Is it possible to stop the government spy agencies and giant information-technology companies like Facebook and Google from scooping up vast quantities of big data? Can the indiscretions of young people addicted to over-sharing and self-disclosure be contained?

A "reasonable expectation of privacy"[364] is, of course, a mandatory requirement for protection under the Fourth Amendment to the Constitution. If there is no such expectation, the Fourth Amendment protection requiring a warrant based upon *probable cause, supported by oath . . . and particularly describing the place to be searched and the persons to be seized*" is not available.[365] If there is no expectation of privacy, evidence obtained would generally be admissible in any court in a civil or criminal proceeding.

Accordingly, if the controlling issue in Secure Democracy is not privacy, then we should examine surveillance. But what is surveillance and what, if anything, is wrong with it? According to the Oxford English Dictionary (OED), the word first appeared in print in 1799 in connection with "Vast *depôts* of . . . property . . . in the rooms belonging to the office of the committee of *Surveillance*." This committee was established during the French Revolution in 1792 "at first to keep watch over suspicious strangers, then to recommend suspects for arrest. Local surveillance committees were started all over the country." According to 19th-century French statesman and historian Adolphe Thiers, during the Reign of Terror, "As the prisons had been just cleared by death, the Committee of Surveillance began to fill them again by issuing fresh orders of arrest."[366] One notorious member was the physician and radical polemicist Jean-Paul Marat. During the brief period of Jacobin rule, he used the Committee of Surveillance to incarcerate and execute enemies of the Revolution, often without trial and with no possibility of appeal. He is quoted as saying, "Five or six hundred [aristocratic] heads cut off would have assured your repose, freedom, and happiness."[367] And perhaps more shocking, "Man has the right to deal with his oppressors by devouring their palpitating hearts."[368] Shades of contemporary Syrian jihadists and the Islamic State executions?

The OED provides two relevant senses of the word surveillance. The first is a "[w]atch or guard kept over a person, etc., esp. over a suspected person, a prisoner, or the like; often, spying, supervision; less commonly, supervision for the purpose of direction or control, superintendence." This definition clearly invokes the original French meaning. The mandate of the Committee of Surveillance was to discover enemies of the state, watch over them, confiscate their property, and imprison them in circumstances that would almost certainly lead to harsh treatment and summary execution. The relationship of surveillance to the Reign of Terror is most revealing. Terror is here conceived as a function of the revolutionary French state, and surveillance as a set of mechanisms through which terror is administered and ultimately achieved, mainly in the form of public beheadings and firing squads.

A similar relationship exists today between state surveillance and targeted killings by remote drone warfare. Persons are selected (no doubt by committee) for surveillance, targeting, and assassination. Because of strict state secrecy, it is "unclear who is involved in the process, how the chain of command works, and who is ultimately responsible for strikes."[369] The connection between Robespierre and the Terror conducted by the Committee on Surveillance during the French Revolution was likewise obscure and attenuated.[370] Like President Obama, Robespierre spoke of high democratic principles and sought to distance himself from the mechanisms of state terror.

The rationale for the execution of these people by remote control is that they are known "terrorists," mistaken identity and murder of innocent bystanders to the contrary notwithstanding. This mushy term pits the *state as terrorist* against a person or group it labels terrorist. The executions are accomplished through the mechanism of surveillance followed by state-sponsored, targeted killings. The ethical and moral contradictions involved in state-sponsored episodic terrorism are made manifest in the difficulty authorities have in recruiting and retaining drone operators. A 2013 Defense Department study "found that pilots of drone aircraft experience mental health problems like depression, anxiety, and post-traumatic stress at the same rate as pilots of manned aircraft who are deployed to Iraq or Afghanistan."[371] For this reason, the U.S. Air Force planned to cut the number of armed drone flights per day from 65 to 60 by October of 2015, even though the battle against the Islamic State was heating up and U.S. military planners had hoped to field 70 drone missions per day.[372]

These numbers, if correctly reported by *The New York Times*, are truly staggering. They would indicate that drone warfare has been normalized, because the number of such flights would be on the order of 23,750 per year. Extensive use of armed drones is likely the prelude to robotic warfare. We could only hope that it is like a video game where drones of one nation or group battle those of another. But the reality is far different, both in the control rooms and on the ground. The greater likelihood is that robotic weapons will be used to kill people who cannot defend themselves. As drone technology deepens and spreads inexorably around the globe, we should ponder a simple question: What would be the political and military response if a foreign nation or group launched a drone strike against a terrorist group like the Ku Klux Klan or the Animal Liberation Front in United States? From an ethical standpoint, it is clear that drone warfare is incompatible with liberal democratic principles.[373]

Most digital data collection can be classified as surveillance. And appropriately, the second OED definition has to do with devices used in police or military activity such as surveillance drones, radar surveillance, and surveillance satellites. It reads, "*attrib.*, esp. of devices, vessels, etc., used in military or police surveillance." The first English-language usage of this aspect of the term dates to 1947: "It recommended that surveillance radar be developed as an adjunct to airport traffic control. . . . Surveillance radar could be used by control tower personnel to . . . locate planes [etc.]." This newer meaning of the term "surveillance" is clearly attached to military and police hardware and technologies. It is embedded in the military acronym C[4]ISR and networks, where "S" has long stood for "surveillance" and is a critical link in military planning, target acquisition, and the overall conduct of electronically enhanced warfare.[374] From the perspectives here provided, it is impossible to say that surveillance is a neutral activity, or that the violation of personal privacy is its most malevolent aspect.

Surveillance also connotes control. This attribute can be arrayed as a continuum or spectrum with largely benign activities such as inventory control systems in grocery stores and hotel loyalty cards at one extreme. To compile big data, sometimes called data analytics, grocery chains like Kroger and Safeway issue discount cards that link the purchase of specific items to the preferences and identity of individual customers. The same systems control the inventory of the store. Many shoppers do not realize that by using a discount card, they are creating a dossier on their likes and eating habits that can be analyzed over time and combined with other data sources to compile remarkably detailed personal profiles. In many respects, this form of digital profiling and control of individuals creates efficiencies that have little direct impact on the millions of persons who are involved because it attaches mainly to things. But there is also a potential for annoyance if advertisers use grocery store data to target advertisements to consumers, and for abuse—for example, if health-insurance providers used discount-card surveillance data to adjust premiums or penalize persons who eat irresponsibly. Surveillance of the browsing habits of Internet users would also fall into this category.

Other forms of surveillance occupy the middle range of the spectrum of control. Consider the digital bracelets that are attached to the ankles of some residents in rest homes. The bracelets alert the staff to the location and likely activities of the person to whom it is issued. An alarm sounds when the person opens a door or attempts to leave the rest-home facility. In many but not all instances, such bracelets are clearly for the protection of residents who may lack mental competency. But sometimes they are placed on ankles or wrists for the convenience of the staff. Or as an economy measure to enable larger resident-to-staff ratios, thus increasing profits for the owners and investors in the rest home. This kind of surveillance verges on direct control and may even be imposed against the will of the individual as a form of soft imprisonment.

At the other extreme of the continuum, modern for-profit prisons are now constructed and fitted with surveillance devices to control all aspects of a prisoner's day-to-day behavior. Closed-circuit cameras abound. Automatic doors, lights, and temperature controls determine the location and environment of prisoners. Sophisticated digital surveillance and control systems also regulate access to and egress from dangerous chemical, biological, radiological, and nuclear facilities. They are also used in industry to control cash and valuable merchandise.

In the middle of the spectrum, "smart" elevators and buildings that employ complex surveillance systems govern access and egress not only of the general public. They also control the movements of persons who are employed in the building or have other legitimate reasons to be there. It is very difficult to draw a line where surveillance ends and control of the individual begins. This is manifest in many diplomatic facilities, for example, the U.S. consulate in Munich, Germany. There, security measures are onerous—blast-proof doors, multiple security checkpoints, electronic and physical searches, and temporary confiscation of electronic media and devices. Indeed, a theoretical or even a practical distinction between the concepts of surveillance and control simply cannot be sustained because they interact, change, and reinforce one another.

The implications of the relationship between surveillance and control are more far-reaching in the context of government surveillance under conditions of Secure Democracy. By incremental degrees, cameras have populated stores, street corners, gathering places, and the like. As has been shown, the intelligence agencies record all manner of metadata, phone conversations, and other electronic communications. An increasing number of municipalities use surveillance cameras and other devices to affect traffic control. This is an unpopular development, as most drivers honor traffic rules, especially speed limits, in the breach. Could most people honestly say they never speed on the interstate highways or in areas where speed limits seem unreasonable? This society-wide deceit flies in the face of the old bromide: "If you have nothing to hide, you have nothing to fear." Does society really want to enforce, through surveillance, all of the bad laws that are still on the books, for example the vast array of laws governing adultery, sexual orientation, and even the physical positions in which sex is permissible? Indeed, in the United States, the "number and variety of laws regulating sex are staggering."[375]

Technology and the Law

The transition to Secure Democracy occurred in the context of the digital revolution. Here we find a constant refrain: Technology continuously outpaces the law. Twenty-five years ago, very few people owned cell phones and no one possessed a personal computer even approaching the capability of a Samsung Galaxy or an Apple iPhone. Today, it is estimated that between 1.5 and 2 billion smart phones are in use globally. Moreover, they are increasingly able to run the 3.7 million existing apps.[376] During this same time period, the Internet and the number of persons with access to it expanded globally and exponentially.

Because of these developments, it became possible for public- and private-sector organizations to conduct surveillance in ways the law could not anticipate or control. Another example: 25 years ago, most people stored their data on disc drives and local computers. Today, they copy their work to remote servers, collectively known as the "cloud," primarily although not exclusively owned by companies in the digital sector. People generally believe that their communications, their data, and their identities are safe. But of course the opposite is true: Data-mining algorithms continuously investigate and probe even the most private aspects of our lives. States, military organizations, and criminals continuously hack into computer systems. Even Mark Zuckerberg places a sticker over the camera and microphone embedded in his computer, just in case the National Security Agency, a competitor, or some hacker succeeds in turning the device on remotely.

In the decade following 9/11, it became clear that the U.S. government was deeply engaged in penetrating the cloud and intercepting Internet traffic. By 2015, the digital-technology companies began to see complicity with government surveillance as a threat to their business. European competitors took out ads extolling the greater privacy of their networks. Indeed, many companies share vast amounts of data with the government and have done so for many years. But after Edward Snowden expropriated a reported 1.7 million secret files from the National Security Agency and released 200,000 intelligence documents[377] detailing widespread government surveillance, more and more companies began to encrypt their software and networks. They did so to bolster public confidence and protect the flow of valuable marketing data.[378]

The issue of unbreakable encryption at the level of the digital device—such as tablets, smart phones, and computers—caused considerable consternation among leaders of intelligence agencies and even heads of state. Indeed, "[t]he F.B.I., the intelligence agencies, and David Cameron, the British prime minister, have all tried to stop Google, Apple, and other companies from using encryption technology that the firms themselves cannot break into."[379] When devices are encrypted, it means that intelligence agencies and the police have to obey the law. They must obtain a warrant and present it to the owner of the information in order to obtain access to it—something they have often been able to circumvent in the past. Indeed, most such surveillance is kept secret from suspected persons or groups. It is a criminal offense to reveal government demands for information to persons under investigation.

Apple was among the first to encrypt information at the level of the individual device, in theory placing emails, photos, text messages, call logs, contacts, and other data beyond the government's reach, and importantly, beyond the reach of the police and intelligence agencies. The response from the Federal Bureau of Investigation was swift and unequivocal. Director Comey, who was holding a press conference devoted largely to the Islamic State of Iraq and Syria, complained, "What concerns me about this is companies marketing something [the iPhone 6] expressly to allow people to hold themselves beyond the law." This was, of course, a privilege that had traditionally been reserved for secret government agencies. Comey predicted dire consequences.[380] He talked about the web "going dark."

His counterpart at the U.K. Government Communications Headquarters, Robert Hannigan, was even more dramatic. He accused the American technology companies of providing "command-and-control networks of choice for terrorists and criminals."[381] He asserted that the militant Islamic State group was "exploiting the power of the web to create a jihadi threat with near-global reach." He called for "a new deal between democratic governments and the technology companies in the area of protecting our citizens."[382] Any such "deal" would of course make available the private correspondence of ordinary people to law enforcement and intelligence agencies.

Historically, the U.S. government worked closely with the telecommunications industry, gaining ready access to phone conversations and other forms of telephony data. In 1994, for example, the U.S. Congress passed the Communications Assistance for Law Enforcement Act (CALEA). It mandates that telecommunications companies create an encryption key or "back door" to their otherwise encrypted networks so that law-enforcement and intelligence agencies can conduct electronic surveillance pursuant to a court order or other legal authority.[383] In theory, the requirement for legal process ought to be sufficient to protect citizens from indiscriminate wiretapping by government agencies. But under conditions of Secure Democracy, the intelligence agencies have not been content to follow legal process, as numerous investigative reports and leaked intelligence documents attest.

Initially, the CALEA legislation did not apply to Internet-based communications services and digital companies that handle Internet traffic. In fact, in the 1994 act, Congress exempted Internet companies from the "back door" decryption requirement.[384] But in 2004 the government—specifically the Department of Justice, the Federal Bureau of Investigation, and the Drug Enforcement Agency—filed a petition with the Federal Communications Commission to extend the CALEA legislation to a range of Internet service providers. Accordingly, the regulations now cover some broadband Internet access and voice-over Internet protocol (VoIP) providers such as Skype, but not Internet-based email, instant messaging, peer-to-peer services, and social networking.[385]

The government's argument, spearheaded and promoted relentlessly by FBI Director Comey, is that the Internet is "going dark."[386] Advances in encryption can make it impossible for intelligence and law-enforcement agencies to access data in motion (real time) or stored data (held on digital devices), even when they have a search warrant issued by a federal court. In the absence of government intervention, or so the argument goes, Islamist and other militants who use the Internet to plot and carry out acts of terror and criminals—the FBI often cites child-abuse offenders—will run amuck. Public advocacy groups such as the Electronic Frontier Foundation and numerous Internet-based companies counter that mandating the creation of such "back doors" weakens the overall security of telecommunications generally and of the Internet as well. Criminals, states, and military cyber-commands, as well as terrorist organizations, they say, will inevitably learn to exploit legally mandated, built-in encryption keys and other legislatively created vulnerabilities. The only way to secure the Internet from hackers of all stripes (governments, corporations, syndicates, gangs, and tech-savvy lone wolves or wolf packs) is to encase it in increasingly strong encryption technology.

This was a source of major headaches for the Federal Bureau of Investigation and the other intelligence agencies, which continued to push for "back door" access to encrypted technology. Director Comey is reported to have told the Senate Judiciary Committee he was attempting to make arrangements (short of a legislative request) with the Internet companies because, he said, the Islamic State group had succeeded in reaching 21,000 English-speaking persons through social media, particularly Twitter. (How could he possible know this, and is there anyone who could challenge his statement?) As he told the Senators, "This is not your grand-father's al-Qaida. There's a device, almost a devil on their shoulder all day long saying, 'Kill, kill, kill, kill.'"[387] What Comey and Hannigan undoubtedly knew, but would not say, is that in the 21st century the Internet functions as a global surveillance platform, tracking the movements, associations, habits, and personal data of hundreds of millions of individuals. They did not want to impede access to this investigative resource.

It is perhaps ironic that an insatiable lust for markets and valuable personal data at times pits commercial data-mining oper-ations, device makers, and Internet service providers against the intelligence and law-enforcement establishments. Nevertheless, private-sector surveillance continues to mushroom, and pro-tection of privacy is first and foremost a business consideration. Indeed, the protestations of companies in the digital economy are unlikely to preserve fundamental rights. If anything, in a liberal democracy one would expect government to protect the privacy rights of citizens against potent business interests, in much the same way that antitrust, child labor, and food and drug laws were passed to protect workers and consumers in the late 19th and early 20th centuries.

But in the debate over the USA Freedom Act of 2015, the Internet giants banded together to lobby for limitations on government surveillance of the Internet, as well as stronger legal controls on "intelligence agencies seeking to collect or compel the production of information" from Internet service providers. Governments, they said, "should allow companies to publish the number and nature of government demands for user information." They also extolled the virtues of "respecting the free flow in information."[388] If this development can be taken at face value, then it may be that Secure Democracy is not as monolithic as some have suggested. Indeed, the relationship between the digital sector of the economy and the intelligence sector of the state may, at times, be one of confrontation and adversarial power relations. The most positive interpretation is that corporate resistance may impede the progressive spread of Secure Democracy, a point that is the subject of further analysis in the final chapter of this book.

In 2014, the European Court of Justice took steps to impose its privacy standards on Google and other Internet service providers. In a case arising in Spain, the court ruled that individuals have the right to remove adverse or embarrassing information and images from the Internet, even when those images or information is true.[389] It is a positive development, but not one that can be easily enforced or that is necessarily to the liking of the digital giants. Moreover, the court did not say anything about national-security information or digital material that is collected, sold, or otherwise exchanged for marketing or other purposes that is not made public. And it did not address the problem of cooperation and data sharing among intelligence agencies of different states.

As it turns out, the National Security Agency and the General Communications Headquarters have significant relationships with the intelligence communities of many EU member states. They have, for example, thoroughly penetrated the German telecommunications networks, including of course tapping Chancellor Angela Merkel's mobile phone. Despite outrage over U.S. surveillance in the German press, there is no doubt that the German intelligence community freely engages with these foreign agencies, spying on Germans and other EU citizens. One study by the European Parliament put it this way:

> Evidence gathered on the surveillance activities of the German intelligence services also indicate that Germany has been engaging in large-scale surveillance of communications data, and that these activities are linked to a network of exchange and transfer of data with both domestic intelligence and law enforcement agencies as well as with international partners. . . .[390]

German law provides some legal protections for privacy, specifically Article 10 of the Basic Law for the Federal Republic of Germany—Privacy of correspondence, posts, and telecommunications. Part (1) states, "The privacy of correspondence, posts, and telecommunications shall be inviolable."[391] This is the kind of unequivocal language found in the First and Fourth Amendments of the U.S. Constitution. But there is also part (2):

> This right may be restricted only by or pursuant to a law . . . to combat the danger of an epidemic, to respond to a grave accident or natural disaster, to protect young persons from serious neglect, or to prevent crime.

It would appear that Article 10 creates an "inviolable" right in part (1) and then empowers myriad exceptions in part (2), such as "to prevent crime." We know that part (1) is not "inviolable" because the U.S. National Security Agency maintains sophisticated surveillance facilities at Griesheim, Germany, and collaborates with the German intelligence services. Indeed, the National Security Agency has been active in Germany for decades. There are, in fact, more than 240 American intelligence analysts working at U.S. facilities in Germany, capturing and analyzing data flowing into and through most of Europe.[392]

Clearly, privacy legislation and the rulings of various courts are an insufficient foil against the surveillance powers of intelligence agencies that populate liberal democracies. Increasingly, these agencies share intelligence and operate in one another's territory. International collaboration in surveillance is decades old, perhaps originating with the "Five Eyes" intelligence alliance including Australia, Canada, New Zealand, the United Kingdom, and the United States. These countries share signals intelligence under a series of multilateral agreements originating during the Second World War. Moreover, the U.S. intelligence community occupies a singular position in global surveillance analogous to its military position, i.e., it leads by sheer power, size, innovation, technical sophistication, commitment of funds, and the ability to invade many regions of the world.

The Struggle over Surveillance

In 2014, the U.S. Supreme Court ruled unanimously in *Ryley v. California* that police could not search a cell phone without a warrant. The case was remarkably well grounded. It was hailed as a victory by privacy-rights advocates. In its opinion, the Court noted:

> Our cases have recognized that the Fourth Amendment was the founding generation's response to the reviled "general warrants" and "writs of assistance" of the colonial era, which allowed British officers to rummage through homes in an unrestrained search for evidence of criminal activity. Opposition to such searches was in fact one of the driving forces behind the Revolution itself.[393]

Ryley is a landmark case because it incorporates the right to privacy of personal data in handheld devices into the Fourth Amendment as a fundamental principle in the modern era. The case is, however, limited in scope because it restrains only a miniscule segment of the surveillance community.

The courts took up the larger issue of illegal government surveillance in 2006 in a challenge to the President's Surveillance Program, a highly classified operation initiated by the White House in 2001. It was carried out by the National Security Agency with information dissemination coordinated by the Director of National Intelligence. The program authorized not only the collection of metadata but also the content of phone calls, emails, and other electronic communications entering or exiting the United States.[394] It is not possible, of course, to determine in many cases where a call or other electronic communication originates or the place to which it is directed. And so the National Security Agency collected a great deal of data on U.S. persons in contravention of the law. Moreover, many people in the United States have business, social, and even family ties with persons who live abroad. Clearly, these communications should not be fodder for the intelligence agencies. These were nevertheless scooped up as well.

In 2006, a U.S. District Court ruled in *ACLU v. NSA* that the President's Surveillance Program was unconstitutional. But the following year, the Sixth Circuit Court of Appeals overturned the decision. The American Civil Liberties Union and other plaintiffs lacked standing because they could not prove that their communications had been intercepted by the National Security Agency.[395] Talk about a catch-22! In October of that year, the Supreme Court refused to review the case on appeal without comment. In this and similar situations, the Court has made itself less relevant because it often defers to national-security interests, specifically the state-secrets privilege and the Classified Information

Procedures Act—which shield classified information, removing many such cases from the Court's jurisdiction.

The legality of broad-based surveillance programs is and will be the subject of ongoing legislation, litigation, and philosophical debate. One federal judge found that the surveillance programs of the National Security Agency were necessary to confront terrorism and also legal. He "acknowledged that the data collection system is far-reaching, and 'vacuums up information about virtually every telephone call, to, from, or within the United States.'" He wrote, "This blunt tool only works because it collects everything. Such a program if unchecked imperils the civil liberties of every citizen." Nevertheless, he stated his belief that if the surveillance programs had been in effect prior to 9/11, the terrorist plot might have been detected.[396]

This is, of course, a highly speculative supposition. It panders to the fear of terrorism rather than terrorism itself. Another federal judge saw the matter differently. He found the National Security Agency program to be in direct conflict with the Constitution. He wrote, "I cannot imagine a more 'indiscriminate' and 'arbitrary invasion' than this systematic and high-tech collection and retention of personal data on virtually every citizen. . . . Surely, such a program infringes on 'that degree of privacy' that the Founders enshrined in the Fourth Amendment."[397]

Following the release of the initial Snowden documents, the legal authority for the National Security Agency to sweep up metadata on U.S. electronic communications came under even greater scrutiny. Senator Tom Udall of New Mexico led the charge, initiating a review of the agency's domestic spying program by the Privacy and Civil Liberties Oversight Board.[398] The board found that the agency had overstepped its authority. The surveillance programs, it said, were not authorized under Section 215 of the Patriot Act and violated the Electronic Communications Privacy

Act. The "NSA's telephone records program," it stated, "also raises concerns under both the First and Fourth Amendments to the United States Constitution."[399]

In concert with this report, the American Civil Liberties Union again brought suit against the National Security Agency, alleging that its domestic spying programs were illegal and unconstitutional. The District Court found against the ACLU, holding that section 215 was not subject to judicial review. Moreover, the lower court said that statutory claims regarding the scope of 215 would fail on the merits and that 215 did not violate the Constitution. It was a resounding setback for the plaintiffs.

But the U.S. Court of Appeals for the Second Circuit unanimously reversed the lower court. It held "that § 215 and the statutory scheme to which it relates do not preclude judicial review, and that the bulk telephone metadata program is not authorized by § 215."[400] Because it found domestic surveillance conducted under section 215 to be illegal, the court did not address the question of constitutionality. Nevertheless, the timing of this decision was consequential because it immediately preceded and informed the reauthorization debate in Congress over Section 215. Moreover, it set the conditions for passage of the USA Freedom Act of 2015,[401] which reformed the Patriot Act and had languished in the House of Representatives at the end of the previous Congress.

The Freedom Act created significant controversy when it reached the Senate floor in June of 2015. Majority leader Mitch McConnell introduced three amendments that if passed would have further weakened the bill, restoring unrestricted surveillance. Indeed, the bill exposed a rift in the Republican Party, with presidential hopeful Senator Rand Paul using the issue of surveillance to amplify his libertarian credentials, hoping to resuscitate his flagging campaign.[402] In defiance of McConnell, he was able to delay briefly the passage of the Freedom Act, simultaneously sending out numerous fundraising letters and appeals focusing on his opposition to surveillance and the USA Patriot Act.

President Obama intervened in the debate on the eve of the Senate vote. He characterized the Freedom Act as necessary to ensure both the security of the nation and the liberty of the people. He invoked the threat of terrorism, even though it is well documented in Congressional hearings that bulk metadata programs have failed to uncover terrorist plots over a 13-year period.[403] He approached his subject in a deliberate way, attempting to balance liberty and security, but careful not to mention The broad-based surveillance programs that sweep up metadata on telecommunications taking place in the United States and internationally as well. He put it this way:

> Today, when investigating terrorist networks, our national security professionals can seek a court order to obtain certain business records. Our law enforcement professionals can seek a roving wiretap to keep up with terrorists when they switch cell phones. We can seek a wiretap on so-called lone wolves—suspected terrorists who may not be directly tied to a terrorist group. These tools are not controversial. Since 9/11, they have been renewed numerous times. FBI Director James Comey says they are "essential" and that losing them would "severely" impact terrorism investigations. But if Congress doesn't act by tomorrow at midnight, these tools go away as well.[404]

What the president did not say is that the Federal Bureau of Investigation and the National Security Agency had for years usurped authority. Using a broad interpretation of Section 215 of the USA Patriot Act, the intelligence agencies had illegally conducted economy-wide domestic spying operations, ostensibly authorized by secret interpretations of the law and secret warrants issued by the Foreign Intelligence Surveillance Court.

Three days later, Congress passed the Freedom Act. The White House and some media outlets hailed the act as a significant redirection of surveillance policy. So too did Human Rights Watch in an editorial supporting its passage.[405] But some politicians and rights organizations were more ambivalent. The Electronic Frontier Foundation, for example, assessed that the Freedom Act made some advances but that more work needed to be done. In its words: "While the USA Freedom Act may have neutered the phone records surveillance program and provided much needed transparency to the secretive FISA Court overseeing the spying, it didn't solve the broader digital surveillance problem.[406] And Congressman Ted Poe voted against the bill because it had been substantially weakened by amendments, largely accommodations to the intelligence agencies,[407] in the House prior to reaching the Senate. His office issued a press release explaining his position:

> [B]tween the Committee vote and the House floor the bill was changed and it now confused what should have been clarified. The version of the USA Freedom Act that passed the House today leaves room for different interpretations, potentially giving NSA the ability to continue to act outside the intent of Congress and the Constitution. I could not support a bill that may allow abuses of the fourth amendment to continue.[408]

Essentially, the legislation was a direct reflection of President Obama's decision to add privacy protections and retain most of the surveillance capacity put in place following the terrorist attacks of 9/11. It did not, for example, abridge any of the vast powers bestowed on the intelligence agencies by Executive Order 12333 as amended, titled "United States Intelligence Activities."[409] It left roving wiretaps in place, which enable the government to maintain continuous surveillance on criminal and terrorist suspects who frequently switch cell-phone numbers. And it did not stop surveillance of suspected terrorists, labeled as "lone wolves," who are not affiliated with terrorist organizations. But perhaps most important, the act and the surveillance policy of the Obama administration left the Security Industrial Complex fully intact, while bestowing a patina of legitimacy on domestic and international digital surveillance activities. It was a compromise thoroughly acceptable to the intelligence community. Following the Senate action on June 2, President Obama petulantly reiterated his long-held position on security and privacy:

> After a needless delay and inexcusable lapse in important national security authorities, my Administration will work expeditiously to ensure our national security professionals again have the full set of vital tools they need to continue protecting the country. Just as important, enactment of this legislation will strengthen civil liberty safeguards and provide greater public confidence in these programs, including by prohibiting bulk collection through the use of Section 215, FISA pen registers, and National Security Letters and by providing the American people with additional transparency measures.[410]

Even though the Freedom Act changes the way in which certain intelligence is collected and stored, the intelligence agencies can find workarounds—although the use of a traditional warrant or subpoena may be required.[411] In the weeks following the passage of the act, for example, the Federal Bureau of Investigation changed its policy from surveillance of "lone wolf" suspects to arresting them. Fellow traveler Chairman Richard Burr of the Senate Select Committee on Intelligence provided the reasoning. He said that the FBI arrests are "an indication that the increased number of threads of threats . . . is at the highest level that most of us have seen since 9/11."[412] Clearly, the reduced authorities under that act made very little difference in terms of the overall surveillance architecture. But depending on how the law is interpreted, it might possibly require some procedural restraints on government surveillance, a point that is addressed in the conclusion of this book.

It was readily assumed at the time that secret documents leaked by NSA whistleblower Edward Snowden had broadly influenced the American and European publics and their legislatures. He made video appearances and received awards at numerous venues including the Cato Institute, Swedish Television News, Amnesty International in France, the Festival of Liberty in Brussels, and at Princeton University—among many others. But on balance, when we examine the structure of the Security Industrial Complex, its historical insubordination to rule of law and its mushrooming presence in terms of authority, budgets, and sheer numbers of agents, we have to conclude that the Snowden affair was merely an inconvenience, at most an embarrassment to the guardians of the internal security. With respect to the USA Freedom Act, the debate centered on three principal items: the collection of metadata, roving wiretaps, and electronic tracking of suspected "lone wolf" terrorists. All of these techniques are preserved in one form or another.

There are two separate standards and two disparate powers of the government in Secure Democracy. The first takes place in a sphere of transparent openness that is generally responsive to rule of law, indeed creates it, interprets constitutional principles, and so on. This includes the *Riley* case, in which the U.S. Supreme Court banned warrantless searches of cell phones, and the Freedom Act. The other takes place in the clandestine world of intelligence and counterterrorism, typically beyond the reach of the courts, where programs and actions are secret and largely unaccountable to the public and most of the public's representatives.

CHAPTER VIII

FREEDOM IN THE BALANCE

In the end, will Secure Democracy prevail over liberalism? Will our privacy and our freedom ultimately be destroyed by the rise of the surveillance security state?

There can be no doubt: The internal security states in the United Kingdom, continental Europe, and especially the United States have mushroomed in scale and scope far beyond the tolerances of liberal democracy. Politicians and security chiefs maintain and increase power by perpetuating a narrative in which the threat of terrorism is permanent and paramount, when, in reality, terrorism is limited, indeed infinitesimal, compared with other causes of death—events like murder, war, gun accidents, and traffic fatalities. Suspects are held incommunicado and tortured, persons summarily deported, privacy invaded, police powers expanded, the Great Writ compromised, secrecy elevated, and *ex parte* secret courts established. The polity that exists today would be unrecognizable to political philosophers of the 18th century, to those who debated the U.S. Constitution in 1787, and to their colleagues in France who put the finishing touches on the Declaration of the

Rights of Man in 1789, including the Marquis de Lafayette, who was a general in the American Revolution and regularly consulted the U.S. envoy to Paris thereafter, Thomas Jefferson.[413]

Some may argue these foundational documents are embedded in a revolutionary period of enormous intellectual gestation, one in which it was possible, even prudent to elevate the rights of the individual in relation to the powers of kings and the agency of government. But if the rights of a single individual collide with the broader security interests of the society, then the Constitution should be set aside. The catch phrase is that the Constitution is "not a suicide pact." In this view, it is not necessary to follow the letter of the law in extreme cases, particularly if it might compromise national security. This view dates to Justice Robert Jackson's extended dissent in *Terminiello v. City of Chicago*. Jackson served as chief U.S. prosecutor during 1945 and 1946 at the Nuremberg Trials of Nazi war criminals. It is likely the anti-Semitic language Terminiello used to whip up the crowds in Chicago alarmed Jackson. He was acutely aware of the violent, radical speech the National Socialists used to take power and turn Germany into a police state.

Arthur Terminiello was a Catholic priest from Alabama under suspension by the Vatican. He addressed a mass meeting of the Christian Veterans of America in Chicago in 1946, working up the crowd with racist comments. Outside, a Communist rally of some 1,000 persons grew disorderly. They threw brickbats and broke windows to disrupt the meeting. The police were unable to maintain order and a riot ensued. Terminiello was charged with a breach of the peace and fined $100. He claimed a violation of his right to free speech, which the U.S. Supreme Court upheld. In his dissent, however, Justice Jackson laid down a marker. "The choice is not between order and liberty," he wrote. "It is between liberty with order and anarchy without either. There is danger that, if the court does not temper its doctrinaire logic with a little practical wisdom, it will convert the constitutional Bill of Rights into a suicide pact."[414]

Terminiello is a landmark case because it rejected Justice Jackson's view, setting a precedent for the acceptance of outrageous speech, even the kind that we saw in the run-up to the presidential election of 2016. Responding to brutal terrorist attacks in Paris and San Bernardino, presidential candidate Donald Trump engaged in demagoguery reminiscent of Europe's fascist past. He called for registration of Muslims and a total ban on Muslims entering the United States and said in a campaign press release, "It is obvious to anybody the hatred [of Muslims] is beyond comprehension. . . . Until we are able to determine and understand this problem and the dangerous threat it poses, our country cannot be the victims of horrendous attacks by people that believe only in Jihad, and have no sense of reason or respect for human life."[415] With his propensity for radical, irresponsible speech, Trump is lucky that Jackson's dissent did not prevail.

In the cases that followed *Terminiello*, however, the U.S. Supreme Court used the "death pact" phrase as a straw man, setting up Jackson's position and then knocking it down.[416] The phrase, however, has become a kind of shorthand for extending the powers of the internal security state, even if it means suspending the fundamental and foundational laws of liberal democracy. In this view, security must triumph over constitutionalism in the fight against terrorism, because it is the only way to maintain safety and order in a technologically advanced society. The Constitution was written for a simpler, less dangerous time—or so the argument goes—an era when nuclear and biological weapons did not exist. Distant terrorists could not strike the capitals of Western Europe and North America, and criminal hackers could not disrupt commercial payment systems, disable electrical grids, or steal military secrets. And so, they say, the times have changed and we must meet the new security challenges head-on.

But the liberal democratic state is no anachronism. It defines and enables enlightened values and a particular view of governance and human freedom that is timeless. The enduring aspects of liberal democracy are made manifest in more recent incarnations of the liberal spirit, indeed, the Charter of Fundamental Rights of the European Union, which entered into force with the Treaty of Lisbon on December 1, 2009.

Now some may argue that the charter is less relevant because the European Union faces significant challenges, namely serious debt default in Greece, unwonted immigration, a lackluster economy, and, in 2016, the Brexit—the vote in the United Kingdom to leave the European Union. But this perspective ignores the fact that the EU charter still protects some 450 million people, both in prosperity and in economically challenging times. Moreover, as time progresses, responsible leaders of the United Kingdom will come to see that leaving the European Union has many downsides and few benefits. In time, it is likely that arrangements will be made to circumvent the leave vote—which will come to be seen as a symbolic veto, as economic and political realities come into clearer focus.

Fundamentally, the EU charter embraces the same conception of humanity evident in the U.S. Constitution and the French Declaration of the Rights of Man, affirming fundamental rights that "everyone" shall have. Several of its provisions pertain directly to our subject. Article 4 states, "No one shall be subjected to torture or to inhuman or degrading treatment or punishment." Article 7: "Everyone has the right to respect for his or her private and family life, home, and communications." And Article 8, which could not have been envisaged in the 18th century, guarantees the "Protection of personal data." From the preceding chapters we know that Secure Democracy has little use for the principles articulated in these articles. If honored to the letter, they would curtail many of the activities of the surveillance security state.

In the U.S. Constitution (as in Article 4 of the EU charter), "cruel or unusual punishment" is forbidden, but unlike the EU charter, the Constitution does not specifically mention "torture" or "inhuman or degrading treatment." Under Secure Democracy, the Central Intelligence Agency sought and received authorization to commit such acts. The agency sanitized its language, substituting the code words "harsh" and "enhanced" interrogation when what transpired was degradation and torture. Secure Democracy enabled the agency to hide behind secrecy laws and perverse interpretations of the Constitution. Moreover, when illegal detention and torture of suspected terrorists finally came to light, the perpetrators were indemnified; and the Central Intelligence Agency was able to maintain the euphemism "enhanced interrogation," even in the glare of Congressional hearings and investigative reporting by the media. The Central Intelligence Agency had long since destroyed videotapes documenting torture.

The Fourth Amendment of the U.S. Constitution enshrines the "right of the people to be secure in their persons, houses, papers, and effects. . . ." Its modern-day incarnation is Article 7 of the EU charter: "Everyone has the right to respect for his or her private and family life, home, and communications." But with the rise of the surveillance security state, intelligence and law-enforcement agencies routinely invade private and family life and steal or copy all kinds of papers, electronic communications, telephone conversations, and other forms of data. Article 8 of the EU charter is even more specific, far-reaching, and tailored to modern circumstances, conferring as it does the "right to the protection of personal data . . . on the basis of the consent of the person concerned." It places an "independent authority" between the individual and the state to assure "compliance." These powerful provisions pertain both to government and to private-sector data mining, surveillance, and extraterritorial transfer of data.

The EU's highest court, the Court of Justice, upended data-transfer operations of Facebook and other digital giants in 2015, as discussed below.

In some respects, the EU charter echoes the U.S. Constitution, both because it contains clear and unequivocal language protecting fundamental rights and because there is a constant pulling and hauling between federalism and what is called "states' rights" in the United States and "national sovereignty" in the European Union. As the U.K. exit in 2016 has shown, federalism is far more entrenched, even ascendant in the United States—and only an impoverished cousin in Europe. Even great projects may have unsteady beginnings. When Benjamin Franklin emerged from Independence Hall at the conclusion of the Constitutional Convention in 1787, one Mrs. Powell of Philadelphia approached him. She quipped, "Well, Doctor, what have we got, a republic or a monarchy?" He is said to have responded, "A republic, madam, if you can keep it."

We can certainly conceive of Franklin's "republic if you can keep it" as one bookend of an epoch, and of Secure Democracy as the other, and in between a 250-year history of the freest people the world has ever known. But even this seems an unsatisfactory depiction because as free people, we cannot tolerate the usurpation of power at the heart of Secure Democracy and remain free for very long. Indeed, we have a duty to future generations to roll back the tide of Secure Democracy and expose it for the fraud that it is.

This book begins with an exposition of the constituent elements of Secure Democracy. It documents the extent to which they have penetrated the state and the body politic, especially in the United States, but also the United Kingdom and in other Western democracies as well. It concedes that we can and will argue interminably about how to interpret the U.S. Constitution and the other great documents of modern liberalism. We will often disagree, and we may not always be able to live up to them. But we know what they mean. And we do not have to accept bloated intelligence assessments and disinformation about terrorism emanating from politicians focused on the next election and security chiefs eager to consolidate their power. We can—indeed, we must—embrace a different and more compelling narrative. Everyone has rights. Inhumane and humiliating treatment and torture are illegal. Arbitrary imprisonment and cruel punishments are banned. Anyone can think and say or write anything that he or she wishes, no matter how outrageous or contrarian it may seem to others—save shouting "fire" in a crowded theater, threats of assault, and "fighting words." Everyone is entitled to the greatest possible degree of freedom consistent with basic public order, and this can only be limited through due process under law. We know that human dignity is founded on the right to privacy, even if we do not always call it a right, and even if some people intentionally expose their privacy to public scrutiny over the Internet.

I have argued that this conception of liberalism is infringed in many areas by the encroachment of Secure Democracy, which has not made us more secure. It has, instead, created an extended state of emergency, engaged us in prolonged and futile foreign wars, and invoked the ire and hatred of vast populations in many countries of the world. It is a pathological, often militaristic response to the fear of terrorism, which has sparked a growing assertiveness of Islamist militancy and contributed to ruinous disorder in parts of the Middle East, North Africa, and South Asia. Secure Democracy is now lodged in the hard core of a secret surveillance security state, mainly through the agency of intelligence, law enforcement, and paramilitary organizations. It is supported and expanded by the irrational fear mongering of unethical politicians and intelligence "professionals" who stand to gain from its ascendance. They have convinced a great many people that "terrorism" is the ultimate threat when environmental degradation, coastal flooding, over-population, nuclear warfare, nationalism, and scarcity of water are far more serious candidates.

This can be seen in public opinion polls. Forty-nine percent of persons polled in the United States report they are "very worried" or "somewhat worried" that they or someone in their family "will become a victim of terrorism." This number has varied between a high of 59 percent right after 9/11 and a low of 28 percent in 2004.[417] On one level, these data from Gallup may reflect the psychological horror of videos featuring jets crashing into skyscrapers in New York, as well as beheadings, immolations, and crucifixions in the Middle East. But in light of more rational considerations, they are absurd: Over the past 10 years, the average number of terrorist incidents in the United States was approximately 18 per year, and some of them were trumped-up conspiracies inspired by the government—like the Sears Tower and Newburgh Four plots of 2006 and 2009. The number of attacks involving fatalities averaged less than two per year over the same period. There is, accordingly, a monumental discrepancy between the fear of terrorism promulgated by elites (and amplified by the media) and the near total absence of terrorism itself.[418] The whole edifice of internal security is built upon this fallacy. It is instructive to compare these numbers to any other statistic about death. The number of murders by firearms in the United States averaged 13,750 per year, 2007–11.[419] And there was a steep rise in the number of incidents involving an active shooter, defined as "an individual actively engaged in killing or attempting to kill people in a confined and populated area"—with 1,043 casualties for the period 2000–13.[420]

Despite the dearth of terrorism in the United States, fear of terrorism has nevertheless deeply penetrated the body politic. It is difficult to reconcile the fact that terrorism is so limited with widely held beliefs that individuals are vulnerable, that terror is a prevalent, and that it is here to stay. This mistaken view has joined U.S. foreign policy and domestic-security policy; it has led to the greatest transformation of the American political landscape since the New Deal. While the presidency of Franklin Roosevelt created the foundations of a welfare state, the presidencies of George W. Bush and Barack Obama fashioned the surveillance security state, which will be far be more difficult to dismantle than Lincoln's suspension of *habeas corpus*, Roosevelt's internment camps, and Hoover's Cointelpros.

Over the past decade and a half, the Security Industrial Complex has steadily increased in scope and power, insinuating itself into the highest levels of government in Washington and London, and to a somewhat lesser extent into the other leading liberal democracies of the world, especially France and Australia. Political rhetoric and fear mongering have persuaded the public that enhanced internal security powers and enormous security budgets are necessary to preserve democracy when, actually, the opposite is true. When it comes to counterterrorism and internal security, the peoples of North America and Western Europe are about as rational and progressive, which is to say not very, as their governments.

Does this mean Secure Democracy is here to stay?

An irreversible process may be under way, through which liberal democracy will ultimately be compromised and subverted, giving way to more authoritarian forms of governance. Certainly, many of the elements are in place. Political elites and security professionals, as the polls suggest, have persuaded most people that terrorism—whatever that word may mean—must be stopped at any cost. And make no mistake; the costs are very high—even though none of the terrorism shills will specify in public what they actually are. At the same time, a steady stream of classified papers leaked to the media and leveraged under the Freedom of Information Act alarmed and dismayed many. These documents establish that the National Security Agency, the Federal Bureau of Investigation, the Drug Enforcement Agency, and other intelligence and law-enforcement organizations infiltrate society, track and record a multitude of communications, and invade the privacy of innocent persons—sworn testimony of the intelligence chiefs before Congress to the contrary notwithstanding. It is also clear that law-enforcement and intelligence agencies are deeply engaged in spying and "sting" operations that clearly look like entrapment to ordinary citizens, even though it is not recognized as such by the courts or other political authorities. They make a spectacle in the media, with staged "terrorist incidents," arresting persons incapable of planning or executing such actions—without the direct and material assistance of the Federal Bureau of Investigation and/or other agencies of the U.S. government.

There is, in short, a contest of will between those who promote Secure Democracy and those who see it as the end of the liberal democratic arc in history. So far the security advocates appear to be winning, hands down. They have shrouded their activities in secrecy, built bureaucratic empires, and manipulated politics and the law to achieve their ends. They have garnered and expended hundreds of billions of dollars in funding, building the Security Industrial Complex and deepening their political influence. But there are, nevertheless, a number of countervailing trends that could potentially bring greater transparency, accountability, and rationality to the conduct of internal security, possibly slowing our descent into Secure Democracy.

Civil society provides perhaps the strongest element of resistance to Secure Democracy. It includes hundreds of non-governmental organizations and advocates who focus on civil liberties, electronic privacy, freedom of information, rogue intelligence activity, extralegal renditions, torture and assassinations, data protection, intrusive data mining by the private sector, Internet freedom, and the integrity of the media in many countries of the world.[421] These organizations, such as the American Civil Liberties Union, the Electronic Frontier Foundation, the Public Voice Coalition, and the Electronic Privacy Information Center, among many others, work continuously to expose the underside of Secure Democracy. While they perform essential functions, such as monitoring the Security Industrial Complex and leveraging secret documents into the public domain, they are typically not well funded and often do not coordinate their activities.

In 2009, however, over 100 such civil-society groups from many nations of the world did come together on the margins of 31st International Conference of Data Protection and Privacy Commissioners in Madrid, Spain. At that time, they drafted the Madrid Privacy Declaration, which is a powerful statement of principles in support of liberal democracy.[422] If the organizations that signed the Madrid Declaration and allied elements of civil society can survive and even grow, they can do much to counter the narrative of fear and secrecy implicit in the establishment of Secure Democracy. Their task is not an easy one because the institutions of Secure Democracy are deeply rooted and still retain a veneer of legitimacy. Nevertheless, these organizations may present viable challenges through the courts, the media, and other institutions of liberal democracy that still function to some degree, and by organizing likeminded people to protest and engage in nonviolent civil disobedience.

It may also be possible for civil society to influence various legal systems to moderate or even weaken Secure Democracy. Two examples come to mind, one in the United Kingdom and the other in the United States. In the United Kingdom, a tradition of appointing an independent reviewer of terrorism legislation dates to the middle 1970s when the Prevention of Terrorism

(Temporary Provisions) Acts and the Northern Ireland (Emergency Provisions) Acts were passed. The purpose of the independent reviewer is to examine "the statutory powers related to terrorism," and to consider elements in the implementation of terrorism legislation that should be "drawn to the attention of [the U.K.] Parliament."[423] The reviewer has access to classified materials and to authorities within the U.K. intelligence community. As the number and intrusiveness of terrorism statutes expanded after the turn of the century, the independent reviewer was formalized under the U.K. Prevention of Terrorism Act of 2005. It is now referenced in several additional statutes and has an annual budget allocation of £250,000 per year.

The current independent reviewer of terrorism legislation is David Anderson, QC. He has held the part-time position for five years, without staff or assistants, but he has access to chambers in the British Home Office, where he can hold occasional meetings, obtain secretarial assistance, and store classified materials. The independent reviewer also consults a "special advisor" who is a former professor of criminal justice studies at the School of Law, University of Leeds.[424] In 2015, Anderson produced what can only be described as a monumental report titled "A Question of Trust." It is a comprehensive analysis of British terrorism legislation and policy, both with respect to the adequacy of contemporary security arrangements and the protection of civil liberties in the United Kingdom. The report sets forth 119 recommendations, many of them well considered, and audaciously calls for replacing U.K. terrorism legislation with:

> a comprehensive new law, drafted from scratch, which: (a) affirms the privacy of communications; (b) prohibits interference with them by public authorities, save on terms specified; and (c) provides judicial, regulatory, and parliamentary mechanisms for authorisation, audit, and oversight of such interferences.[425]

Anderson, who has announced his decision to retire as the independent reviewer, unabashedly writes, "My task is not to adjudicate, but to design a better system."[426] The report also describes British terrorism legislation as "incomprehensible to all but a tiny band of initiates," which is also true in the United States. It continues, "A multitude of alternative powers, some of them without statutory safeguards, confuse the picture further . . . this state of affairs is undemocratic, unnecessary, and—in the long run—intolerable."[427] Although the independent reviewer has conducted a wide-ranging and commendable analysis, his resources are nevertheless severely limited. Additionally, the U.K. prime minister and Parliament are under no obligation to accept his recommendations. It is, nevertheless, a hopeful sign because the institution of the independent reviewer appears to be growing in stature and influence. A proposal to establish a privacy and civil-liberties board passed Parliament and received royal assent on February 11, 2015. It was to have been chaired by the independent reviewer and would have substantially increased his resources and powers.[428] But after much wrangling, the government of Prime Minister David Cameron decided not to establish it. Instead, the independent reviewer was granted three special assistants and a budget increase of £50,000.[429]

As new terrorism legislation was introduced in 2014 and 2015, then–British Home Secretary Theresa May (now the U.K. prime minister) told Parliament that the government would present "new standards for openness, transparency, and oversight" to U.K. terrorism legislation, a body of law widely criticized as disjointed and unintelligible. She promised that "world-leading oversight arrangements" would be applied to the U.K. intelligence community. But civil-liberties groups derided the proposed legislation as a "breathtaking attack on the Internet security of every man, woman, and child in our country."[430] It included the Anti-Social Behaviour Crime and Policing Act 2014, the Counter-Terrorism and Security

Act 2015, the Criminal Justice and Courts Act 2015, the Serious Crime Act 2015—all passed by the first half of 2015. None is clear or lucid.

It is possible that media attention to extensive spying in Europe by the National Security Agency and various European intelligence units helped to create a climate somewhat more conducive to the protection of liberty and personal information in the United Kingdom—and more so in other parts of Europe.[431] Thanks to Edward Snowden. But it is also clear that a single independent reviewer (even with three advisors and additional funds of £50,000) is hardly a match for the tens of thousands of agents who populate MI5, MI6, the Government Communications Headquarters, and other U.K. intelligence agencies. And in the wake of the Islamic State–inspired attacks in Paris in 2015 and Brussels in 2016, it is likely that European security agencies will gain additional funding and authorities as well.

Terrorism legislation in the United States has also come under closer scrutiny. The USA Freedom Act of 2015 can be read as imposing modest new strictures on the intelligence agencies. For example, it explicitly prohibits bulk data collection under Sections 215 and 702 of the Foreign Intelligence Surveillance Act of 1978, as amended—the very sections that intelligence officials frequently cited as legal authority in the past. Moreover, it would be possible to interpret the Freedom Act as going beyond control of metadata collection to reach all domestic surveillance activity. The act prohibits "bulk data" collection with respect to three specific areas: business records (Title I, Section 103), trap and trace devices (Title II, Section 201), and FBI national security letters (Title V, Section 501). But the language is thick and impenetrable to the uninitiated, that is to say, to everyone accept a few lawyers who serve the intelligence committees of Congress.

Nevertheless, in order to obtain records under the Freedom

Act, the intelligence agencies are instructed to meet a number of requirements set by the Foreign Intelligence Surveillance Court. These include use of a "specific selection term," which means a word or phrase that particularly identifies a person, account, address, or personal device, or any other specific identifier.[432] In addition, the law may require the government to "limit, to the greatest extent reasonably practicable, the scope of tangible things sought consistent with the purpose for seeking the tangible things."[433] In other words, the agency or official requesting surveillance authority from the court cannot go on a fishing expedition, dredging up data on broad categories such as organizations, religions, professions, cities, nationalities, ethnicities, or zip codes.

When the intelligence and law-enforcement agencies petition the court with a specific surveillance request, they are now supposed to show that the records sought are relevant to an authorized investigation,[434] and that there is a reasonable, articulable suspicion that the person in question is associated with a foreign power engaged in international terrorism. This is a far cry from probable cause, yet if it is followed, it would be a step in the right direction. The act also sets forth "minimization" procedures. Accordingly, a request to conduct surveillance must be "designed in light of the purpose and technique of an order for the production of tangible things, to minimize the retention, and prohibit the dissemination, of nonpublicly [sic] available information concerning unconsenting [sic] United States persons."[435]

The Freedom Act, which amends the Patriot Act and the Foreign Intelligence Surveillance Act of 1978, also brings a limited measure of transparency to the still secret court system created under the initial act. If an important law is involved, the court must now publish its opinions or unclassified summaries of them, and it must report to Congress. The secret court is also required to appoint an ombudsman whose job is to see that constitutional and statutory rights of Americans are protected. The ombudsman may ultimately have access to information collected under the authority of the court. Although the proceedings of the court are still non-adversarial, the court can appoint *amicus curiae*, literally "a friend of the court," who can provide additional relevant information but who is not solicited by parties to the proceeding. These are technical improvements at the margins, but they offer little additional protection of privacy and of civil liberties.

Finally, the act bars all evidence that is illegally obtained—something that should not have to be legislated under the most basic principles of liberal democracy. If the secret court finds that the evidence was illegally collected, then "no information obtained or evidence derived" from it "concerning any United States person shall be received in evidence or otherwise disclosed in any trial."[436]

In layman's terms, the Freedom Act set up additional requirements for the intelligence agencies, mostly relating to domestic spying and bulk metadata collection by the National Security Agency. It introduced a limited measure of transparency into the still secret, *ex parte* Foreign Intelligence Surveillance Court system. It established procedural hurdles, but it did not put the telephone records beyond the reach of the Federal Bureau of Investigation and the National Security Agency, or even local law enforcement—just as President Obama had said.

The question going forward, then, turns on how broadly the act will be interpreted. Will it constrain only bulk metadata collection (if that) or will it have wider application to myriad government surveillance programs? Will further presidents decide to issue secret instructions authorizing prohibited internal security activity, as their predecessors have done? Certainly it will take many years to interpret the language and intent of this legislation—a language that is abstruse to an extreme degree—and for the courts to clarify the outcomes. The important issue, not addressed in the debate or in the press, is whether the intelligence agencies will comply with the law, and if the public will know if they do not. How, for example, would they react to decreases in their budgets, or to another 9/11-type terrorist attack? What surveillance, infiltration, and other tactics would they deploy against recent immigrants in the United States, marginalized people, and suspected terrorists abroad? Will they seize additional powers in the wake of the mass shootings in San Bernardino and Orlando by reportedly self-radicalized Islamic State sympathizers in 2016? In the end, will they abide by the Fourth Amendment of the U.S. Constitution—or not?

The Fourth Amendment: "*The right of the people to be secure in their persons, houses, papers, and effects, against unreasonable searches and seizures, shall not be violated, and no Warrants shall issue, but upon probable cause, supported by Oath or affirmation, and particularly describing the place to be searched, and the persons or things to be seized.*" No doubt, this standard of permissible search is routinely flouted under the auspices of Secure Democracy. Clearly, the Federal Bureau of Investigation, the National Security Agency, the Central Intelligence Agency, and others have learned to circumvent the Fourth Amendment—all the while pledging allegiance to it with great solemnity. The same can be said of every presidential administration and the dominant security elements of every Congress of the United States in the 21st century. Even in those liberal democracies where privacy is an acknowledged right, the probing surveillance of secret government agencies, both foreign and domestic, cannot easily be resisted—if it can be detected at all. Nevertheless, the expanded authority of the independent reviewer of terrorism legislation in the United Kingdom and the passage of the Freedom Act in the United States suggest a kind of pushback from civil society against unwarranted surveillance and unaccountable police powers in the United Kingdom and the United States.

The struggle between the United States Congress and the executive branch on one side and the Supreme Court on the other over the legal status and rights of detainees imprisoned at Guantánamo Bay may also be seen as an encouraging sign. It may mean that the principle of divided sovereignty at the heart of the U.S. Constitution will not be so easily disabled in the future. In 2005 and 2006, Congress passed laws to deny Guantánamo prisoners basic rights of due process, even *habeas corpus*, that are fundamental to liberal democracy everywhere.

In three separate cases bearing on incarceration of suspected terrorists at Guantánamo, the Supreme Court found statutory reasons that some privileges should be extended to the prisoners—including to extremely unpopular leaders, adherents, and supporters of al Qaeda. And in a fourth case, *Boumediene v. Bush*, the Court invoked its ultimate power of judicial review, finding the Military Commissions Act of 2006 to be unconstitutional. *Boumediene* appears to place a preliminary check on executive authority, potentially making the writ of *habeas corpus* and other aspects of due process available to Guantánamo detainees, some of whom have been illegally imprisoned for 15 years.

It is clear that the Court proceeded cautiously and with great deference to the other branches. It did not order the release of prisoners at Guantánamo, which given the crimes they are thought to have committed, was arguably a prudent course. And it did not explicitly mandate that *habeas corpus* be extended to them. But the Court did establish the principle that Congress and the president could not arbitrarily abolish or suspend the Great Writ for the Guantánamo inmates, or indeed, for anyone else. The lower courts with jurisdiction over the District of Columbia can receive *habeas* petitions from Guantánamo detainees, and then decide on the legality of incarceration on a case-by-case basis. However, the Court left open even the most basic evidentiary and procedural questions. And the lower court is populated with judges who apparently place political considerations above the Constitution of the United States.

So much so that it is unclear if the prisoners at Guantánamo will ever receive fair trials, trials that would very likely lead to convictions in many cases. The government has too much illegal and unsavory activity to hide, and it has classified most if not all of the evidence against the inmates. And so there is little certainty as to the outcome, except that the inmates have been incarcerated for many years and that their punishment will continue for the indefinite future. It is nevertheless possible that the mistakes of the past will not so easily be repeated. The weight of history may force future presidents and their henchmen to consider the likely consequences when they are tempted to round up people and torture suspects in defiance of rule of law.

There is even an emerging precedent: During the Obama presidency, suspected terrorists were routinely charged with criminal offenses and tried in courts throughout the United States. We may not like the sleazy tactics of the Federal Bureau of Investigation. Its unethical use of informants to engage, motivate, and lure unwitting persons into terrorist plots is certainly repugnant to liberalism. But at least defendants receive their day in court, even if they eventually serve mandatory 25-year sentences under draconian federal terrorism laws. But perhaps even these practices can be moderated if enough people stand up and see that their freedoms and liberal democracy are wavering in the balance.

There is as well ground for cautious optimism regarding the control of personal data in Europe. The laws and legal institutions of the European Union have reached a far better understanding of the threat to privacy—an essential element of liberal democracy—than the weary courts and contentious legislatures in the United States. We have already touched on the privacy provisions in Articles 7 and 8 of the Charter of Fundamental Rights of the European Union. In September 2015, EU Advocate General Yves Bot delivered an opinion bearing on data-privacy rights to the Court of Justice, the highest court in the European Union. He contends that Facebook (in Ireland) violated the EU charter by transferring personal data on EU citizens to Facebook servers in the United States, where privacy standards are less rigorous. The opinion specifically cited the revelations of whistleblower Edward Snowden and the PRISM digital surveillance program operated by the U.S. National Security Agency.

Bot advised the court that the EU directive that establishes "safe harbor privacy principles" for data transferred to the United States is inadequate and should not bind the national privacy authorities of the EU member states. He argued that the privacy of personal data of EU citizens cannot be guaranteed when it is transferred to the United States.[437] The U.S. intelligence agencies, he said, routinely scoop up personal data on everyone and use it in ways that are prohibited under the EU charter, specifically Articles 7, 8 (discussed above), and 47, which concerns the "Right to an effective remedy and to a fair trial." As he put it:

> [O]nce personal data is transferred to the United States, the NSA and other United States security agencies such as the Federal Bureau of Investigation (FBI) are able to access it in the course of a mass and indiscriminate surveillance and interception of such data . . . [compromising] . . . the essence of the fundamental right to respect for privacy and the other rights enshrined in Article 7 of the Charter.[438]

Bot's opinion caused alarm, not just among intelligence agencies, but also to Apple, Facebook, Google, Amazon, Microsoft, and some 400 other information-technology companies that move personal data from Europe to the United States and back in the course of business, often for analysis or advertising purposes. A representative from the industry trade association DigitalEurope said, "We are concerned about the potential disruption to international data flows if the court follows today's opinion,"[439] and in short order, that is exactly what the court did.

The Court of Justice rendered the European Commission's 2000 "safe harbor" directive that regulates data transfer to the United States invalid. The U.S. intelligence agencies, the court found, arbitrarily compromise the privacy of EU citizens. "The United States safe harbour scheme," the court said in a press release, "thus enables interference by United States public authorities, with the fundamental rights of [EU] persons."[440] The decision set aside the relevant directives of the European Commission. It also instructed the privacy regulators of the 28 EU member states to review their policies and comply with the privacy mandates of the EU charter, even if it meant prohibiting Facebook from transferring personal data from its Irish subsidiary to its data centers in the United States.

One lawyer who helped to negotiate the original safe-harbor data provisions for the United States said, "We can't assume that anything is now safe. The ruling is so sweepingly broad that any mechanism used to transfer data from Europe could be under threat." The technology companies appeared to be less alarmed, even playing down the significance of the court's opinion.[441] For the time being, they continued to transfer personal data on EU citizens to the United States. It was clear, however, that they would soon have to look for workarounds and that they would likely focus lobbying efforts on privacy authorities of the different national governments of Europe. Facebook said, "We have done nothing wrong," which is debatable considering that they collaborated with the National Security Agency in the PRISM surveillance program until they were exposed in the media and feared loss of business due to the privacy concerns of their customers. And in a matter of months, in February 2016, the European Union and the United States negotiated a new safe-harbor data deal, complete with assurances from the U.S. government that its intelligence agencies would henceforth respect EU data-privacy requirements.[442] So much for the privacy of EU citizens, whose data is once again subject to the tender mercy of the U.S. National Security Agency.

Another challenge, possibly more telling to Secure Democracy, stems from the diverging interests of the intelligence agencies and the software companies and device makers. The technology itself presents a double-edged sword. While the Internet enables access by governments and digital enterprises to personal information on virtually everyone who uses a computer (and almost everyone does), it also conveys significant liabilities. As the contemporary Internet emerged in the early 1980s, so too did computer viruses, worms, Trojan horses, rootkits, and all manner of malicious programming designed to attack computer systems as well as the broader Internet and compromise the security of data.

Today, any unencrypted computer is certain to contract viruses and entertain unauthorized access. Even systems with sophisticated encryption are vulnerable, as successful attacks on Target, eBay, JPMorgan Chase, the U.S. Office of Personnel Management, UPS, Home Depot, the Democratic National Committee, the Clinton campaign, and countless others attest. As the threats to financial institutions, the U.S. electoral process, government secrecy, utility infrastructure, commercial transactions, and personal data have escalated, so too has the power of encryption programs designed to defeat criminal hackers, hacktivists, governments, and other security threats.

As a result, law-enforcement and intelligence agencies became concerned that they would lose access to personal data. This is not a new problem. In 1995, Congress passed the Communications Assistance for Law Enforcement Act (CALEA). It requires telecommunications companies to configure their overall communications architecture to "enable law enforcement officials to conduct electronic surveillance pursuant to court order or other lawful authorization." In other words, the law is designed to empower the government to listen in on telephone conversations, even if they are encrypted. In May 2006, the Federal Communications Commission expanded the CALEA regulations to cover some broadband Internet access providers as well as other data handlers.[443] But it should be noted that this law is antiquated and cannot be applied to personal digital devices such as iPhones, computers, and tablets.

As the development of new software applications for computer systems and the Internet began to escalate in the late 1990s, an energetic debate ensued in which the U.S. government proposed to mandate a "Clipper Chip." The purpose of this chipset was to give intelligence and law-enforcement agencies covert "extraordinary access" to all kinds of data. It would keep the networks from "going dark" (an interesting phrase), no matter how powerful encryption might become. The idea was to design "encryption keys" for software applications and build "escrow systems" that would store the "keys" until the government wanted to "unlock" the data. It was an absurd idea. Some of the most brilliant computer scientists and cryptologists of the time vigorously opposed it. They concluded it would be prohibitively expensive, would introduce unacceptable security risks to the Internet, and was beyond the technical competence of contemporary software engineers.[444]

Twenty years later, Apple, Google, and other companies began to design strong encryption into computer networks and personal digital devices. The same debate began to gather storm. This time, both U.S. and British intelligence authorities accused the companies of creating secure command and control networks for terrorists and criminals. FBI Director Comey rode it like a hobbyhorse into Congressional hearings, think tanks, and the media. He argued the need for back-door, exceptional access to keep the Internet from (again, 20 years later) "going dark." But experts at MIT and several major computer companies waded into the debate. They noted that law-enforcement and intelligence agencies have far greater access to the Internet today than 20 years ago. Moreover, they wrote, "if all information applications had had to be designed and certified for exceptional access, it is doubtful that companies like Facebook and Twitter would even exist."[445] They concluded that establishing exceptional access or special access keys for the government would introduce unacceptable vulnerabilities to the Internet because foreign governments, industrial spies, and hackers would discover the decryption keys and exploit them. Moreover, there appeared to be insurmountable jurisdictional, financial, and technological challenges. The only way to secure computer systems and the Internet more generally, they concluded, would be to continue to develop currently unbreakable "forward secrecy" and "authenticated encryption" systems, and design them into software and digital devices—placing them beyond the reach of terrorists, criminals, and intelligence agencies, both foreign and domestic.[446]

But here we must add a caveat. It may in fact not be necessary to build back doors or encryption keys that enable the government exceptional access to computers and personal digital devices. The National Security Agency appears to be in the business of creating such vulnerabilities. Sometime prior to the summer of 2016, the agency lost control of some of its most sophisticated digital espionage tools and hacking software. The agency uses it to break into the computer networks of governments, corporations, and other NSA targets. According to media reports, a "cache of hacking tools with code names such as Epicbanana, Buzzdirection and Egregiousblunder" mysteriously spilled out of the National Security Agency and into the public domain.[447] These top-secret tools, which were developed at great cost by the NSA, can now be used to compromise the security of U.S. government agencies, multinational corporate networks, and any other organizations that operate computer systems. A group calling itself the "Shadow Boxers" claimed responsibility. Their identity, affiliation, purpose, and objectives could not immediately be determined.

For most of its first seven years, the Obama administration jousted with companies like Apple, Google, Facebook, and Microsoft, attempting to persuade them to provide government access to software applications with strong encryption. It became the kind of cause célèbre that Apple CEO Timothy Cook could really sink his teeth into. He told the Electronic Privacy Information Center, "Like many of you, we at Apple reject the idea that our customers should have to make tradeoffs between privacy and security. . . . We believe that people have a fundamental right to privacy. The American people demand it, the constitution demands it, morality demands it."[448] But he reserved his most confrontational language for other companies in the digital economy:

> I'm speaking to you from Silicon Valley, where some of the most prominent and successful companies have built their businesses by lulling their customers into complacency about their personal information. They're gobbling up everything they can learn about you and trying to monetize it. We think that's wrong. And it's not the kind of company that Apple wants to be.[449]

Cook's privacy campaign was good for business. As a device maker, Apple's profits do not depend on data mining, data analysis, and targeted advertising. Its main business is selling computers, software, personal digital devices, and financial services. In fact, providing encryption and greater privacy to the users of Apple products in the United States and Europe meant only one thing: more sales for Apple. But the situation in China is quite different, where Apple is reported to have disabled its news app[450] and to have censored iPhone apps related to the Dalia Lama.[451] Cook also reportedly agreed to permit "China's State Internet Information Office to carry out security audits of Apple products sold in the country."[452] It will be interesting to see if Apple can maintain its high rhetorical and ethical stance if Chinese authorities insist on exceptional access to its products to keep their end of the Internet from "going dark."

In the fall of late 2015, the Obama administration announced that it would not seek legislation to compel access to encrypted computers and other devices *at that time*, a decision that upset the intelligence agencies as well as Silicon Valley. The U.S.-based tech giants hoped to be able to tell Chinese authorities that the United States would never legislate back-door access for the government, setting a forward-facing precedent. For their part, the Federal Bureau of Investigation and the National Security Agency wanted unfettered access to all kinds of digital communications.[453] The Obama decision suggested that, for the time being at least, intelligence and law-enforcement agencies would not have direct access to personal data stored on or transmitted by encrypted smartphones and other personal devices. But that says nothing about access by companies and the National Security Agency to myriad other sources of personal data, including, for example, documents stored in the Google or Apple "clouds," and other data centers operated by hundreds of high-tech companies.

As new applications for the Internet and computing rapidly evolved, many experts took issue with the "going dark" thesis. As one technology policy specialist put it, "Embedding surveillance capabilities deeply into communications infrastructures squarely pits surveillance against security, and may, in fact, [en]danger us far more than it serves us."[454] Legal experts agreed, "Strong encryption should be deployed widely because it is essential for the Internet and computing. The logic of this position was so overwhelming that it remained firmly in place after September 11, 2001."[455] Despite the gathering muscle of Internet and computer encryption, new technologies related to the "Internet of things" continued to expand the ability of government agencies and the information-technology industries to surveil personal information. One study that convened experts from academia, industry, and the intelligence agencies argued that access to personal information would increasingly be available through expanding Internet connectivity. This included "appliances and products ranging from televisions and toasters to bed sheets, light bulbs, cameras, toothbrushes, door locks, cars, watches and other wearables [that] are being packed with sensors and wireless connectivity. Numerous companies are developing platforms and products in these areas."[456]

The Apple Corporation is, of course, at the forefront of these developments, and it was not long before the issue of encryption of personal communications devices again generated a major conflict and public debate. In December 2015, after the attack at a San Bernardino County recreation center, President Obama characterized it as an act of terrorism, and shortly thereafter the FBI opened an investigation. They soon learned the correspondence of the San Bernardino terrorist was locked up in an iPhone.

It is here that Tim Cook's role as high-tech icon and privacy advocate reached a crescendo. He took the principled position that the Apple Corporation would not build software to enable the Federal Bureau of Investigation to unlock the iPhone used by one of the attackers, and he did so in defiance of a court order. In an open letter addressed to Apple customers, Cook wrote, "The government is asking Apple to hack our own users and undermine decades of security advancements that protect our customers—including tens of millions of American citizens—from sophisticated hackers and cybercriminals." He concluded, "it would be wrong for the government to force us to build a backdoor into our products. And ultimately, we fear that this demand would undermine the very freedoms and liberty our government is meant to protect."[457]

It was a perfect storm. The world's most highly valuated corporation faced off with the world's most powerful law-enforcement agency. The U.S. Department of Justice geared up to force compliance. Apple braced for bruising public relations and legal battles. The intelligence community, the media, and privacy advocates everywhere staked out positions. FBI Director Comey told the Senate Select Committee on Intelligence, "The growing use of encryption both to lock devices when they sit there and to cover communications . . . is actually overwhelmingly affecting law enforcement."[458] It seemed as though the question of whether to provide a back door to defeat iPhone encryption would finally be resolved. But just as quickly as it had appeared on the horizon, the storm abated. The FBI found another source to unlock the shooter's iPhone, a source it refused to reveal, and the case against Apple was dropped.

The case is an important one because it shows that there is at least a segment of the digital economy that is willing to fight for privacy, even if the motivation cannot be separated from public-relations campaigns that seek to sell more products. And true, device makers and Internet service providers like Google, Facebook, Microsoft, AOL, and Yahoo have at times joined forces to call for reform of government surveillance. Indeed, they have enunciated a set of principles to limit government access to their customers' data.[459] But on the flip side, it is just as true that a hundred-billion-dollar market for surveillance software and equipment has sprung up, and companies are rushing to supply all comers, especially government intelligence and military units. It is a certainty: We cannot depend on the private sector to secure the rights and liberties that Americans and EU citizens claim to cherish.

So in the end, we find privacy, a cornerstone of freedom and liberal democracy, teetering in the balance.

It is not a balance that can indefinitely be sustained, because economy-wide surveillance and expansive internal security powers exert a corrosive force on liberty in the 21st century. Indeed, the scale, scope, and intrusiveness of the Security Industrial Complex are breathtaking. It is difficult to see how the modern democracies can scale back outsized law enforcement and intelligence operations, having built them up and armed them in the name of counterterrorism and patriotism over the past two decades. While all predictions about the course of international affairs are inherently hazardous, it seems unlikely that the disorder associated with Islamist militancy and weak or failed states will fade anytime in the foreseeable future. And even if it did, the American foreign policy of counterterrorism—and the fear of terrorism at home—would likely persist. And yet, we can assess with assurance that the Security Industrial Complex is at least an order of magnitude larger and more powerful than it needs to be. It is not the place for special interests to hold sway, and it should not function as a jobs program for college graduates.

Having ceded to government extraordinary powers "to control the governed" under Secure Democracy, we must now take steps to "oblige it to control itself," as James Madison once cautioned. Citizens and consumers can empower corporations and those elements of civil society that already take issue with the scope and reach of Secure Democracy; they can demand privacy and generally oppose government incursion against rights that are enshrined in fundamental law. The media can moderate its obsessive and prurient coverage of the few terrorist incidents that actually do occur. Professors of security studies and international affairs can help their students gain a more sophisticated understanding of the threat to liberty posed by the surveillance security state. But we cannot be naïve. We must assume that public agencies will continue to spy on us, and that the tech giants will continue to build "their businesses by lulling their customers into complacency about their personal information," just as the Apple CEO said. But it is still possible that the interests of the private sector will continue to diverge from those of the security agencies of government, especially when citizens advocate their rights, demanding privacy through encryption that no one can break. Just as 9/11 was a wakeup call to the security establishment, the establishment of Secure Democracy should be a wakeup call for freedom in the body politic.

Certainly the political and bureaucratic rationalizations to defend and even expand the surveillance security state will remain. There will be terrorist incidents from time to time that can be exploited by unprincipled politicians and overly ambitious intelligence officials. It may, indeed, be analogous to the military situation in the United States; like the military establishment, it may already be a permanent feature of pseudo-democratic governance. If so, internal security itself becomes the enemy within. We will have reached the limits of liberal tolerance pushed aside by the security mandates of the state. And in that case, freedom will be substantially diminished, as well as our conception of individual rights and of the idea of progress associated with liberal democracy from the 18th to the 21st century.

But it does not have to go that way.

We can, indeed we must, shine the light and prominence of the people into the dark spaces of fear, anxiety, and secrecy that characterize Secure Democracy. Whatever terrorism may be—and it is nothing new—we must not permit it to undermine our most cherished values. In the contest between liberty and security, there will never be a balance. Liberty must always be privileged over security. Let the great arc of history record not the demise of the open society but rather a new era in which the rights of individual expression are restored, and our most personal feelings, associations, and ideas will never again be fodder in the machinery of the surveillance security state.

ENDNOTES

CHAPTER I: THE CHALLENGE TO LIBERAL DEMOCRACY

1. "Data brokers collect and store a vast amount of data on almost every U.S. household and commercial transaction. Of the nine data brokers [examined in this study], one data broker's database has information on 1.4 billion consumer transactions and over 700 billion aggregated data elements." Federal Trade Commission, "Data Brokers: A Call for Transparency and Accountability," May 2014, p. iv. Accessed at www.ftc.gov/system/files/documents/reports/data-brokers-call-transparency-accountability-report-federal-trade-commission-may-2014/140527databrokerreport.pdf on July 25, 2014.

2. William W. Keller, The Liberals and J. Edgar Hoover: Rise and Fall of a Domestic Intelligence State (Princeton, NY: Princeton Univ. Press, 1989), pp. 9 and 34.

3. Stephen Breyer, America's Supreme Court: Making Democracy Work (Oxford, England: Oxford University Press, 2010), p. 193.

4. Op. cit., Keller, The Liberals and J. Edgar Hoover, passim.

5. Betty Medsger, The Burglary: The Discovery of J. Edgar Hoover's Secret FBI (New York: Random House, 2014), pp. 6–8.

6. See the reports of Select Committee to Study Governmental Operations with Respect to Intelligence Activities. Accessed at www.intelligence.senate.gov/churchcommittee.html on June 16, 2014. See also, Loch K. Johnson, A Season of Inquiry Revisited: The Church Committee Confronts America's Spy Agencies (Lawrence, Kansas: Univ. of Kansas Press, 2015) passim.

7. The phrase "the liberal tradition in American" refers directly to the Lochean liberal consensus expressed so eloquently by Louis Hartz, The Liberal Tradition in America (New York: Harcourt, Brace & Company, 1955), passim.

8. Many of the most important documents can be found at the Snowden Digital Library, which can be accessed at https://snowdenarchive.cjfe.org/greenstone/cgi-bin/library.cgi. See also NBC Exclusive with Brian Williams, "Inside the Mind of Edward Snowden," May 28, 2014. Accessed at www.nbcnews.com/feature/

edward-snowden-interview/exclusive-edward-snowden-tells-brian-williams-i-was-trained-spy-n115746 on June 16, 2014.

9. See Thomas L. Friedman, "Blowing the Whistle," The New York Times, June 11, 2013. Accessed at www.nytimes.com/2013/06/12/opinion/friedman-blowing-a-whistle.html?_r=0 on October 8, 2015. See also Bill Keller, "Living With the Surveillance State," The New York Times, June 16, 2013. Accessed at www.nytimes.com/2013/06/17/opinion/keller-living-with-the-surveillance-state.html on October 8, 2015.

10. Episodic terror typically involves only a few fatalities and is largely indistinguishable from serious crime; in contrast, catastrophic or existential terror involves thousands, even tens or hundreds of thousands of deaths. To date, 9/11 is the only event perpetrated by non-state actors that even approaches catastrophic terror.

11. Ariane Chebel D'Appollonia, Frontiers of Fear: Immigration and Insecurity in the United States (Ithaca, New York: Cornell University Press, 2012), p. 5.

12. CNN/ORC poll, June 1, 2015, question 20, p. 4. Accessed at http://i2.cdn.turner.com/cnn/2015/images/06/01/cnnorcpollnsa.pdf on June 4, 2015.

13. Pew Research Center for the People & the Press, "Majority Views NSA Phone Tracking as Acceptable Anti-terror Tactic," June 10, 2013. Accessed at www.people-press.org/2013/06/10/majority-views-nsa-phone-tracking-as-acceptable-anti-terror-tactic on February 15, 2015.

14. Ibid.

15. Ibid.

16. "Obama's NSA Speech Has Little Impact on Skeptical Public," Pew Research Center, January 20, 2014. Accessed at www.people-press.org/2014/01/20/obamas-nsa-speech-has-little-impact-on-skeptical-public on February 15, 2015.

17. John McCain and Lindsey Graham, "Stop Dithering, Confront ISIS Now," The New York Times, August 29, 2014. Accessed at www.nytimes.com/2014/08/30/opinion/john-mccain-and-lindsey-graham-confront-isis.html on August 29, 2014.

18. See U.K. Government, "Terrorism and national emergencies," May 11, 2016. Accessed at https://www.gov.uk/terrorism-national-emergency/print on September 8, 2016.

19. John McCain and Lindsey Graham, "Stop Dithering, Confront ISIS Now," The New York Times, August 29, 2014. Accessed at www.nytimes.com/2014/08/30/opinion/john-mccain-and-lindsey-graham-confront-isis.html on August 29, 2014.

20. Nicholas Watt and Alan Travis, "David Cameron promises new UK powers to tackle Isis terror threat," The Guardian, August 29, 2014. Accessed at www.theguardian.com/politics/2014/aug/29/david-cameron-uk-security-powers-isis-threat on August 30, 2014.

21. Australian Parliament: David Cameron's speech, November 14, 2014. Accessed at www.gov.uk/government/speeches/australian-parliament-david-camerons-speech on November 24, 2014.

22. The bill and related documents can be found at the U.K. Parliament website http://services.parliament.uk/bills/2014-15/counterterrorismandsecurity/documents.html.

23. David Cameron, "Oral statement to Parliament, Syria: refugees and counter-terrorism - Prime Minister's statement," September 7, 2015. Accessed at www.gov.uk/government/speeches/syria-refugees-and-counter-terrorism-prime-ministers-statement on September 9, 2015.

24. Quoted by Stephen Castle, "Britain Won't 'Hesitate' on Drone Strikes in Syria," The New York Times, September 8, 2015. Accessed at www.nytimes.com/2015/09/09/world/europe/britain-isis-syria-drone-strike.html?_r=0 on September 9, 2015.

25. The White House, Office of the Press Secretary, "Statement by the President on ISIL," September 10, 2014. Accessed at www.whitehouse.gov/the-press-office/2014/09/10/statement-president-isil-1 on December 26, 2014.

26. Ryan Teague Beckwith, "Read the CIA Director's Thoughts on the Paris Attacks" (transcript), Time, November 16, 2015. Accessed at http://time.com/4114870/paris-attacks-cia-john-brennan/ on November 18, 2015.

27. New York Times editorial board, "Mass Surveillance Isn't the Answer to Fighting Terrorism," November 17, 2015. Accessed at www.nytimes.com/2015/11/18/opinion/mass-surveillance-isnt-the-answer-to-fighting-terrorism.html on November 19, 2015.

28. National Public Radio, "Former CIA Chief on ISIS: 'We Have to Go After Them in Their Homeland,'" November 15, 2015. Accessed at www.npr.org/2015/11/15/456132192/former-cia-chief-on-isis-we-have-to-go-after-them-in-their-homeland on November 19, 2015.

29. Aaron Y Zelin, "Abu Bakr al-Baghdadi: Islamic State's driving force," BBC News, Middle East, July 30, 2014. Accessed at www.bbc.com/news/world-middle-east-28560449 on August 30, 2014.

30. Kristina Sgueglia, "Chattanooga Shootings 'Inspired' by Terrorists, FBI Chief Says," CNN, December 16, 2015. Accessed at www.cnn.com/2015/12/16/us/chattanooga-shooting-terrorist-inspiration on June 15, 2016.

31. John Adams, Letter to Thomas Jefferson, July 15, 1817. Accessed at http://quotes.liberty-tree.ca/quotes/individual+rights on August 30, 2014.

32. Ted Britis, "Obama administration sets new record for withholding FOIA requests," Associated Press, March 18, 2015. Accessed at www.pbs.org/newshour/rundown/obama-administration-sets-new-record-withholding-foia-requests on December 9, 2015.

33. The Takeaway with John Hockenberry, "'A New Level of Secrecy and Control': Jill Abramson on the Obama White House," Thursday, April 10, 2014. Accessed at www.thetakeaway.org/story/new-level-secrecy-and-control-nytimes-chief-jill-abramson-obama-white-house on June 2, 2014.

34. Mark Berman, "The Supreme Court won't intervene in the James Risen case. What's next?" The Washington Post, June 2, 2014. Accessed at www.washington-post.com/news/post-nation/wp/2014/06/02/the-supreme-court-wont-intervene-in-the-james-risen-case-whats-next on August 17, 2014.

35. Kaspersky Lab, "Equation Group: Questions and Answers," version 1.5, February 2015, p. 3. Accessed at http://securelist.com/files/2015/02/Equation_group_questions_and_answers.pdf on February 20, 2015.

36. "The Kaspersky equation," The Economist, February 21, 2015. Accessed at www.economist.com/news/business/21644154-russian-antivirus-firm-impresses-sceptics-again-kaspersky-equation on February 20, 2015.

37. Thomas Fox-Brewster, "NSA Hacked? 'Shadow Brokers' Crew Claims Compromise of Surveillance Op," Forbes, August 15, 2016. Accessed at www.forbes.com/sites/thomasbrewster/2016/08/15/nsa-hacked-shadow-brokers-equation-group-leak/#6a01b30977f9 on August 30, 2016.

38. Brad Heath, "Exclusive: FBI allowed informants to commit 5,600 crimes," USA Today, August 4, 2013. Accessed at www.usatoday.com/story/news/nation/2013/08/04/fbi-informant-crimes-report/2613305/ on August 20, 2014.

39. Ryan J. Reilly, "FBI Allowed Informants to Commit More Crimes in 2012 Than Year Before," The Huffington Post, December 23, 2013. Accessed at www.huffing-tonpost.com/2013/12/27/fbi-otherwise-illegal-activity-report_ n_4506385.html on August 20, 2014.

40. Brad Heath and Kevin Johnson, "Crimes by ATF and DEA informants not tracked by feds," USA Today, October 20, 2012. Accessed at www.usatoday.com/story/news/2012/10/07/informants-justice-crime/1600323 on August 20, 2014.

41. U.S. Department of Justice, Office of the Inspector General, Audit Division, "The Drug Enforcement Administration's Payments for Confidential Sources," n.d., but certainly after 2003. Accessed at www.justice.gov/oig/reports/DEA/a05/final.pdf on August 20, 2014.

42. Op. cit., Brad Heath and Kevin Johnson.

43. U.S. Department of Justice, "The Attorney General's Guidelines for Domestic FBI Operations," n.d. Accessed at www.justice.gov/ag/readingroom/guidelines.pdf on August 20, 2014.

44. Peter B. Kraska, "Militarization and Policing—Its Relevance to 21st Century Police," Oxford University Press, December 13, 2007, p. 11. Accessed at http://cjmasters.eku.edu/sites/cjmasters.eku.edu/files/21stmilitarization.pdf on July 5, 2014.

45. Thomas Michael McDonnell, The United States, International Law and the Struggle Against Terrorism (London and New York: Routledge, 2010), pp. 211–214.

46. Louise Cainkar, "Post 9/11 Domestic Policies Affecting U.S. Arabs and Muslims: A Brief Review," Comparative Studies of South Asia, Africa and the Middle East, Volume 24, Number 1, 2004, p. 245–248. Accessed at http://muse.jhu.edu/journals/cst/summary/v024/24.1cainkar02.html on September 9, 2014.

47. American Civil Liberties Union, "Fact Sheet: Extraordinary Rendition," December 6, 2005. Accessed at www.aclu.org/national-security/fact-sheet-extraordinary-rendition on June 2, 2014.

48. Open Society Justice Initiative, "Globalizing Torture: CIA Secret Detention and Extraordinary Rendition," Open Society Foundations, 2013, p. 5. Accessed at www.opensocietyfoundations.org/sites/default/files/globalizing-torture-20120205.pdf on June 2, 2014.

49. U.S. Department of Justice, Office of the Inspector General, "A Review of the Federal Bureau of Investigation's Use of National Security Letters," March 2007, p. xviii. Accessed at www.justice.gov/oig/special/s0703b/final.pdf on June 2, 2014.

50. Radley Balko, "Shedding light on the use of SWAT teams," The Washington Post, February 17, 2014. Accessed at www.washingtonpost.com/news/the-watch/wp/2014/02/17/shedding-light-on-the-use-of-swat-teams on July 5, 2014; Balko, "Rise of the Warrior Cop," The Wall Street Journal, August 7, 2013. Accessed at http://online.wsj.com/news/articles/SB10001424127887323848804578608040780519904 on July 5, 2014. Maryland Statistical Analysis Center, Governor's Office of Crime Control & Prevention, "Fifth Report to the State of Maryland Under Public Safety Article § 3-507," Fiscal Year 2014 SWAT Team Deployment Data Analysis MSAR # 7790, September 2, 2014. Accessed at http://goccp.maryland.gov/wp-content/uploads/swat-report-fy2014.pdf on October 10, 2016.

51. ACLU, "War Comes Home: The Excessive Militarization of American Policing," June 2014. Accessed at www.aclu.org/sites/default/files/assets/jus14-warcomeshome-report-web-rel1.pdf on September 8, 2016.

52. The Economist, "Paramilitary police. Cops or soldiers? America's police have become too militarized," March 22, 2014. Accessed at www.economist.com/news/united-states/21599349-americas-police-have-become-too-militarised-cops-or-soldiers on July 5, 2014.

CHAPTER II: DIMENSIONS OF THE SECURITY INDUSTRIAL COMPLEX

53. The speech can be viewed at www.youtube.com/watch?v=R_w3VHbYVZA. Accessed on September 9, 2014.

54. See Figure II.6: US Defense Spending 1948–2020 (constant 2016 dollars in billions).

55. Marcy Gordon and Marcia Mendoza, "AT&T, Verizon and Sprint Push Back Against the NSA, Too," The Huffington Post, March 3, 2014. Accessed at www.huffingtonpost.com/2014/03/03/att-verizon-sprint-nsa_n_4891533.html on August 29, 2015; and Glenn Greenwald and Ewen MacAskill, "NSA Prism program taps in to user data of Apple, Google and others," The Guardian, June 7, 2013. Accessed at www.theguardian.com/world/2013/jun/06/us-tech-giants-nsa-data on January 2, 2015.

56. Press release, Statement of Chairman Bennie G. Thompson "Responsibility in Federal Homeland Security Contracting," accessed at http://chsdemocrats.house.gov/SiteDocuments/20070420152226-55782.pdf on May 6, 2014.

57. See Figure II.3.

58. Steve Morgan, "Cybersecurity Market Reaches $75 Billion in 2015; Expected to Reach $170 Billion by 2020," Forbes, December 20, 2015. Accessed at www.forbes.com/sites/stevemorgan/2015/12/20/cybersecurity%E2%80%8B-%E2%80%8Bmarket-reaches-75-billion-in-2015%E2%80%8B%E2%80%8B-%E2%80%8Bexpected-to-reach-170-billion-by-2020/#68c4cf072191 on May 30, 2016.

59. Markets and Markets, "Video Surveillance Market Global Forecast to 2022," n.d. Accessed at www.marketsandmarkets.com/Market-Reports/video-surveillance- market-645.html on May 30, 2016.

60. Gartner, "Gartner Says Worldwide Information Security Spending Will Grow Almost 4.7 Percent to Reach $75.4 Billion in 2015," September 23, 2015. Accessed at www.gartner.com/newsroom/id/3135617 on May 30, 2016.

61. Jim Dwyer, "City Police Spied Broadly Before G.O.P. Convention," The New York Times, March 25, 2007, p. A1.

62. See for example Dana Priest and William M. Arkin, Top Secret America: The Rise of the New American Security State (New York: Back Bay Books, Little Brown and Company 2011), passim; and Mark Mazzetti, The Way of the Knife (New York: Penguin Books 2014). These authors are investigative journalists associated with The Washington Post and The New York Times, respectively.

63. The White House, Office of the Press Secretary, "Weekly Address: Pass the USA Freedom Act," May 30, 2015. Accessed at www.whitehouse.gov/the-press-office/2015/05/29/weekly-address-pass-usa-freedom-act on June 1, 2015.

64. In re Application of the FBI, Docket Number BR 13-80, United States Foreign Intelligence Surveillance Court, Washington, D.C. Accessed at www.theguardian.com/world/interactive/2013/jun/06/verizon-telephone-data-court-order on November 20, 2015. In fact, such broad-based collections had been going on since 2006. See also In re Application of the FBI, Docket Number BR 06-05, United States Foreign Intelligence Surveillance Court, Washington, D.C. Accessed at www.eff.org/sites/default/files/filenode/docket_ 06-05_1dec201_ redacted.ex_-_ocr_0.pdf.

65. Section 1861 (b)(2).

66. See BRIEF FOR THE UNITED STATES IN OPPOSITION, In Re Electronic Privacy Information Center, Petitioner, United States Supreme Court Case No. 13-58.

67. ACLU v. Clapper 785 F3rd 787 (2nd Cir., 2015) p. 97.

68. Evan Perez, "Secret Court's Oversight Gets Scrutiny," The Wall Street Journal, June 9, 2013. Accessed at http://www.wsj.com/articles/SB10001424127887324904004578535670310514616 on October 4, 2016.

69. Charlie Savage, "Roberts's Picks Reshaping Secret Surveillance Court," The New York Times, July 25, 2013. Accessed at www.nytimes.com/2013/07/26/us/politics/robertss-picks-reshaping-secret-surveillance-court.html on Nov-ember 20, 2015;

and "Changing Makeup of Surveillance Courts," The New York Times, 2013. Accessed at www.nytimes.com/interactive/2013/07/26/us/changing-makeup-of-surveillance-court.html on November 20, 2015.

70. Zeninjor Enwemeka, "What We Know About Usaamah Rahim, the Boston Man Fatally Shot by Law Enforcement," WBUR News, June 3, 2015. Accessed at www.wbur.org/news/2015/06/03/what-we-know-about-usaama-rahim on August 30, 2016.

71. The White House, Office of the Press Secretary, "Weekly Address: Pass the USA Freedom Act," May 30, 2015. Accessed at www.whitehouse.gov/the-press-office/2015/05/29/weekly-address-pass-usa-freedom-act on June 1, 2015.

72. Charlie Savage, "A Gap in Surveillance, but Ways Around It," The New York Times, May 31, 2015. Accessed at www.nytimes.com/2015/06/01/us/a-gap-in-surveillance-but-ways-around-it.html on June 1, 2015.

73. Josh Rogin and Eli Lake, "FBI Rounding Up Islamic State Suspects," Bloomberg View, June 25, 2015. Accessed at www.bloombergview.com/articles/2015-06-25/fbi-rounding-up-islamic-state-suspects on June 25, 2015.

74. Greenwald, G., & MacAskill, E. "NSA Prism program taps in to user data of Apple, Google and others," The Guardian, June 7, 2013. Accessed at http://www.theguardian.com/world/2013/jun/06/us-tech-giants-nsa-data on September 27, 2016.

75. IC Off the Record, NSA Global Access Operation, "Boundless Informant: Describing Mission Capabilities from Metadata Records," July 13, 2012. Accessed at https://nsa.gov1.info/dni/boundless-informant.html on September 26, 2016.

76. Glenn Greenwald and Ewen MacAskill, "Boundless Informant: the NSA's secret tool to track global surveillance data," The Guardian, June 11, 2013. Accessed at https://www.theguardian.com/world/2013/jun/08/nsa-boundless-informant-global-datamining on September 27, 2016.

77. James Risen and Laura Poitras, "N.S.A. Gathers Data on Social Connections of U.S. Citizens," The New York Times, September 28, 2013. Accessed at http://www.nytimes.com/2013/09/29/us/nsa-examines-social-networks-of-us-citizens.html?_r=0 on September 27, 2016.

78. James Ball, "NSA stores metadata of millions of web users for up to a year, secret files show," The Guardian, September 30, 2013. Accessed at https://www.theguardian.com/world/2013/sep/30/nsa-americans-metadata-year-documents on September 26, 2016.

79. Grace Eden, "Tempora," Digital Citizenship and Surveillance Society, May 6, 2015, Accessed at http://www.dcssproject.net/tempora/ on September 24, 2016.

80. Ewen MacAskill, Julian Borger, Nick Hopkins, Nick Davies and James Ball, "GCHQ taps fibre-optic cables for secret access to world's communications," The Guardian, June 21, 2013. Accessed at https://www.theguardian.com/uk/2013/jun/21/gchq-cables-secret-world-communications-nsa on September 27, 2016.

81. Morgan Marquis-Boire, Glenn Greenwald, and Micah Lee, "XKeyscore: NSA's Google for the World's Communications," The Intercept, July 1, 2015. Accessed at https://theintercept.com/2015/07/01/nsas-google-worlds-private-communications/ on September 24, 2016.

82. "Snowden-Interview: Transcript, NDR.de, January 26, 2014. Accessed at https://web.archive.org/web/20140128224439/http://www.ndr.de/ratgeber/netzwelt/snowden277_page-3.html on September 24, 2016.

83. Ryan W. Neal, "Edward Snowden Reveals Secret Decryption Programs: 10 Things You Need To Know About Bullrun And Edgehill," International Business Times, September 6, 2013. Accessed at http://www.ibtimes.com/edward-snowden-reveals-secret-decryption-programs-10-things-you-need-know-about-bullrun-edgehill?amp=1 on September 27, 2016.

84. Joe Mullin, "New docs show NSA taps Google, Yahoo data center links," Ars Technia, October 30, 2013. Accessed at http://arstechnica.com/tech-policy/2013/10/new-docs-show-nsa-taps-google-yahoo-data-center-links/ on September 24, 2016.

85. Barton Gellman and Ashkan Soltani, "NSA tracking cellphone locations worldwide, Snowden documents show," The Washington Post, December 4, 2013. Accessed at https://www.washingtonpost.com/world/national-security/nsa-tracking-cellphone-locations-worldwide-snowden-documents-show/2013/12/04/5492873a-5cf2-11e3-bc56-c6ca94801fac_story.html on September 24, 2016.

86. April Glaser and Kurt Opsahl, "Meet CO-TRAVELER: The NSA's Cell Phone Location Tracking Program," December 5, 2013. Accessed at https://www.eff.org/deeplinks/2013/12/meet-co-traveler-nsas-cell-phone-location-tracking-program on September 24, 2016.

87. Nicholas Weaver, "A Close Look at the NSA's Most Powerful Internet Attack Tool," Wired, March 13, 2014. Accessed at https://www.wired.com/2014/03/quantum/ on September 26, 2016..

88. David E. Sanger and Thom Shanker, "N.S.A. Devises Radio Pathway Into Computers," The New York Times, January 14, 2014. Accessed at http://www.nytimes.com/2014/01/15/us/nsa-effort-pries-open-computers-not-connected-to-internet.html on September 26, 2016.

89. GCHQ report on 'MULLENIZE' program to 'stain' anonymous electronic traffic," The Washington Post, n.d. Accessed at https://www.washingtonpost.com/apps/g/page/world/gchq-report-on-mullenize-program-to-stain-anonymous-electronic-traffic/502/ on September 27, 2016.

90. Matthew Cole, Richard Esposito, and Glen Greenwald, "Snowden Docs: British Spies Used Sex and 'Dirty Tricks,'" NBC News. Accessed at www.nbcnews.com/news/investigations/snowden-docs-british-spies-used-sex-dirty-tricks-n23091 on May 20, 2014.

91. James Ball, "NSA collects millions of text messages daily in 'untargeted' global sweep," The Guardian, January 16, 2014. Accessed at https://www.theguardian.com/world/2014/jan/16/nsa-collects-millions-text-messages-daily-untargeted-global-sweep on September 27, 2016.

92. Charlie Savage, "Obama Administration Set to Expand Sharing of Data That N.S.A. Intercepts," *The New York Times,* February 25, 2016. Accessed at www.nytimes.com/2016/02/26/us/politics/obama-administration-set-to-expand-sharing-of-data-that-nsa-intercepts.html on May 30, 2016.

93. Matthew Jaffe, "Eric Holder says Edward Snowden performed a 'public service,'" CNN Politics, May 30, 2016. Accessed at www.cnn.com/2016/05/30/politics/axe-files-axelrod-eric-holder/index.html on May 30, 2016.

94. As it turns out, the legal action was subsequently terminated because the German government could not prove that Chancellor Merkel's mobile phone had been compromised. Apparently, President Obama had not been informed about this surveillance. Mark Mazzetti and Mark Lander, "Spying Case Left Obama in Dark, U.S. Officials," The New York Times, July 8, 2014. Accessed at www.nytimes.com/2014/07/09/world/europe/spying-case-left-obama-in-dark-us-officials-say.html on December 21, 2014.

95. Op. cit. U.S. Government, Office of the Director of National Intelligence, "2013 Report on Security Clearance Determinations," p. 4.

96. Dana Priest and William M. Arken, "Top Secret America: A Washington Post Investigation," The Washington Post, June 19, 20, and 21, 2010. See also Dana Priest and William M. Arken, Top Secret America: The Rise of the New American Security State (New York: Back Bay Books, 2011), passim.

97. Mark Mazzetti et al., "SEAL Team 6: A Secret History of Quiet Killings and Blurred Lines," June 6, 2015, The New York Times. Accessed at www.nytimes.com/2015/06/07/world/asia/the-secret-history-of-seal-team-6.html?_r=0 on June 8, 2015.

98. Central Intelligence Agency, Office of the CIA, Clandestine Service. Accessed at www.cia.gov/offices-of-cia/clandestine-service/index.html on May 27, 2015.

99. Mark Mazzetti, "C.I.A. to Be Overhauled to Fight Modern Threats," The New York Times, March 6, 2015. Accessed at www.nytimes.com/2015/03/07/us/major-overhaul-set-for-cia-with-thousands-to-be-reassigned.html?_r=0 on March 8, 2015; and "Unclassified Version of March 6, 2015 Message to the Workforce from CIA Director John Brennan: Our Agency's Blueprint for the Future." Accessed at www.cia.gov/news-information/press-releases-statements/2015-press-releases-statements/message-to-workforce-agencys-blueprint-for-the-future.html on March 8, 2015.

100. These data are not presented in this book because they are still classified, even though they can easily be obtained by anyone with an Internet connection, for example, "FY 2013 Congressional Budget Justification, Vol.1, National Intelligence Program Summary, February 2012," available at http://cryptome.org/2013/08/spy-budget-fy13.pdf.

101. Micah Zenko, "Transferring CIA Drone Strikes to the Pentagon," Policy Innovation Memorandum No. 31, Council on Foreign Relations, April 2013. Accessed at www.cfr.org/drones/transferring-cia-drone-strikes-pentagon/p30434 on May 27, 2015.

102. In the run-up to the Iraq War, the George W. Bush administration gave many reasons for invading Iraq including prominently the existence of weapons of mass destruction and the alleged connection of the Saddam Hussein regime to terrorists. Neither claim was proved. Instead of bringing peace and security, after a decade of war the region disintegrated into greater chaos and violence, witnessing even the deployment of chemical weapons against Syrian civilians and the rise of the Islamic State of Iraq and Syria insurgent group.

103. For a description of government sponsorship of military innovation, see U.S. Congress, Office of Technology Assessment, "Holding the Edge: Maintaining the Defense Technology Base," OTA-ISC-420 (Washington, DC: U.S. Government Printing Office, April 1989), passim.

104. SIPRI Fact Sheet, "Trends in World Military Expenditure, 2013," April 2014. Accessed at http://books.sipri.org/files/FS/SIPRIFS1404.pdf on November 24, 2014.

105. Nick Turse, "America's Secret War in 134 Countries," The Nation, January 16, 2014. Accessed at www.thenation.com/article/177964/americas-secret-war-134-countries on May 7, 2014.

106. Chelsea Manning, "The Fog Machine of War," The New York Times, June 15, 2014, Sunday Review, p. 4. At this writing Manning, a former U.S. Army intelligence analyst, was serving a 25-year term in prison for unauthorized disclosure of information.

107. Associated Press, "Pentagon lifts ban on coffin photos," NBC News, February 26, 2009. Available at www.nbcnews.com/id/29410258/ns/us_news-military/t/pentagon-lifts-media-ban-coffin-photos/. Accessed June 16, 2014. Dana Priest and Anne Hull, "Soldiers Face Neglect, Frustration at Army's Top Medical Facility," The Washington Post, February 18, 2007. Accessed at www.washingtonpost.com/wp-dyn/content/article/2007/02/17/AR2007021701172.html on June 18, 2007.

108. Pew Research Center, "Iraq and Public Opinion: The Troops Come Home," December 16–19, 2012. Accessed at www.pewresearch.org/2011/12/14/iraq-and-public-opinion-the-troops-come-home on May 6, 2014. See also Dana Priest and Anne Hull, "Soldiers Face Neglect, Frustration at Army's Top Medical Facility," The Washington Post, February 18, 2007. Accessed at www.washingtonpost.com/wp-dyn/content/article/2007/02/17/AR2007021701172.html on June 10, 2014.

109. Pew Research Center, "Iraq and Public Opinion: The Troops Come Home, December 16–19, 2012." Accessed at http://www.pewresearch.org/2011/12/14/iraq-and-public-opinion-the-troops-come-home on May 6, 2014.

110. The Insurrection Act (1809) and the Posse Comitatus Act (1878) substantially limit the powers of the federal government to use the military for law enforcement within the United States.

111. See Craig Horowitz, "The NYPD's War on Terror," New York Magazine, February 3, 2003. Accessed at http://nymag.com/nymetro/news/features/n_8286 on June 11, 2014; Darwin Bond-Graham and Ali Winston, "Forget the NSA, the LAPD Spies on Millions of Innocent Folks," LA Weekly, February 27, 2014. Accessed at www.laweekly.com/2014-02-27/news/forget-the-nsa-la-cops-spy-on-millions-of-innocent-folks on June 11, 2014; Michael P. Downing, "Policing Terrorism in the United States: The Los Angeles Police Department's Convergence Strategy," The Police Chief, vol. LXXVI, no. 2, February 2009. Accessed at www.policechiefmagazine.org/magazine/index.cfm?fuseaction=display_arch&article_id=1729&issue_id=22009 on June 11, 2014.

112. The expansion of police power is evident in the USA Patriot Act. See Ralph Neas, "Two Years After 9/11: Ashcroft's Assault on the Constitution," People for the American Way Foundation, September 9, 2003, p. 4.

113. Anil Kalhan, "Immigration Enforcement and Federalism after September 11, 2001," in Ariane Chebel d'Appollonia and Simon Reich, Immigration, Integration and Security: Europe and America in Comparative Perspective (University of Pittsburgh Press, 2007).

114. "The Police and the Spy Unit," The New York Times, March 27, 2007, editorial.

115. Craig Horowitz, "The NYPD's War on Terror," New York Magazine, n.d. Accessed at http://nymag.com/nymetro/news/features/n_8286/index2.html. Accessed on June 18, 2014.

116. J. David Goodman, "With Permanent Squad, New York Police Step Up Fight on Terrorism," The New York Times, November 20, 2015. Accessed at www.nytimes.com/2015/11/21/nyregion/new-york-police-form-counterterrorism-force-with-more-firepower-and-training.html on November 21, 2015.

117. Darwin Bond-Graham and Ali Winston, "Forget the NSA, the LAPD Spies on Millions of Innocent Folks," LA Weekly, February 27, 2014. Accessed at www.laweekly.com/2014-02-27/news/forget-the-nsa-la-cops-spy-on-millions-of-innocent-folks on June 18, 2014.

118. Michael P. Downing, "Policing Terrorism in the United States: The Los Angeles Police Department's Convergence Strategy," Police Chief: The Professional Voice of Law Enforcement, June 2014, p. 1. Accessed at www.policechiefmagazine.org/magazine/index.cfm?fuseaction=display_arch&article_id=1729&issue_id=22009 on June 18, 2014.

119. "According to Pentagon data. . . . The equipment has been added to police forces that already look and act like military units. SWAT teams are deployed tens of thousands of times each year, increasingly for routine jobs. Masked, heavily armed police officers in Louisiana raided a nightclub in 2006 as part of a liquor inspection. In Florida, officers in SWAT gear carried out barbershop license inspections with guns drawn in 2010." Matt Apuzzo, "War Gear Flows to Local Police Departments," The New York Times, Times Digest, June 9, 2014, p.1.

120. USA Today and KSDK-TV St. Louis, "Timeline: Michael Brown shooting in Ferguson, Mo.," August 19, 2014. Accessed at www.usatoday.com/story/news/nation/2014/08/14/michael-brown-ferguson-missouri-timeline/14051827 on August 19, 2014.

121. AP, "Police Targeted Media With No-Fly Over Ferguson, Tapes Show," The New York Times, November 3, 2014, p. A12.

122. David Jackson, "Obama treads fine line on Ferguson," USA Today, August 19, 2014. Accessed at www.usatoday.com/story/theoval/2014/08/19/obama-ferguson-michael-brown/14277483 on August 19, 2014.

123. AP, "US cities brace for protests off Ferguson Decision," The Wall Street Journal, November 15, 2014.

124. Matt Apuzzo and Michael S. Schmidt, "In Washington, Second Thoughts on Arming Police," The New York Times, August 24, 2014, p. 1.

125. Executive Office of the President, "Review: Federal Support for Local Law Enforcement Equipment Acquisition," December 2014, pp. 7–18. Accessed at www.whitehouse.gov/sites/default/files/docs/federal_support_for_local_law_enforcement_equipment_acquisition.pdf on December 2, 2014.

126. Mark Lander, "Obama Offers New Standards on Police Gear: Militarized Tactics at Issue After Ferguson," The New York Times, December 2, 2014, p. 1.

127. John Mueller, Overblown (New York: Free Press, 2006), pp. 13–14.

128. Emmarie Heutteman, "Perry Says Terrorists Could Be Entering the U.S. From Mexico," The New York Times, August 21, 2015. Accessed at www.nytimes.com/2014/08/22/us/politics/rick-perry-says-terrorists-could-be-entering-us-along-mexico-border.html?_r=0 on August 23, 2014. See also Erin Kelley, "Rick Perry calls for more airstikes against Islamic State," USA Today, August 21, 2014. Accessed at www.usatoday.com/story/news/politics/2014/08/21/perry-isis-border-obama/14399579 on August 23, 2014.

129. http://clatl.com/freshloaf/archives/2014/09/03/us-sen-johnny-isakson-on-isis-weve-got-to-kill-em-and-exterminate-em-so-theyre-gone-and-destroyed.

130. Chalmers Johnson, Blowback: The Costs and Consequences of American Empire (New York: Metropolitan Books, 2000).

CHAPTER III: IRRATIONAL SECURITY

131. Terrorism experts agree that no acceptable and unambiguous definition of terrorism is likely to emerge. See for example, Bruce Hoffman, Inside Terrorism, 2nd ed. (New York: Columbia University Press, 2006), p. 34.

132. "The failure to find a widely acceptable definition of terrorism is tied to the political use of the word. Fundamentally, 'terrorism' is a pejorative term with a range of negative meanings. For this reason, many media organisations such as the BBC and Reuters are extremely reluctant to describe any individual or group in their reports as 'terrorists', preferring instead to use terms such as 'militant', 'insurgents'

or 'guerrillas.'" Andrew Silke, ed., The Psychology of Counter Terrorism (London and New York: Routledge, 2011), p. 2.

133. Jessica Stern, The Ultimate Terrorists (Cambridge, MA: Harvard University Press, 1999), pp. 11–17.

134. Justice Potter Stewart, concurring opinion in Jacobellis v. Ohio 378 U.S. 184 (1964), regarding possible obscenity in the 1958 French film Les Amants.

135. David L. Altheide, "Terrorism and the Politics of Fear," Cultural Studies ? Critical Methodologies, November 2006, pp. 415–16.

136. Cincinnati, Ohio, October 7, 2002.

137. VFW National Convention, August 26, 2002.

138. UN Security Council, February 5, 2003.

139. ABC's This Week With George Stephanopoulos, March 30, 2003.

140. "Colin Powell's Presentation to the UN Security Council on Iraq's WMD Program," September 3, 2003. Accessed at www.youtube.com/watch?v=ErlDSJHRVMA on July 19, 2016.

141. As Delivered, Briefing of the Security Council, February, 2003, Executive Chairman of UNMOVIC, Dr. Hans Blix. Accessed at www.un.org/Depts/unmovic/blix14Febasdel.htm on June 22, 2014.

142. See Iraq Body Count, "Total Violent Deaths Including Combatants 202,000." Accessed at www.iraqbodycount.org/ on November 30, 2014, and Iraq Body Count Database, "Documented Civilian Deaths From Violence." Accessed at /www.iraqbodycount.org/database on September 14, 2015; World Health Organization, "New study estimates 151,000 violent Iraqi deaths since 2003 invasion," January 9, 2008. Accessed at www.who.int/mediacentre/news/releases/2008/pr02/en on November 30, 2014; and the U.K firm Opinion Business Research estimated "that over 1,000,000 Iraqi citizens have died as a result of the conflict which started in 2003," Hannah Fischer, "Iraq Casualties: U.S. Military Forces and Iraqi Civilians, Police, and Security Forces," Congressional Research Service, October 7, 2010. Accessed at www.fas.org/sgp/crs/mideast/R40824.pdfm on November 30, 201.

143. World Public Opinion, "The American Public on International Issues," March 1–6, 2006, p. 7. Accessed at worldpublicopinion.org/pipa/pdf/mar06/USIraq_Mar06-quaire.pdf on November 30, 2014.

144. University of Maryland, The Global Terrorism Database, "Data Collection Methodology," last updated June 2015. Accessed at www.start.umd.edu/gtd/using-gtd on September 12, 2015.

145. Edith M. Lederer, "UN report: More than 25,000 foreigners fight with terrorists," AP, April 2, 2015. Accessed at http://bigstory.ap.org/article/cec52a0dbfab-4c00b89bc543badf6c20/un-report-more-25000-foreigners-fight-terrorists on September 10, 2015.

146. United States Census, "Table 1103. Motor Vehicle Accidents—Number and Deaths: 1990 to 2009." Accessed at www.census.gov/compendia/statab/2012/tables/12s1103.pdf on September 29, 2015.

147. Ibid., pp. 6 and 20.

148. The University of Chicago, Chicago Project on Security and Terrorism, Suicide Attack Database. Accessed at http://cpostdata.uchicago.edu/search_new.php on June 24, 2014.

149. The number of suicide attacks in Afghanistan for the period 1982–2013 is also very high compared with in the United States, but much smaller compared with in Iraq: 859 attacks, 3,951 dead and 9.458 wounded. Ibid.

150. Mass Shooting Tracker. Accessed at http://shootingtracker.com/wiki/Main_Page on September 10, 2015.

151. Centers for Disease Control and Prevention, FastStats, Mortality, All firearm deaths, 2013. Accessed at www.cdc.gov/nchs/fastats/injury.htm on September 11, 2015.

152. Les Neuhaus, "Soldiers become detectives in Operation Pericles," Stars and Stripes, August 16, 2007. Accessed at www.stripes.com/news/soldiers-become-detectives-in-operation-pericles-1.67728 on July 30, 2014.

153. Stephen I. Schwartz, Atomic Audit: The Costs and Consequences of U.S. Nuclear Weapons Since 1940 (Washington, DC: Brookings Institution Press, 1998). See also Stephen I. Schwartz, "The Costs of Nuclear Weapons," October 1, 2008. Accessed through the Nuclear Threat website at www.nti.org/analysis/articles/costs-us-nuclear-weapons on June 22, 2014.

154. This number includes the total of U.S. and U.S.S.R. weapons plus 973 weapons held by the U.K., France, China, and Israel. Hans M. Kristensen and Robert S. Norris, "Global nuclear weapons inventories, 1945–2013," in Bulletin of the Atomic Scientists, 69(5) 75–81. Accessed at http://bos.sagepub.com/content/69/5/75.full.pdf on June 22, 2014. The U.S. stockpile reached its highest point (31,255 weapons) in 1967, while the Soviet Union continued to build production, reaching its highest point (40,159 weapons) in 1986. States closely guard information on the number and disposition of nuclear weapons, and so the figures quoted above are educated guesses. See also Natural Resource Defense Council, "Table of Global Nuclear Weapons Stockpiles, 1945–2002," accessed at www.nrdc.org/nuclear/nudb/datab19.asp on May 6, 2014.

155. "Deployed warheads are defined as warheads that are on missiles or at bases with operational launchers." Ibid., Kristensen and Norris.

156. Lynn Eden, Whole World on Fire: Organizations, Knowledge, and Nuclear Weapons Devastation (Ithaca, NY: Cornell University Press, 2005), pp. 2–3.

157. Op. cit., Kristensen and Norris.

158. George P. Shultz, William J. Perry, Henry A. Kissinger, and Sam Nunn, Nuclear Security Project, Wall Street Journal op-eds. Accessed at www.nuclearsecurity-project.org/publications/wall-street-journal-op-eds on June 26, 2014.

159. William J. Broad and David E. Sanger, "U.S. Ramping Up Major Renewal in Nuclear Arms." The New York Times, September 21, 2014. Accessed at http://www.nytimes.com/2014/09/22/us/us-ramping-up-major-renewal-in-nuclear-arms.html on September 26, 2014.

160. Remarks as prepared by Michael McCaul, House Committee on Homeland Security, "Beyond Bin Laden's Caves and Couriers to a New Generation of Terrorists: Confronting the Challenges in a Post 9/11 World," September 8, 2015. Accessed at http://homeland.house.gov/sites/homeland.house.gov/files/documents/09-08-15-McCaul-Open.pdf on September 13, 2015.

161. "Donald Trump on Terrorism," Fox & Friends interview, December 2, 2015. Accessed at http://2016.presidential-candidates.org/Trump/?on=terrorism on May 24, 2016.

162. Nolan D. McCaskill, "Trump: I may ask Congress to formally declare war to fight terror," Politico, May 23, 2016. Accessed at www.politico.com/story/2016/05/trump-terror-declaration-war-223497 on May 24, 2016.

163. Mark Mazzetti, "Spy Agencies Say Iraq War Worsens Terrorism Threat," The New York Times, September 24, 2006. Accessed at www.nytimes.com/2006/09/24/world/middleeast/24terror.html?_r=0 on August 20, 2016. See also "Declassified Key Judgments of the National Intelligence Estimate Trends in Global Terrorism: Implications for the United States" (National Intelligence Estimate, April 2006), accessed at www.dni.gov/press_releases/Declassified_NIE_Key_Judgments.pdf on May 31, 2007; Daniel Benjamin and Steven Simon, "Of Course Iraq Made It Worse," The Washington Post, September 29, 2006. Accessed at www.washingtonpost.com/wp-dyn/content/article/2006/09/28/AR2006092801455.html on June 1, 2007.

164. The Center for International Trade and Security at the University of Georgia has developed methodologies to improve the safety and security cultures at dangerous CBRN facilities. For more information, see http://cits.uga.edu. The extensive work of Igor Khripunov is instructive. See for example: "Legal Framework for Strengthening Nuclear Security and Combating Nuclear Terrorism," (Amsterdam: AOL Press, 2012), Co-editor, 2012; and "2012 Nuclear Security Summit in Seoul: Achieving Sustainable Nuclear Security Culture," Public Interest Report, Federation of American Scientists, Fall 2011.

CHAPTER IV: CATASTROPHIC TERROR

165. U.S. Department of State, Bureau of Counterterrorism, Country Reports on Terrorism 2014, "Chapter 3: State Sponsors of Terrorism Overview." Accessed at www.state.gov/j/ct/rls/crt/2014/239410.htm on June 9, 2016.

166. Jayshree Bajoria and Eben Kaplan, "The ISI and Terrorism: Behind the Accusations," Council on Foreign Relations, May 4, 2011. Accessed at www.cfr.org/pakistan/isi-terrorism-behind-accusations/p11644 on June 9, 2016.

167. "Summary of Information Regarding U.S. Counterterrorism Strikes Outside Areas of Active Hostilities," Office of the Director of National Intelligence, n.d. Accessed at https://content.govdelivery.com/attachments/USODNI/2016/07/01/ file_attachments/579487/DNI%2BRelease%2Bon%2BCT%2BStrikes%2BOutsi de%2BAreas%2Bof%2BActive%2BHostilities_FINAL.PDF on July 20, 2016.

168. Rachael Stohl, "Halfway to Transparency on Drone Strikes," Breaking Defense, July 12, 2016. Accessed at http://breakingdefense.com/2016/07/halfway-to-transparency-on-drone-strikes on July 21, 2016.

169. Chris Woods, "Drone strikes in Pakistan: Drone War Exposed—the complete picture of CIA strikes in Pakistan," the Bureau of Investigative Journalism, August 10, 2011. Accessed at www.thebureauinvestigates.com/2011/08/10/ most-complete-picture-yet-of-cia-drone-strikes/?version=meter+at+0&modu le=meter-Links&pgtype=article&contentId=&mediaId=&referrer=http%3A %2F%2Fwww.theatlantic.com%2Fpolitics%2Farchive%2F2016%2F03%2Fthe-obama-administrations-drone-strike-dissembling%2F473541%2F&priority=tr ue&action=click&contentCollection=meter-links-click on May 29, 2016.

170. Michael T. Kaufman, "Idi Amin, Murderous and Erratic Ruler of Uganda in the 70's, Dies in Exile," The New York Times, August 17, 2003.

171. ABC News, "List of Saddam's Crimes Is Long," December 30, 2006. Accessed at http://abcnews.go.com/WNT/IraqCoverage/story?id=2761722&page=1 on June 9, 2016.

172. Graham T. Alison, Nuclear Terrorism: The Ultimate Preventable Catastrophe (New York: Times Books, 2004), passim.

173. CTBTO Preparatory Commission, "Manhattan Project," n.d. Accessed at www. ctbto.org/nuclear-testing/history-of-nuclear-testing/manhattan-project on May 24, 2016.

174. Arms Control Association, "U.S. Nuclear Modernization Programs," December 2015. Accessed at www.armscontrol.org/factsheets/USNuclear Modernization on May 29, 2016.

175. William J. Broad and David E. Sanger, "As U.S. Modernizes Nuclear Weapons, 'Smaller' Leaves Some Uneasy," The New York Times, January 11, 2016. Accessed at www.nytimes.com/2016/01/12/science/as-us-modernizes-nuclear-weapons-smaller-leaves-some-uneasy.html on May 29, 2016.

176. Oliver Burkeman, "How two students built an A-bomb," The Guardian, June 24, 2003. Accessed at www.theguardian.com/world/2003/jun/24/usa.science on May 24, 2016.

177. Richard K. Rein, "A Princeton Tiger Designs an Atomic Bomb in a Physics Class," People Magazine, October 25, 1976. Accessed at www.people.com/peo ple/archive/article/0,,20067027,00.html on May 24, 2016.

178. Donald L. Barlett and James B. Steele, "The Oily Americans," Time, May 13, 2003. Accessed at http://content.time.com/time/magazine/article/0,9171,450997-92,00.html on May 27, 2016,

179. David Wood, "For Civilian Airliners, Shoulder-Fired Missiles Still a Global Threat," The Huffington Post, July 23, 2014. Accessed at www.huffingtonpost.com/2014/07/23/civilian-airplanes-missiles_n_5614040.html on May 27, 2016.

180. Srinivas Laxman, "'Smiling Buddha' had caught US off-guard in 1974," The Times of India, December 7, 2011. Accessed at http://timesofindia.indiatimes.com/india/amp39Smiling-Buddhaamp39-had-caught-US-off-guard-in-1974/articleshow/11013437.cms on May 27, 2016.

181. David E. Sanger, "Obama Order Sped Up Wave of Cyberattacks Against Iran," The New York Times, June 1, 2012. Accessed at www.nytimes.com/2012/06/01/world/middleeast/obama-ordered-wave-of-cyberattacksagainst-iran.html?pagewanted=2&_r=2&seid=auto&smid=tw-nytimespolitics&pagewanted=all on May 27, 2016.

182. Kim Setter, "An unprecedented look at the Stuxnet, the world's first digital weapon," Wired, November 3, 2014. Accessed at www.wired.com/2014/11/countdown-to-zero-day-stuxnet on May 27, 2016.

183. Arms Control Association, "Timeline of Nuclear Diplomacy With Iran," September 18, 2015. Accessed at www.armscontrol.org/factsheet/Timeline-of-Nuclear-Diplomacy-With-Iran on May 27, 2016.

184. The President's Budget FY2016, "Middle Class Economics: Cybersecurity," n.d. Accessed at www.whitehouse.gov/sites/default/files/omb/budget/fy2016/assets/fact_sheets/cybersecurity.pdf on June 1, 2016; and Aliya Sternstein, "The Military's Cybersecurity Budget in 4 Charts," Defense One, March 9, 2016. Accessed at www.defenseone.com/management/2015/03/militarys-cybersecurity-budget-4-charts/107679 on June 1, 2016.

185. Pauline Jelinek, "Nuclear Bombs Mistakenly Flown Over U.S.," September 6, 2007, Associated Press. Accessed at www.washingtonpost.com/wp-dyn/content/article/2007/09/05/AR2007090501683.html on June 22, 2016.

186. Union of Concerned Scientists, "Top American Scientists Urge Obama to Take Nuclear Missiles off Hair-Trigger Alert," June 21, 2016. Accessed at www.ucsusa.org/news/press_release/Scientists-Hair-Trigger-Letter-to-Obama#.V2rnxpMrKV7 on June 22, 2016. The letter the scientists sent to President Obama is located at www.ucsusa.org/sites/default/files/attach/2016/06/Scientists-to-Obama-security-letter.pdf. Accessed on June 22, 2016.

187. This policy was changed after the end of the Cold War. Nuclear-armed aircraft were taken off-line and the vast majority of U.S. land- and sea-based nuclear weapons were de-alerted. See Arms Control Association, "Text of Nov. 28 E-mail from Strategic Command responding to ACT's questions on the alert status of U.S. nuclear weapons," November 2007. Accessed at www.armscontrol.org/interviews/20071204_STRATCOM on June 22, 2016.

188. William M. Arkin and Joshua M. Handler, "Nuclear disasters as sea, then and now," Bulletin of the Atomic Scientists, July 1989, p. 20.

189. NPR, "For 50 Years, Nuclear Bomb Lost in Watery Grave," February 3, 2008. Accessed at www.npr.org/templates/story/story.php?storyId=18587608 on May 26, 2016.

190. Eyewitness account by an officer on one of the ships.

191. Justin Bresolin, "Fact Sheet: The Nunn-Lugar Cooperative Threat Reduction Program," Center for Arms Control and Non-Proliferation, June 1, 2014. Accessed at armscontrolcenter.org/fact-sheet-the-nunn-lugar-cooperative-threat-reduction-program on May 26, 2016. See also Defense Threat Reduction Agency, Cooperative Threat Reduction Programs. Accessed at http://web.archive.org/web/20070927215354/http:/www.dtra.mil/oe/ctr/programs on May 26, 2016.

192. Mary Beth D. Nikitin and Amy F. Woolf, "The Evolution of Cooperative Threat Reduction: Issues for Congress," Congressional Research Service, June 13, 2014. Accessed at https://www.fas.org/sgp/crs/nuke/R43143.pdf on May 26, 2016.

193. David Albright and Serena Kelleher-Vergantini, "Plutonium and Highly Enriched Uranium 2015; Summary Tables and Charts," Tables 1 and 3, Institute for Science and International Security, December 1, 2015. Accessed at http://isis-online.org/uploads/isis-reports/documents/Summary_Tables_and_Charts_FINAL.pdf on May 29, 2016.

194. William W. Keller, Arm in Arm: The Political Economy of the Global Arms Trade (New York, NY: Basic Books, 1995), p.178.

195. The American Presidency Project, quotation from the president's news conference of March 21, 1963. Accessed at www.presidency.ucsb.edu/ws/?pid=9124 on June 29, 2014.

CHAPTER V: EPISODIC TERROR

196. Halimah Abdullah and Jim Miklaszewski, "Pentagon: Live Anthrax Sent to 52 Labs in 18 States, 3 Countries," ABC News, June 4, 2015. Accessed at www.nbcnews.com/news/veterans/pentagon-live-anthrax-sent-51-labs-17-states-3-countries-n369306 on June 11, 2016.

197. Sourcebook of Criminal Justice Statistics 2003, Table 3.170, p. 337. Accessed at www.albany.edu/sourcebook/pdf/t3170.pdf on August 9, 2014.

198. FBI, Unified Crime Reports, Expanded Homicide Table 8, "Murder Victims by Weapon, 2008–2012." Accessed at www.fbi.gov/about-us/cjis/ucr/crime-in-the-u.s/2012/crime-in-the-u.s.-2012/offenses-known-to-law-enforcement/expanded-homicide/expanded_homicide_data_table_8_murder_victims_by_weapon_2008-2012.xls on July 3, 2014.

199. Michael Winter, "MLK Day bomb in Spokane contained rat poison, shrapnel" USA Today, January 27, 2011. Accessed at http://content.usatoday.com/communities/ondeadline/post/2011/01/mlk-day-bomb-in-spokane-wash-

contained-rat-poison-shrapnel/1#.Vg8MnhNVhBc on October 2, 2015; Jason Ryan, "FBI: Pipe Bomb Found on MLK Parade Route," The Spokesman-Review, September 8, 2011. Accessed at http://abcnews.go.com/Blotter/fbi-pipe-bomb-found-spokane-washington-mlk-parade/story?id=12642275 on October 2, 2015; Dave Cotton, "MLK Bomber Harpham Gets Max Sentence: 32 Years," KHQ6 News, December 20, 2011. Accessed at www.khq.com/story/16361188/mlk-bomber-set-to-be-sentenced-today on October 2, 2015.

200. Southern Poverty Law Center. Accessed at www.splcenter.org on June 1, 2014.

201. Pam Belluck, "Threats and Responses: The Bomb Plot; Unrepentant Shoe Bomber Is Given a Life Sentence for Trying to Blow Up Jet," The New York Times, January 31, 2003. Accessed at www.nytimes.com/2003/01/31/us/threats-responses-bomb-plot-unrepentant-shoe-bomber-given-life-sentence-for.html on October 2, 2015.

202. Mark Hosenball, "Islamic Radicalization: Umar Farouk Abdulmutallab," Newsweek, January 1, 2010. Accessed at www.newsweek.com/islamic-radicalization-umar-farouk-abdulmutallab-70905 on October 2, 2015; Fox News,"Father of Terror Suspect Reportedly Warned U.S. About Son," December 26, 2009. Accessed at www.foxnews.com/story/2009/12/26/father-terror-suspect-reportedly-warned-us-about-so-1157956136.html on October 2, 2015; CBS News, "Did Abdulmutallab Talk to Radical Cleric?," CBS, December 29, 2009. Accessed at http://www.cbsnews.com/news/did-abdulmutallab-talk-to-radical-cleric/ on October 2, 2015.

203. CBS News, "Faisal Shahzad Kept Low Profile in U.S.," May 4, 2010. Accessed at www.cbsnews.com/news/faisal-shahzad-kept-low-profile-in-us on October 2, 2015; Greg Miller and Jerry Markon, "Radicalization of Times Square suspect was gradual, investigators say," The Washington Post, May 7, 2010. Accessed at www.washingtonpost.com/wp-dyn/content/article/2010/05/07/AR2010050700194.html on October 2, 2015; Richard A. Serrano and David S. Cloud, "Times Square bomb suspect had ties to key Pakistani militants," Los Angeles Times, May 8, 2010. Accessed at http://articles.latimes.com/2010/may/08/nation/la-na-bomb-motive-20100508 on October 2, 2015; Yochi J. Dreazan and Evan Perez, "Suspect Cites Radical Imam's Writings," The Wall Street Journal. Accessed at www.wsj.com/articles/SB10001424052748704370704575228150116907566 on October 2, 2015.

204. Steven Vogel, Sari Horwitz, and David A. Fahrenthold, "Sandy Hook Elementary shooting leaves 28 dead, law enforcement sources say," The Washington Post, December 14, 2012. Accessed at www.washingtonpost.com/politics/sandy-hook-elementary-school-shooting-leaves-students-staff-dead/2012/12/14/24334570-461e-11e2-8e70-e1993528222d_story.html on July 2 2014.

205. AP News Archive, "Newspapers Publish Excerpts of Unabomber's Manifesto," August 2, 1995. Accessed at www.apnewsarchive.com/1995/Newspapers-Publish-Excerpts-of-Unabomber-s-Manifesto/id-076a0f3d3fd238a3e85b-887f5a71ec75 on July 2, 2014. The full text of "Industrial Science and Its Future"

can be found at www.washingtonpost.com/wp-srv/national/longterm/una-bomber/manifesto.text.htm.

206. Tim McGirk, "Hasan's Therapy: Could 'Secondary Trauma' Have Driven Him to Shooting?," Time, November 7, 2009. Accessed at http://content.time.com/time/nation/article/0,8599,1936407,00.html on July 2, 2014.

207. Molly Hennessy-Fiske, "Ft. Hood jury resumes deliberations in Nidal Malik Hasan case," Los Angeles Times, August 23, 2013. Accessed at http://articles.latimes.com/2013/aug/23/nation/la-na-nn-fort-hood-jury-20130823 on July 2, 2014.

208. Allen G. Breed and Ramit Plushnick-Masti, "Terror Act or Workplace Violence? Hasan Trial Raises Sensitive Issue," Arizona Daily Star, August 11, 2013. Accessed at http://azstarnet.com/news/national/terror-act-or-workplace-violence-hasan-trial-raises-sensitiveissue/article_be513c51-a35d-5b4f-b3a0-13654f019ea6.htm on June 24, 2014. See also Ryan J. Reilly, "Mukasey Says Fort Hood Attack Was Terrorism," Main Justice, November 9, 2009. Accessed at www.mainjustice.com/2009/11/09/mukasey-says-fort-hood-attack-was-terrorism on June 24, 2014.

209. Mark Mazzetti and Eric Schmitt, "In the Age of ISIS, Who's a Terrorist, and Who's Simply Deranged?," The New York Times, July 17, 2016. Accessed at www.nytimes.com/2016/07/18/world/europe/in-the-age-of-isis-whos-a-terrorist-and-whos-simply-deranged.html?smid=nytcore-ipad-share&smprod=nytcore-ipad&_r=0 on July 22, 2016.

210. Time, "Top 10 Manhunts: The Beltway Snipers," October 20, 2011. Accessed at http://content.time.com/time/specials/packages/article/0,28804,2002407_2002427_2002418,00.html on July 9, 2014.

211. Radley Balko, "Was the police response to the Boston bombing really appropriate?," Washington Post, April 22, 2014. Accessed at http://www.washingtonpost.com/news/the-watch/wp/2014/04/22/the-police-response-to-the-boston-marathon-bombing on July 9, 2014.

212. Conor Friedersdorf, "The Alarming Mistakes Police Made After the Boston Bombing," The Atlantic, October 17, 2014. Accessed at http://www.theatlantic.com/national/archive/2013/10/the-alarming-mistakes-police-made-after-the-boston-bombing/280635 on July 9, 2014.

213. Nate Rawlings, "Was Boston Actually on Lockdown?," Time, April 19, 2013. Accessed at http://nation.time.com/2013/04/19/was-boston-actually-on-lockdown on July 22, 2016.

214. FBI Unified Crime Reports, Expanded Homicide Data Table 11, 2011. Accessed at www.fbi.gov/about-us/cjis/ucr/crime-in-the-u.s/2011/crime-in-the-u.s.-2011/tables/expanded-homicide-data-table-11 on May 6, 2014.

215. U.S. Department of Transportation, National Highway and Traffic Safety Administration, "Passenger Vehicle Occupant Fatalities: The Decline for Six

Years in a Row from 2005 to 2011." The figure for 2005 was 43,510. Accessed at www-nrd.nhtsa.dot.gov/Pubs/812034.pdf on June 20, 2014.

216. Rong-Gong Lin II and Richard Winton, "San Bernardino suspects 'sprayed the room with bullets,' police chief says," Los Angeles Times, December 4, 2016. Accessed at www.latimes.com/local/lanow/la-me-ln-san-bernardino-suspects-sprayed-the-room-with-bullets-20151203-story.html on June 11, 2016.

217. Team Fix, "5th Republican debate transcript, annotated: Who said what and what it meant," The Washington Post, December 15, 2015. Accessed at www.washingtonpost.com/news/the-fix/wp/2015/12/15/who-said-what-and-what-it-meant-the-fifth-gop-debate-annotated on December 16, 2015.

218. David E. Sanger and Nicole Perlroth, "F.B.I. Chief Says Texas Gunman Used Encryption to Text Overseas Terrorist," The New York Times, December 9, 2015. Accessed at www.nytimes.com/2015/12/10/us/politics/fbi-chief-says-texas-gun-man-used-encryption-to-text-overseas-terrorist.html on January 10, 2016.

219. W.J. Hennigan, "Air Force proposes $3-billion plan to vastly expand its drone program," Los Angeles Times, December 10, 2015. Accessed at www.latimes.com/world/middleeast/la-fg-drone-pilots-20151210-story.html on January 10, 2016.

220. FBI News, "Latest Hate Crime Statistics Available: Report Contains Info on Offenses, Victims, and Offenders," November 15, 2015. Accessed at www.fbi.gov/news/stories/latest-hate-crime-statistics-available on July 23, 2016.

221. Southern Poverty Law Center, "Ku Klux Klan," n.d. Accessed at www.splcenter.org/fighting-hate/extremist-files/ideology/ku-klux-klan on July 23, 2016.

222. "An Overview of Bombing and Arson Attacks by Environmental and Animal Rights Extremists in the United States, 1995–2010," Final Report to the Resilient Systems Division, Science and Technology Directorate, U.S. Department of Homeland Security, May 2013. Accessed at www.start.umd.edu/sites/default/files/files/publications/START_Bombing on July 22, 2016.

223. Leighton Woodhouse, "How The Pursuit of Animal Liberation Activists Became Among the FBI's 'Highest Domestic Terrorism Priorities,'" The Huffington Post, October 25, 2012. Accessed at www.huffingtonpost.com/leighton-wood-house/animal-liberation_b_2012426.html on July 23, 2016.

224. Federal Bureau of Investigation, "Operation Backfire: Help Find Four Eco-Terrorists," November 19, 2008. Accessed at https://archives.fbi.gov/archives/news/stories/2008/november/backfire_11908 on July 22, 2016.

225. "US Domestic Terrorism: Earth Liberation Front," History Commons. Accessed at http://www.historycommons.org/timeline.jsp?timeline=us_domestic_terrorism_tmln&haitian_elite_2021_organizations=us_domestic_terrorism_tmln_earth_liberation_front on August 21, 2016.

226. "Who Is the ALF?" Accessed at http://animalliberationfront.com/ALFront/ALF_leaflet_biteback.pdf on July 22, 2016.

227. Richard Faussett, "For Robert Dear, Religion and Rage Before Planned Parenthood Attack," *The New York Times*, December 1, 2015. Accessed at http://www.nytimes.com/2015/12/02/us/robert-dear-planned-parenthood-shooting.html on October 1, 2016.

228. Accessed at http://www.armyofgod.com/. Accessed on October 3, 2016.

229. David Paul, "Why Robert Lewis Dear Is Terrifying But Not a Terrorist," The Huffington Post, December 3, 2015. Accessed at http://www.huffingtonpost.com/david-paul/robert-lewis-dear-is-terr_b_8697202.html on October 3, 2016.

230. Nathaniel Sheppard, Jr., "Abortion Doctor and Wife Are Freed," *The New York Times*, August 21, 1982. Accessed at http://www.nytimes.com/1982/08/21/us/abortion-doctor-and-wife-are-freed.html on September 30, 2016.

231. Aylish Cotter, "Jennifer Jefferis. Armed for Life: The Army of God and Anti-Abortion Terror in the United States. Santa Barbara, CA: Praeger. 2011," Perspectives on Terrorism, Vol 5, No 5-6 (2011). Accessed at http://www.terrorismanalysts.com/pt/index.php/pot/issue/view/32 on September 30, 2016.

232. National Abortion Federation, "Anti-Abortion Extremists," n.d. Accessed at https://prochoice.org/education-and-advocacy/violence/anti-abortion-extremists/ on September 30, 2016.

233. Anne Bower, "Army of God: Still Marching," *The Body Politic*, Vol. 5, No. 11, December 1995, p. 8. Accessed at http://www.publiceye.org/body_politic/mag/back/art/0511pg08.htm on October 3, 2016.

234. Steven G. Bradbury, Principal Deputy Assistant Attorney General, U.S. Department of Justice, Office of Legal Counsel, "Memorandum for John A. Rizzo, Senior Deputy General Counsel, Central Intelligence Agency," May 30, 2005. Accessed at http://ccrjustice.org/files/05-30-2005_bradbury_40pg_OLC%20torture%20memos.pdf on July 25, 2014.

235. ABC News, "Thwarted Terrorist Plots Since Sept. 11, February 6, 2006. Accessed at http://abcnews.go.com/Politics/story?id=1599331 on June 1, 2014. See also UPI, "Bush: Al-Qaida plots have been thwarted," Oct. 6, 2005. Accessed at www.upi.com/Top_News/2005/10/06/Bush-Al-Qaida-plots-have-been-thwarted/UPI-83141128613293 on June 1, 2014.

236. White House Press Release, "President Discusses Progress in War on Terror to National Guard," February 9, 2006. Accessed at http://2001-2009.state.gov/r/pa/ei/wh/rem/60873.htm on July 21, 2014.

237. Office of the White House Press Secretary, "Press Briefing on the West Coast Terrorist Plot by Frances Fragos Townsend, Assistant to the President for Homeland Security and Counterterrorism," February 9, 2006. Accessed at http://georgewbush-whitehouse.archives.gov/news/releases/2006/02/20060209-4.html on July 21, 2014.

238. James Risen and Eric Lightblau, "Bush Lets U.S. Spy on Callers Without Courts." The New York Times. Accessed at www.nytimes.com/2005/12/16/politics/16program.html?pagewanted=all&_r=0 on July 25, 2014.

239. Joel Roberts, "Bush Defends Domestic Spying at NSA." CBS News, January 25, 2006. Accessed at www.cbsnews.com/news/bush-defends-domestic-spying-at-nsa on August 27, 2014.

240. "Unclassified Report on the President's Surveillance Program," July 10, 2009. Authored by Offices of the Inspector General of several intelligence agencies. Accessed at http://fas.org/irp/eprint/psp.pdf on October 17, 2014.

241. Electronic Frontier Foundation, "NSA Spying on Americans." Accessed at www.eff.org/nsa-spying on July 25, 2014.

242. "Declaration of William E. Binney," CASE NO. CV-08-04373-JSW, U.S. District Court for the Northern District of California, September 28, 2012. Accessed at https://info.publicintelligence.net/NSA-WilliamBinneyDeclaration.pdf on August 30, 2014.

243. The White House, Office of the Press Secretary, "Statement by the President on Airstrikes in Syria," September 23, 2014. Accessed at www.whitehouse.gov/the-press-office/2014/09/23/statement-president-airstrikes-syria on September 27, 2014.

244. Terrence McCoy, "Khorasan and leader Muhsin al-Fadhli: who are they?," The Sidney Morning Herald, September 24, 2014. Accessed at www.smh.com.au/world/khorasan-and-leader-muhsin-alfadhli-who-are-they-20140924-10l59a.html on September 27, 2014.

245. Mark Mazzetti, "A Terror Cell That Avoided the Spotlight," The New York Times, September 24, 2014. Accessed at www.nytimes.com/2014/09/25/world/middleeast/khorasan-a-terror-cell-that-avoided-the-spotlight.html on September 27, 2014.

246. Zack Beauchamp, "Khorasan, explained: why the US is bombing an al-Qaeda group you've never heard of," Vox, September 27, 2014. Accessed at www.vox.com/2014/9/26/6836491/khorasan-isis-syria-al-qaeda on September 27, 2014.

247. Sean Alfano, "Details Emerge in Sears Tower Plot," CBS, AP, June 29, 2006.

248. Walter Pincus, "FBI Role in Terror Probe Questioned," The Washington Post, September 2, 2006. Accessed at www.washingtonpost.com/wp-dyn/content/article/2006/09/01/AR2006090101764.html on May 6, 2014.

249. US Department of Justice press release, "Seven Florida Men Charged with Conspiring to Support al Qaeda, Attack Targets in the United States," June 23, 2006.

250. USA Today, "FBI says suspects sought to form own army," June 23, 2006. Accessed at http://usatoday30.usatoday.com/news/nation/2006-06-22-terror-ism-investigation_x.htm on September 27, 2015.

251. FBI Director Robert S. Mueller III, Citizens Crime Commission James Fox Memorial Lecture, New York, April 26, 2006.

252. Columbia Law School, Human Rights Institute and Human Rights Watch, "Illusion of Justice: Human Rights Abuses in US Terrorism Prosecutions," July

2014, pp. 12–13. Accessed at www.hrw.org/sites/default/files/reports/usterror-ism0714_ForUpload_0_0_0.pdf on September 22, 2015.

253. Ibid., p. 2.

254. Paul Harris, "Newburgh Four: poor, black, and jailed under FBI 'entrapment' tactics," The Guardian, December 12, 2011. Accessed at www.theguardian.com/world/2011/dec/12/newburgh-four-fbi-entrapment-terror on September 27, 2015.

255. Ibid.

256. Ted Conover, "The Pathetic Newburgh Four: Should the FBI really be baiting sad-sack homegrown terrorists?," Slate, November 23, 2010. Accessed at www.slate.com/articles/news_and_politics/jurisprudence/2010/11/the_pathetic_newburgh_four.html on September 27, 2015.

257. Federal Bureau of Investigation, New York Office, "Four Men Found Guilty of Plotting to Bomb New York Synagogue and Jewish Community Center and to Shoot Military Planes with Stinger Missiles," October 18, 2010. Accessed at www.fbi.gov/newyork/press-releases/2010/nyfo101810.htm on September 28, 2015.

258. Kate Davis and David Heilbroner, directors, The Newburgh Sting, an HBO documentary. Accessed at www.hbo.com/documentaries/the-newburgh-sting on September 27, 2015.

259. Al Baker and Javier C. Hernandez, "4 Accused of Bombing Plot at Bronx Synagogues," The New York Times, May 20, 2009. Accessed at www.nytimes.com/2009/05/21/nyregion/21arrests.html on September 27, 2015.

260. Officer Down Memorial Page. Accessed at www.odmp.org/search/year on July 23, 2016.

261. Andy Kiersz and Brett LoGiurato, "Obama was right when he said 'this type of mass violence does not happen in other developed countries,'" Business Insider, June 18, 2015. Accessed at www.businessinsider.com/oecd-homicide-rates-chart-2015-6 on July 23, 2016.

262. Risa Brooks, "Muslim 'Homegrown' Terrorism in the United States: How Serious Is the Threat?" Accessed at http://belfercenter.ksg.harvard.edu/publication/21390/muslim_homegrown_terrorism_in_the_united_states.html on July 11, 2014.

263. Risa Brooks, "Muslim 'Homegrown' Terrorism in the United States: How Serious Is the Threat?," International Security 36:2 8, pp. 29–29. Accessed at http://belfercenter.ksg.harvard.edu/publication/21390/muslim_homegrown_terrorism_in_the_united_states.html on July 11, 2014.

264. New America Foundation, "Deadly Attacks Since 9/11." Accessed at http://securitydata.newamerica.net/extremists/deadly-attacks.html on June 23, 2015.

265. Tim Arango and Eric Schmitt, "U.S. Actions in Iraq Fueled Rise of a Rebel," The New York Times, August 11, 2014, p. 1.

266. Jason Ukman, "New estimate of U.S. war costs: $4 trillion," The Washington Post, June 29, 2011. Accessed at www.washingtonpost.com/blogs/checkpoint-washington/post/new-estimate-of-us-war-costs-4-trillion/2011/06/29/AGnolfqH_blog.html on June 26, 2014. See also Ernesto Londono, "Study: Iraq, Afghan war costs to top $4 trillion," The Washington Post, March 28, 2013. Accessed at www.washingtonpost.com/world/national-security/study-iraq-afghan-war-costs-to-top-4-trillion/2013/03/28/b82a5dce-97ed-11e2-814b-063623d80a60_story.html on June 26, 2014.

267. U.S. Department of Defense, "Casualty Status." Accessed at www.defense.gov/casualty.pdf on September 2, 2016.

CHAPTER VI: TORTURE AND DETENTION

268. Torture FOIA—Torture Documents Released 4/15/2010, Part 1, p. 3. Accessed at www.aclu.org/files/assets/cia_release20100415_p01-09.pdf on July 29, 2015.

269. Ibid., Part 2, p. 23. Accessed at www.aclu.org/files/assets/cia_release20100415_p10-18.pdf on July 29, 2015.

270. Ibid., Part 3, p. 1. Accessed at www.aclu.org/files/assets/cia_release20100415_p19-27.pdf on July 29, 2015.

271. Peter Finn and Julie Tate, "2005 destruction of interrogation tapes caused concern at CIA, e-mails show," The Washington Post, April 16, 2012. Accessed at www.washingtonpost.com/wp-dyn/content/article/2010/04/15/AR2010041505854.html on April 30, 2015.

272. Johnson v. Eisentrager, 339 U.S. 763, 798, 70 S.Ct. 936, 954, 94 L.Ed. 1255 (1950).

273. The definition and usage are from the Oxford English Dictionary.

274. Pub. L. 107-40, codified at 115 Stat. 224, was passed as S.J.Res. 23 by the U.S. Congress on September 14, 2001. It authorizes the use of U.S. Armed Forces against those responsible for 9/11 attacks.

275. See Jay S. Bybee, U.S. Department of Justice, Office of Legal Counsel, Office of the Assistant Attorney General, Memorandum for John Rizzo, Acting General Counsel of the Central Intelligence Agency, "Interrogation of al Qaeda Operative," August 1, 2002; Bybee, Memorandum for Alberto R. Gonzales, Counsel to the President, "Re: Standards of Conduct for Interrogation under 18 U.S.C.2340-234-A," August 1, 2002.

276. Yoo became a law professor at Berkeley and an unrepentant advocate of torture, and Bybee a federal judge on the U.S. Court of Appeals for the Ninth Circuit.

277. John C. Yoo, U.S. Department of Justice, Office of Legal Counsel, Office of the Deputy Assistant Attorney General, Memorandum for William J. Haynes II, General Counsel of the Department of Defense, "Re: Military Interrogation of Alien Unlawful Combatants Held Outside the United States," March 14, 2003.

278. "Unclassified Report on the President's Surveillance Program," July 10, 2009. Authored by Offices of the Inspector General of several intelligence agencies. Accessed at http://fas.org/irp/eprint/psp.pdf on October 17, 2014.

279. UN Committee Against Torture, "Concluding observations on the third to fifth periodic reports of United States of America," November 28, 2014, p. 3. Accessed at http://tbinternet.ohchr.org/Treaties/CAT/Shared%20Documents/USA/INT_CAT_COC_USA_18893_E.pdf on November 30, 2014.

280. Greg Miller and Adam Goldman, "Public feud between CIA, Senate panel follows years of tension over interrogation report," The Washington Post. The quotation is taken from a video available at this source of Senator Dianne Feinstein making a public statement about the resistance of the Central Intelligence Agency for the record in the Senate Chamber. Accessed at www.washingtonpost.com/world/national-security/public-feud-between-cia-senate-panel-follows-years-of-tension-over-interrogation-report/2014/03/12/f0633d1c-aa1d-11e3-b61e-8051b8b52d06_story.html on June 18, 2014.

281. CIA, Office of the Inspector General, "Final Report of the Rendition, Detention, and Interrogation, Network Agency Accountability Board," approved for release January 14, 2014, p. 35. Accessed at https://www.cia.gov/library/reports/Redacted-December-2014-Agency-Accountability-Board-Report.pdf on January 17, 2015; and Matt Apuzzo and Mark Mazzetti, "Panel to Advise Against Penalty for C.I.A.'s Computer Search," The New York Times, December 20, 2014.

282. Siobhan Gorman, "Top Spy Battles Congress Over Classified Report," The Wall Street Journal, July 3, 2014, pp. A1 and A10.

283. Black was in charge of the design and implementation of the CIA torture program at "black sites" in secret CIA detention centers located in various countries. He later served as vice-chairman of Blackwater USA (2005–present), a mercenary firm engaged in the wars in Iraq and Afghanistan. The Center for Torture Accountability, "Cofer Black, Torture Connection: 'The gloves come off.'" Accessed at http://tortureaccountability.org/cofer_black on August 6, 2014. See also "US Firm Offers Private Army," Greater Talent Network. Accessed at www.greatertalent.com/speaker-news/cofer-black-vicechairman-of-the-leading-us-security-firm-blackwater-usa-has-offered-to-provide-forces-for-counterinsurgency-mission-around-the-world on August 6, 2014.

284. Mark Mazzetti, "Ex-Chief of C.I.A. Shapes Response to Detention Report," The New York Times, July 25, 2014.

285. Major General Antonio M. Taguba (U.S. Army, rtd.), "Stop the C.I.A. Spin on the Senate Torture Report," The New York Times, August 5, 2014. Taguba conducted the investigation and wrote the report on the detainee abuses at the Abu Ghraib prison in Bagdad.

286. Senator Dianne Feinstein, "Statement on Intel Committee's CIA Detention, Interrogation Report," March 11, 2014, official transcript. Accessed at www.feinstein.senate.gov/public/index.cfm/press-releases?ID=db84e844-01bb-4eb6-b318-31486374a895 on December 22, 2014.

287. Council on Foreign Relations, transcript, "CIA Director Brennan Denies Hacking Allegations, A Conversation with John O. Brennan," MSNBC,

March 11, 2014. Accessed at www.cfr.org/intelligence/cia-director-brennan-denies-hacking-allegations/p32563 on December 22, 2014. For a video of Brennan's remarks, see www.youtube.com/watch?v=6apC6jN0TZo&t=16m38s. Accessed on November 19, 2015. See also Dustin Volz, "CIA Director: We Are Not Spying on Congress," National Journal, March 11, 2014. Accessed at www.nationaljournal.com/tech/cia-director-we-are-not-spying-on-congress-20140311 on December 22, 2014.

288. CIA, Office of the Inspector General, "Summary of Report Prepared at the Request of the Congressional Intelligence Committees," July 31, 2014. Accessed at www.washingtonpost.com/r/2010-2019/WashingtonPost/2014/07/31/National-Security/Graphics/Cleaned2014-07-30%20Unclass%20Summary%20of%20RDI%20ROI%2031%20Jul%2014.pdf on December 30, 2014.

289. CIA, Office of the Inspector General, "Final Report of the Rendition, Detention, and Interrogation, Network Agency Accountability Board," approved for release January 14, 2014. Accessed at https://www.cia.gov/library/reports/Redacted-December-2014-Agency-Accountability-Board-Report.pdf on January 17, 2015.

290. Jonathan S. Landay and Ali Watkins, "CIA admits it broke into Senate computers; senators call for spy chief's ouster," McClatchy Washington Bureau, July 31, 2014. Accessed at www.mcclatchydc.com/2014/07/31/234997/cia-staffers-accessed-senate.html#storylink=cpy on December 30, 2014.

291. Mark Mazzetti, "C.I.A. Admits Penetrating Senate Intelligence Computers," The New York Times, July 31, 2014.

292. Ibid.

293. Senate Select Committee on Intelligence, Committee Study of the Central Intelligence Agency's Detention and Interrogation Program, Foreword by Senate Select Committee on Intelligence Chairman Dianne Feinstein, Findings and Conclusions, Executive Summary, December 2014. Accessed at www.intelligence.senate.gov/study2014/sscistudy1.pdf on December 29, 2014.

294. Mark Mazzetti and Carl Hulse, "Senate Panel Faces New Obstacle to Release of Torture," The New York Times, December 5, 2014. Accessed at www.nytimes.com/2014/12/06/us/politics/new-obstacle-to-senate-panels-release-of-cia-torture-report.html on December 21, 2014.

295. Josh Rogin, "Kerry Puts Brakes on CIA Torture Report," Bloomberg View, December 5, 2014. Accessed at www.bloombergview.com/articles/2014-12-05/kerry-puts-brakes-on-cia-torture-report on December 21, 2014.

296. Peter Baker and Mark Mazzetti, "Brennan Draws on Bond With Obama in Backing C.I.A.," The New York Times, December 14, 2014. Accessed at www.nytimes.com/2014/12/15/us/politics/cia-chief-and-president-walk-fine-line-.html on December 21, 2014.

297. Peter Baker, "Obama Catches Blame on Tactics of Torture That He Ended," The New York Times, December 10, 2014. Accessed at www.nytimes.com/2014/12/11/us/politics/obama-effectiveness-cia-torture.html on Dec-ember 21, 2014.

298. Washington Post/ABC News Poll December 11–14, 2014, "Majority says CIA harsh interrogations justified," January 4, 2015. Accessed at www.washingtonpost.com/page/2010-2019/WashingtonPost/2014/12/16/National-Politics/Polling/release_376.xml on July 30, 2015.

299. Remarks as Prepared for Delivery CIA Director John O. Brennan Response to SSCI Study on the Former Detention and Interrogation Program. Accessed at www.cia.gov/news-information/speeches-testimony/2014-speeches-testimony/remarks-as-prepared-for-delivery-cia-director-john-o-brennan-response-to-ssci-study-on-the-former-detention-and-interrogation-program.html on December 21, 2014.

300. "Additional Views," Senate Select Committee on Intelligence, Committee Study of the Central Intelligence Agency's Detention and Interrogation Program, December 2014. Accessed at www.intelligence.senate.gov/study2014/sscistudy2.pdf on December 29, 2014.

301. Douglas A. Johnson et al., "The Strategic Costs of Torture," Foreign Affairs, September/October 2016, p. 130.

302. Scott Shane, "Backing C.I.A., Cheney Revisits Torture Debate From Bush Era," The New York Times, December 14, 2014. Accessed at www.nytimes.com/2014/12/15/us/politics/cheney-senate-report-on-torture.html on December 21, 2014.

303. CNN Press Room, "Bush refutes CIA torture report to CNN's Candy Crowley," December 8, 2014. Accessed at http://cnnpressroom.blogs.cnn.com/2014/12/08/bush-refutes-cia-torture-report-to-cnns-candy-crowley on December 21, 2014.

304. Rowan Scarborough, "George Tenet, Michael Hayden—other former CIA chiefs—say enhanced interrogations helped," Washington Times, December 10, 2014. Accessed at www.washingtontimes.com/news/2014/dec/10/george-tenet-michael-hayden-former-cia-chiefs on December 21, 2014. The website was accessed at http://ciasavedlives.com on December 21, 2014.

305. The release was accompanied by a minority report that attacked the methodology and many other aspects of the report. See Senate Select Committee on Intelligence, Committee Study of the Central Intelligence Agency's Detention and Interrogation Program, Minority Views of Vice Chairman Chambliss, Joined by Senators Burr, Risch, Coats, Rubio, and Coburn, June 20, 2014. Accessed at www.feinstein.senate.gov/public/index.cfm/files/serve/?File_id=db587bbf-f52d-47eb-b90c-a60ff3f92484 on December 29, 2014.

306. Executive Order 13491—Ensuring Lawful Interrogations, January 22, 2009. Accessed at www.whitehouse.gov/the_press_office/EnsuringLawful Interrogationson December 23, 2014.

307. Both men are cited in Mark Mazzetti, "Panel Faults C.I.A. Over Brutality and Deceit in Terrorism Interrogations," The New York Times, December 9, 2014, accessed at www.nytimes.com/2014/12/10/world/senate-intelligence-committee-cia-torture-report.html on December 23, 2014; and in Robert Windrem, "CIA Paid Torture Teachers More Than $80 Million," NBC News, December

16, 2014, accessed at www.nbcnews.com/storyline/cia-torture-report/majority-americans-believe-cias-harsh-interrogation-tactics-were-acceptable-n269211 on December 23, 2014.

308. Editorial Board, "Prosecute Torturers and Their Bosses," The New York Times, December 21, 2014. Accessed at www.nytimes.com/2014/12/22/opinion/prosecute-torturers-and-their-bosses.html?_r=0 on December 23, 2014.

309. The author wishes to express his appreciation to Ren Keller for legal research he conducted that helps to inform this section.

310. "Convention (III) relative to the Treatment of Prisoners of War. Geneva, 12 August 1949." Accessed at www.icrc.org/ihl/WebART/375-590006 on May 18, 2015.

311. United Nations General Assembly, A/RES/39/46, 10 December 1984, Meeting no. 93. Accessed at www.un.org/documents/ga/res/39/a39r046.htm on May 18, 2015.

312. 18 U.S. Code § 2441. See Legal Information Institute, Cornell University, "War Crimes," n.d. Accessed at www.law.cornell.edu/uscode/text/18/2441 on July 31, 2015.

313. "Torture: The Guantanamo Guidebook," 2005. Accessed at www.youtube.com/watch?v=HCUzHnVeI10 on September 23, 2015.

314. George Tenet, "Guidelines on Interrogations Conducted Pursuant to the (redacted)," January 28, 2003, in IG Special Review, Appendix E, p. 1.

315. Central Intelligence Agency Inspector General, Special Review, "Counterterrorism Detention and Interrogation Activities" (September 2001–October 2003) (2003-7123-IG), May 7, 2004, p. 15. Accessed at http://fas.org/irp/cia/product/ig-interrog.pdf on September 23, 2015.

316. Online Oxford English Dictionary.

317. English translation of the Magna Carta. Accessed at www.bl.uk/magna-carta/articles/magna-carta-english-translation on September 1, 2015. "+" means the article was incorporated into the 1225 version of the Magna Carta.

318. 79 Eng. Rep. 746 K.B. 1629. Accessed at http://press-pubs.uchicago.edu/founders/documents/a1_9_2s1.html on July 24, 2016.

319. Court of the Star Chamber, legal documents in the trial of Richard Chambers, [1629?]. Accessed at http://orbexpress.library.yale.edu/vwebv/ on July 24, 2016.

320. See Select Pleas of the Crown (Selden Soc., Vol. 1), 67 referencing 1214.

321. A. Raymond Randolph, "The Guantanamo Mess," Joseph Story Distinguished Lecture—2010. Accessed at www.heritage.org/events/2010/10/guantanamo-mess on August 24, 2015.

322. 12 Stat. 755.

323. 339 U.S. 763; 70 S. Ct. 936; 94 L. Ed. 1255; (1950).

324. Eisentrager at 778.

325. Eisentrager at 798.

326. Boumediene v. Bush 553 U.S. 723 (2008), quoting Hamilton C. Rossiter ed., p. 512 (1961) (quoting 1 Blackstone *136, 4 id., at *438). p. 724,3; accessed at http://files.libertyfund.org/files/2140/Blackstone_1387-01_EBk_v6.0.pdf.

327. 115 Stat. 224 Public Law 107–40—Sept. 18, 2001. Accessed at www.gpo.gov/fdsys/pkg/PLAW-107publ40/pdf/PLAW-107publ40.pdf on August 11, 2015.

328. Ibid.

329. "Military Order of November 13, 2001, "Detention, Treatment, and Trial of Certain Non-Citizens in the War Against Terrorism." Accessed at http://fas.org/irp/offdocs/eo/mo-111301.htm on August 11, 2015.

330. 107th Congress Public Law 243. Accessed at www.gpo.gov/fdsys/pkg/PLAW-107publ243/html/PLAW-107publ243.htm on August 11, 2015.

331. 542 U.S. 466 (2004), 124 S. Ct. 2686; 159 L. Ed. 2d 548.

332. Stephen Breyer, America's Supreme Court: Making Democracy Work (Oxford, England: Oxford University Press, 2010), p. 198.

333. Rasul at 484.

334. 542 U.S. 507 (2004), 124 S. Ct. 2633; 159 L. Ed. 2d 578.

335. Hamdi at 533.

336. "Human Intelligence Collector Operations," Headquarters, Department of the Army, FM 2-22.3 (FM 34-52), September 2006. Accessed at http://fas.org/irp/doddir/army/fm2-22-3.pdf on October 5, 2015.

337. Section 1005(e) of 28 U. S. C. §2241, as amended.

338. 42 U.S. Code § 2000dd–1 - Protection of United States Government personnel engaged in authorized interrogations. Accessed at https://www.law.cornell.edu/uscode/text/42/2000dd%E2%80%931# on June 24, 2016.

339. 548 U.S. 557 (2006), 124 S.Ct. 2633, 2650, 159 L.Ed.2d 578.

340. Hamdan v. Rumsfeld, Opinion of STEVENS, J., June 29, 2006. Accessed at www.law.cornell.edu/supct/pdf/05-184P.ZO on October 5, 2015.

341. See "Military Order of November 13, 2001," Federal Register: November 16, 2001 (Volume 66, Number 222), Presidential Documents, pp. 57831–57836. Accessed at http://fas.org/irp/offdocs/eo/mo-111301.htm on October 5, 2015.

342. 553 U.S. 723 (2008), 128 S. Ct. 2229.

343. Ibid. at 739.

344. Op. cit., Breyer, p. 209.

345. Boumediene at 787.

346. Military Commissions Act of 2009, Sec. 1802, §§ 948a(7), 948b(a), 948c.

347. See id. § 948a(6).

348. For a good review of the differences between the Military Commissions Act of 2006 and the Military Commissions Act of 2009, see Jennifer K. Elsea, "The

Military Commissions Act of 2009 (MCA 2009): Overview and Legal Issues," Congressional Research Service, August 4, 2014. Accessed at https://www.fas.org/sgp/crs/natsec/R41163.pdf on September 28, 2015.

349. NPR Staff, "Guantanamo Defense Lawyer Resigns, Says U.S. Case Is 'Stacked.'" National Public Radio, August 30, 2014. Accessed at www.npr.org/2014/08/31/344576895/guantanamo-defense-lawyer-resigns-says-u-s-case-is-stacked on August 30, 2014.

350. Laura Pitter, "13 Years On, Will 9/11 Ever Go to Trial?" Foreign Policy, August 27, 2014. Accessed at www.foreignpolicy.com/articles/2014/08/27/13_years_on_will_911_ever_go_to_trial_guantanamo_obama on August 30, 2014.

351. Op. cit., NPR Staff.

CHAPTER VII: SURVEILLANCE AND CONTROL

352. "Moore's Law" is the observation that the logic density of silicon integrated circuits closely follows the curve bits per square inch = $2(t-1962)$, where t is time measured in calendar years. That is, the amount of information that can be stored on a given area of silicon has roughly doubled every two years since the technology was invented. See Gordon E. Moore, "Cramming more components onto integrated circuits," Electronics, Volume 38, Number 8, April 19, 1965.

353. Martha Crenshaw, "Counterterrorism Policy and the Political Process," Studies in Conflict & Terrorism, vol. 24, 2001, pp. 329 and 335.

354. See Bruce Ackerman, Before the Next Attack: Preserving Civil Liberties in an Age of Terrorism (New Haven, CT: Yale University Press, 2006), pp. 2–4.

355. Joel Roberts, "Bush Defends Domestic Spying at NSA," CBS News, May 31, 2007. Accessed at www.cbsnews.com/stories/2006/01/25/politics/main1236272.shtml on August 27, 2014. On the USA Patriot Act, see Chris Doyle, "The USA Patriot Act: A Sketch," CRS Report for Congress, Order Code RS21203, April 18, 2002, pp. 1–5. Accessed at www.fas.org/irp/crs/RS21203.pdf on May 31, 2007.

356. George W. Bush, "Address to a Joint Session of Congress and the American People," September 20, 2001. Accessed at www.whitehouse.gov/news/releases/2001/09/20010920-8.html on May 31, 2007.

357. NPR, "Transcript: Obama Addresses Counterterrorism, Drones," May 23, 2013. Accessed at www.npr.org/2013/05/23/186305171/transcript-obama-addresses-counterterrorism-drones on May 19, 2014. See also Peter Baker, "Pivoting From a War Footing, Obama Acts to Curtail Drones," The New York Times, May 23, 2013.

358. Michael S. Schmidt, "At FBI, Change in Leaders Didn't Change Focus on Terror," The New York Times, May 18, 2014.

359. James B. Comey, Director, Federal Bureau of Investigation, "Statement Before the Senate Committee on Homeland Security and Governmental Affairs," Washington, D.C., November 14, 2013. Accessed at www.fbi.gov/news/testimony/homeland-threats-and-the-fbis-response on September 7, 2014.

360. Bruce Livesey, "The Salafist Movement," PBS Frontline, January 25, 2005. Accessed at www.pbs.org/wgbh/pages/frontline/shows/front/special/sala.html on June 1, 2007. For more information on the Salafist ideology and its global threat, see Quintan Wiktorowicz, "A Genealogy of Radical Islam," Studies in Conflict and Terrorism, Vol. 28, No. 2, February 2005, pp. 75–97 and "The New Global Threat: Transnational Salafis and Jihad," Middle East Policy, Vol. VIII, No. 4, December 2001, pp. 18–38.

361. See Lorenzo Vidino, "The Hofstad Group: The New Face of Terrorist Networks in Europe," Studies in Conflict and Terrorism, Vol. 30, No. 7, July 2007, pp. 579–590.

362. See Michael Ignatieff, The Lesser Evil (Princeton: Princeton University Press, 2004), pp. 58–59.

363. Manes, Stephen, "Private Lives? Not Ours!," PC World, April 18, 2000. Accessed at www.computerworld.com.au/article/20046/full_disclosure_private_lives_ ours_ on July 14, 2015.

364. See entry under "Search and Seizure," The Free Legal Dictionary. Accessed at http://legal-dictionary.thefreedictionary.com/Reasonable+expectation+of+pri vacy on August 24, 2015.

365. Fourth Amendment to the United States Constitution.

366. BBC News, Magazine Monitor, The Vocabularist, "The very French history of the word 'surveillance,'" July 14, 2015. Accessed at www.bbc.com/news/blogs-magazine-monitor-33464368 on July 14, 2015.

367. Jean-Paul Marat. Accessed at www.brainyquote.com/quotes/quotes/j/jean-paulm329305.html on July 17, 2015.

368. A-Z quotes. Accessed at www.azquotes.com/quote/801685 on July 17, 2015.

369. Rachel Stohl, "All the President's Drones: Obama's Targeted-Killing Problem," The National Interest, April 20, 2015. Accessed at http://nationalinterest.org/ feature/all-the-president%E2%80%99s-drones-obama%E2%80%99s-target-ed-killing-problem-12663 on July 19, 2015.

370. Thomas Henry Dyer, Modern Europe, Volume 4 (London: George Bell, 1877), p. 411.

371. James Dao, "Drone Pilots Are Found to Get Stress Disorders Much as Those in Combat Do," The New York Times, February 22, 2013. Accessed at www. nytimes.com/2013/02/23/us/drone-pilots-found-to-get-stress-disorders-much-as-those-in-combat-do.html?_r=0 on July 19, 2015.

372. Christopher Drew and Dave Philipps, "As Stress Drives Off Drone Operators, Air Force Must Cut Flights." The New York Times, June 16, 2015. Accessed at www.nytimes.com/2015/06/17/us/as-stress-drives-off-drone-operators-air-force-must-cut-flights.html on July 19, 2015.

373. Firmin Debrabander, "Drones and the Democracy Disconnect," The New York Times, September 14, 2014. Accessed at http://opinionator.blogs.nytimes. com/2014/09/14/drones-and-the-democracy-disconnect/ on July 20, 2015.

374. C⁴ISR stands for "Command, Control, Communications, Computers, Intelligence, Surveillance, and Reconnaissance."

375. Richard A. Posner and Katharine B. Silbaugh, A Guide to America's Sex Laws (Chicago: University of Chicago Press, 1996), p. 2.

376. Statista: The Statistics Portal, "Number of apps available in leading app stores as of May 2015." Accessed at www.statista.com/statistics/276623/number-of-apps-available-in-leading-app-stores on July 19, 2015.

377. Michael B. Kelley, "NSA: Snowden Stole 1.7 MILLION Classified Documents and Still Has Access to Most of Them," Business Insider, Dec. 13, 2013. Accessed at www.businessinsider.com/how-many-docs-did-snowden-take-2013-12 on August 24, 2015.

378. David E. Sanger and Nicole Perlroth, "Internet Giants Erect Barriers to Spy Agencies," The New York Times, June 7, 2014, p. 1. See also Elena Schneider, "Technology Companies Are Pressing Congress to Bolster Privacy Protections," The New York Times, May 27, 2014, p. A14.

379. David E. Sanger and Nicole Perlroth, "Obama Heads to Tech Security Talks Amid Tensions," The New York Times, February 12, 2015. Accessed at www.nytimes.com/2015/02/13/business/obama-heads-to-security-talks-amid-tensions.html?_r=0 on February 13, 2015.

380. Davis E. Sanger and Brian X. Cheng, "Signaling Post-Snowden Era, New iPhone Locks Out N.S.A.," The New York Times, September 27, 2014. Accessed at www.nytimes.com/2014/09/27/technology/iphone-locks-out-the-nsa-signaling-a-post-snowden-era-.html?_r=0 on September 27, 2014.

381. Robert Hannigan, "The web is a terrorist's command-and-control network of choice," Financial Times, November 3, 2014. Accessed at www.ft.com/cms/s/2/c89b6c58-6342-11e4-8a63-00144feabdc0.html#axzz3I2BdS7rE on December 21, 2014.

382. Alan Cowell and Mark Scott, "Top British Spy Warns of Terrorists' Use of Social Media," The New York Times, November 6, 2014.

383. Federal Communications Agency, "Communications Assistance for Law Enforcement Act." Accessed at www.fcc.gov/encyclopedia/communications-assistance-law-enforcement-act on September 27, 2014.

384. Electronic Frontier Foundation, "The Communications Assistance for Law Enforcement Act (CALEA) of 1994." Accessed at www.eff.org/issues/calea on September 13, 2015.

385. [Cite FBI/DOJ here.]

386. James B. Comey, "Joint Statement with Deputy Attorney General Sally Quillian Yates Before the Senate Judiciary Committee," Washington, D.C., July 8, 2015. Accessed at www.fbi.gov/news/testimony/going-dark-encryption-technology-and-the-balances-between-public-safety-and-privacy on September 13, 2015.

387. Dustin Volz, "FBI Director Warns Lawmakers ISIS Is Using Encryption to Order Killings," National Journal, July 8, 2015. Accessed at www.defenseone.

com/technology/2015/07/fbi-director-warns-lawmakers-isis-using-encryption-order-killings/117247 on July 9, 2015.

388. "Open Letter to the Senate on the USA Freedom Act," May 19, 2015, signed by the CEOs of AOL, Apple, Dropbox, Evernote, Facebook, Google, LinkedIn, Microsoft, Twitter, and Yahoo. Accessed at www.reformgovernmentsurveillance.com/index.html on August 3, 2015.

389. Craig Timberg and Michael Birnbaum, "In Google case, EU court says people are entitled to control their own online histories," The Washington Post, May 13, 2014. Accessed at www.washingtonpost.com/business/technology/eu-court-people-entitled-to-control-own-online-h%20istories/2014/05/13/8e4495d6-dabf-11e3-8009-71de85b9c527_story.html on June 10, 2013.

390. EU Parliament, D-G for Internal Policies, Citizens' Rights and Constitutional Affairs, "National Programmes for Mass Surveillance of Personal Data in EU Member States and Their Compatibility with EU Law," 2013. Accessed at www.europarl.europa.eu/RegData/etudes/etudes/join/2013/493032/IPOL-LIBE_ET(2013)493032_EN.pdf on October 20, 2014.

391. Article X, "Basic Law for the Federal Republic of Germany." Accessed at www.gesetze-im-internet.de/englisch_gg/englisch_gg.html on October 21, 2014.

392. Deutsche Welle, "Germany admits Europe's spy agencies cooperate on surveillance," November 2, 2013. Accessed at www.dw.de/germany-admits-europes-spy-agencies-cooperate-on-surveillance/a-17200903 on October 20, 2014; David Francis, "Germany's Hypocrisy on NSA Surveillance: The country has rallied around Snowden, but its government isn't innocent." Slate, February 25, 2014. Accessed at www.slate.com/articles/technology/future_tense/2014/02/angela_merkel_surveillance_proposal_germany_is_hypocritical_about_the_nsa.html on October 20, 2014; Spiegel Online International, "Indispensable Exchange: Germany Cooperates Closely with NSA," July 8, 2013. Accessed at www.spiegel.de/international/world/spiegel-reveals-cooperation-between-nsa-and-german-bnd-a-909954.html on October 21, 2014.

393. Ryley v. California, No. 13–132. Argued April 29, 2014—Decided June 25, 2014. Accessed at www.supremecourt.gov/opinions/13pdf/13-132_8l9c.pdf on June 25, 2014.

394. "Unclassified Report on the President's Surveillance Program," July 10, 2009. Authored by Offices of the Inspector General of several intelligence agencies. Accessed at http://fas.org/irp/eprint/psp.pdf on October 17, 2014.

395. ACLU v. NSA, Nos. 06-2095/2140, p.2. Accessed at www.ca6.uscourts.gov/opinions.pdf/07a0253p-06.pdf on December 6, 2014. See also "ACLU v. NSA: The Challenge to Illegal Spying." Accessed at www.aclu.org/national-security/aclu-v-nsa-challenge-illegal-spying on December 6, 2014.

396. Doug Stanglin, "Federal judge: NSA phone surveillance legal," USA Today, December 27, 2013. Accessed at www.usatoday.com/story/news/nation/2013/12/27/new-york-nsa-phone-surveillance/4219055 on September 3, 2014.

397. Bill Mears and Evan Perez, "Judge: NSA domestic phone data-mining unconstitutional," CNN News, December 16, 2013. Accessed at www.cnn.com/2013/12/16/justice/nsa-surveillance-court-ruling on September 3, 2014.

398. Letter from Senator Udall et al. to the Privacy and Civil Liberties Oversight Board requesting a review of NSA surveillance programs conducted under Section 215 of the Patriot Act and section 702 of the Foreign Intelligence Surveillance Act, June 12, 2013. Assessed at www.scribd.com/doc/147446726/2013-Letter-to-Privacy-and-Civil-Liberties-Oversight-Board on July 20, 2015.

399. Privacy and Civil Liberties Oversight Board, "Report on the Telephone Records Program Conducted Under Section 215 of the USA PATRIOT Act and on the Operations of the Foreign Intelligence Surveillance Court," January 23, 2014. Accessed at www.pclob.gov/library/215-Report_on_the_Telephone_Records_Program.pdf on July 20, 2015.

400. ACLU v. Clapper, May 7, 2015. Accessed at http://justsecurity.org/wp-content/uploads/2015/05/14-42.majority.pdf on July 20, 2015.

401. From a drafting standpoint, the Freedom Act is a series of amendments to the Foreign Intelligence Surveillance Act of 1978.

402. Jonathan Weisman, "Rand Paul Takes On 'Eye Roll' Caucus to Oppose Data Gathering in Patriot Act," The New York Times, May 31, 2015. Accessed at www.nytimes.com/2015/06/01/us/politics/rand-paul-takes-on-eye-roll-caucus-to-oppose-data-gathering-in-patriot-act.html on June 1, 2015.

403. Bailey Cahall, David Sterman, Emily Schneider and Peter Bergen, "Do NSA's Bulk Surveillance Programs Stop Terrorists?" New America Foundation policy paper, January 13, 2013. Accessed at www.newamerica.org/international-security/do-nsas-bulk-surveillance-programs-stop-terrorists on June 1, 2015.

404. The White House, Office of the Press Secretary, "Weekly Address: Pass the USA Freedom Act," May 30, 2015. Accessed at www.whitehouse.gov/the-press-office/2015/05/29/weekly-address-pass-usa-freedom-act on June 1, 2015.

405. Human Rights Watch, "US: Pass USA Freedom Act—Congress Should Take First Step Toward Reform," April 30, 2015. Accessed at www.hrw.org/news/2015/04/30/us-pass-usa-freedom-act on July 23, 2015.

406. Cindy Cohn and Rainey Reitman, "USA Freedom Act Passes: What We Celebrate, What We Mourn, and Where We Go From Here," June 2, 2015. Accessed at www.eff.org/deeplinks/2015/05/usa-freedom-act-passes-what-we-celebrate-what-we-mourn-and-where-we-go-here on July 22, 2015.

407. [Cite needed here.]

408. Office of U.S. Congressman Ted Poe, press release, "Poe Votes No on USA Freedom Act," May 22, 2014. Accessed at http://poe.house.gov/2014/5/poe-votes-no-on-the-usa-freedom-act on July 22, 2015.

409. Executive Order 12333, United States Intelligence Activities (as amended by Executive Orders 13284 (2003), 13355 (2004) and 13470 (2008)). Accessed

at http://fas.org/irp/offdocs/eo/eo-12333-2008.pdf on June 4, 2015. For an analysis, see Mark Jaycox, "A Primer on Executive Order 12333: The Mass Surveillance Starlet," June 2, 2014, Electronic Frontier Foundation. Accessed at www.eff.org/deeplinks/2014/06/primer-executive-order-12333-mass-surveillance-starlet on June 4, 2015.

410. The White House, Office of the Press Secretary, "Statement by the President on the USA FREEDOM Act," June 2, 2015. Accessed at www.whitehouse.gov/the-press-office/2015/06/02/statement-president-usa-freedom-act on July 22, 2015.

411. Charlie Savage, "A Gap in Surveillance, but Ways Around It," The New York Times, May 31, 2015. Accessed at www.nytimes.com/2015/06/01/us/a-gap-in-surveillance-but-ways-around-it.html on June 1, 2015.

412. Josh Rogin and Eli Lake, "FBI Rounding Up Islamic State Suspects," Bloomberg View, June 25, 2015. Accessed at www.bloombergview.com/articles/2015-06-25/fbi-rounding-up-islamic-state-suspects on June 25, 2015.

CHAPTER VIII: FREEDOM IN THE BALANCE

413. Gregory Fremont-Barnes, ed., Encyclopedia of the Age of Political Revolutions and New Ideologies, 1760–1815 Vol. I, (Westport, CT: Green-wood Press, 2007), p. 190.

414. Terminiello v. City of Chicago, 337 U.S. 1 (1949).

415. "Donald Trump Statement on Preventing Muslim Immigration," December 7, 2015. Accessed at www.donaldjtrump.com/press-releases/donald-j.-trump-statement-on-preventing-muslim-immigration on December 7, 2015.

416. George P. Fletcher, "The Cliché That 'The Constitution Is Not a Suicide Pact': Why It Is Actually Pro-, not Anti-, Civil Liberties," Find Law, January 7, 2003. Accessed at http://writ.news.findlaw.com/commentary/20030107_fletcher.html on November 9, 2015.

417. "Terrorism in the United States," Gallup, n.d. Accessed at www.gallup.com/poll/4909/terrorism-united-states.aspx on September 29, 2015.

418. There is a strong argument that police brutality and active shooting incidents against African Americans constitute terrorism, but are not counted as such by the authorities. See Rick Gladstone, "Many Ask, Why Not Call Church Shooting Terrorism?," The New York Times, June 18 2015. Accessed at www.nytimes.com/2015/06/19/us/charleston-shooting-terrorism-or-hate-crime.html?_r=0 on October 24, 2015. See also Adam Hudson, "1 Black Man Is Killed Every 28 Hours by Police or Vigilantes," May 28, 2013, Alternet. Accessed at www.alternet.org/news-amp-politics/1-black-man-killed-every-28-hours-police-or-vigilantes-america-perpetually-war-its on October 24, 2015.

419. FBI, "Unified Crime Statistics, 2011," Expanded Homicide Data Table 8. Accessed at www.fbi.gov/about-us/cjis/ucr/crime-in-the.u.s/2011/crime-in-the-u.s.-2011/tables/expanded-homicide-data-table-8 on September 29, 2015.

420. U.S. Department of Justice, Federal Bureau of Investigation, "A Study of Active Shooter Incidents in the United States Between 2000 and 2013," pp. 5–6, September 16, 2013, Washington Navy Yard, Washington, D.C. Accessed at www.fbi.gov/news/stories/2014/september/fbi-releases-study-on-active-shooter-incidents/pdfs/a-study-of-active-shooter-incidents-in-the-u.s.-between-2000-and-2013 on October 14, 2015.

421. See "Privacy Advocates List," PrivacyAdvocates.ca: Resisting the Spread of Surveillance. Accessed at www.privacyadvocates.ca/privacy-advocates/list on September 30, 2015.

422. "The Madrid Privacy Declaration," November 3, 2009, Madrid, Spain. Accessed at http://thepublicvoice.org/TheMadridPrivacyDeclaration.pdf on September 30, 2015.

423. Independent Reviewer of Terrorism, "History." Accessed at https://terrorismlegislationreviewer.independent.gov.uk/history on October 1, 2015.

424. Independent Reviewer of Terrorism Legislation, "The Independent Reviewer's role." Accessed at https://terrorismlegislationreviewer.independent.gov.uk/about-me/#special_adviser on October 2, 2015.

425. David Anderson, Q.C., Independent Reviewer of Terrorism Legislation, "A Question of Trust: Report of the Investigatory Powers Review," June 2015, p. 285. Presented to the Prime Minister pursuant to Section 7 of the Data Retention and Investigatory Powers Act 2014. Accessed at https://terrorismlegislationreviewer.independent.gov.uk/wp-content/uploads/2015/06/IPR-Report-Print-Version.pdf on October 1, 2015.

426. Ibid.

427. Stephen Erlanger and Stephen Bishop, "Britain Will Present Legislation to Increase Oversight of Surveillance," The New York Times, November 3, 2015. Accessed at www.nytimes.com/2015/11/04/world/europe/britain-will-present-legislation-to-increase-oversight-of-surveillance.html?emc=edit_tnt_20151104&nlid=29585879&tntemail0=y&_r=0 on November 4, 2015.

428. Impact Assessment, "Counter-Terrorism and Security Act 2015 – Privacy and Civil Liberties Board – Royal Assent," February 11, 2015. Accessed at www.gov.uk/government/uploads/system/uploads/attachment_data/file/403559/PCLB_IA_Royal_Assent_MASTER_COPY.pdf on October 1, 2015.

429. Independent Reviewer of Terrorism Legislation, "Posts Tagged: Privacy and Civil Liberties Board," March 31, 2016. Accessed at https://terrorismlegislationreviewer.independent.gov.uk/tag/privacy-and-civil-liberties-board on June 9, 2016.

430. Stephen Castle, "Britain Announces Plan to Update Surveillance Laws," The New York Times, November 4, 2015. Accessed at www.nytimes.com/2015/11/05/world/europe/uk-britain-surveillance-laws.html?emc=edit_tnt_20151105&nlid=29585879&tntemail0=y&_r=0 on November 9, 2015.

431. Court of Justice of the European Union, "Advocate General's Opinion in Case C-362/14 Maximillian Schrems v Data Protection Commissioner,"

Press Release No. 106/15, Luxembourg, September 23, 2015, p. 1. Accessed at http://curia.europa.eu/jcms/upload/docs/application/pdf/2015-09/cp150106 en.pdf on October 1, 2015.

432. USA Freedom Act, Section 107 (k)(4)(A) and (B). Hereafter, Freedom Act.

433. Freedom Act, Section 101 C.

434. Ibid.

435. 50 USC sec.1861(g)

436. Freedom Act, Sections 301 (D), 102(a)(5).

437. Court of Justice of the European Union, Press Release No. 106/15, Luxembourg, September 23, 2015, Advocate General's Opinion in Case C-362/14, Maximillian Schrems v. Data Protection Commissioner. Accessed at http://curia.europa.eu/ jcms/upload/docs/application/pdf/2015-09/cp150106en.pdf on October 13, 2015.

438. Opinion of Advocate General Bot, delivered on September 23, 2015 (1) Case C?362/14, Maximillian Schrems v. Data Protection Commissioner, paragraphs 36 and 77. Accessed at http://curia.europa.eu/juris/document/document.jsf;jse ssionid=9ea7d0f130d5752c7b853f0040e48b25a67e8953820b.e34KaxiLc3eQc40 LaxqMbN4ObNqOe0?text=&docid=168421&pageIndex=0&doclang=EN&mo de=req&dir=&occ=first&part=1&cid=405603 on October 13, 2015.

439. Mark Scott, "European Court Adviser Calls Trans-Atlantic Data-Sharing Pact Insufficient," The New York Times, September 23, 2015. Accessed at www. nytimes.com/2015/09/24/business/international/adviser-to-europes-top-court-calls-data-transfer-pact-insufficient.html?emc=edit_tnt_20150923&nlid =29585879&tntemail0=y&_r=1 on October 13, 2015.

440. Court of Justice of the European Union, Press Release No. 117/15, Luxembourg, October 6, 2015, Judgment in Case C-362/14, Maximillian Schrems v. Data Protection Commissioner. Accessed at http://curia.europa.eu/jcms/upload/docs/ application/pdf/2015-10/cp150117en.pdf on October 13, 2015.

441. Mark Scott, "Data Transfer Pact Between U.S. and Europe Is Ruled Invalid," The New York Times, October 13, 2015. Accessed at www.nytimes.com/2015/10/07/ technology/european-union-us-data-collection.html on October 13, 2015.

442. Mark Scott, "U.S. and Europe in 'Safe Harbor' Data Deal, but Legal Fight May Await," The New York Times, February 2, 2016. Accessed at www.nytimes.com/2016/02/03/ technology/us-europe-safe-harbor-data-deal.html on June 9, 2016.

443. Federal Communications Commission, "Communications Assistance for Law Enforcement Act." Accessed at www.fcc.gov/encyclopedia/communications-assistance-law-enforcement-act#CCSBI on October 16, 2015.

444. Hal Abelson et al., "The Risks of Key Recovery, Key Escrow, and Trusted Third-Party Encryption," May 27, 1997, Final Report, pp. 3 and 19. Accessed at http:// academiccommons.columbia.edu/catalog/ac:127127 on October 16, 2015.

445. MIT, Computer Science and Artificial Intelligence Laboratory Technical Report, "Keys Under Doormats: Mandating insecurity by requiring government access

to all data and communications" (MIT-CSAIL-TR-2015-0), July 6, 2015, p. 1. Accessed at http://dspace.mit.edu/bitstream/handle/1721.1/97690/MIT-CSAIL-TR-2015-026.pdf on October 15, 2015.

446. Ibid., pp. 1–3.

447. Ellen Nakashima, "Powerful NSA hacking tools have been revealed online," The Washington Post, August 16, 2016. Accessed at www.washingtonpost.com/world/national-security/powerful-nsa-hacking-tools-have-been-revealed-online/2016/08/16/bce4f974-63c7-11e6-96c0-37533479f3f5_story.html on September 6, 2016.

448. Matthew Panzarino, "Apple's Tim Cook Delivers Blistering Speech On Encryption, Privacy," Tech Crunch Newsletter, June 2, 2015. Accessed at http://techcrunch.com/2015/06/02/apples-tim-cook-delivers-blistering-speech-on-encryption-privacy/#.ned5rv:kVGu on October 17, 2015.

449. Ibid.

450. Paul Mozur and Katie Benner, "Apple Is Said to Deactivate Its News App in China," The New York Times, October 10, 2015. Accessed at www.nytimes.com/2015/10/12/technology/apple-is-said-to-deactivate-its-news-app-in-china.html?partner=rss&emc=rss&_r=2 on October 24, 2015.

451. Owen Fletcher, "Apple Censors Dalai Lama IPhone Apps in China," PCWorld, n.d. Accessed at www.pcworld.com/article/185604/article.html on October 24, 201. See also Charles Arthur, "iPhone apps about Dalai Lama blocked in China," The Guardian, December 31, 2009. Accessed at www.theguardian.com/world/2009/dec/31/iphone-china-blocks-dalai-lama on October 24, 2015.

452. Ben Lovejoy, "Tim Cook agreed to allow Chinese government to conduct security audits on Apple devices – local media," 9to5Mac, January 23, 2015. Accessed at http://9to5mac.com/2015/01/23/china-apple-government-security-audits on October 24, 2015. See also "Apple to Allow Chinese Government Product Security Inspections, But What Does It Mean?," iDigitalTimes, January 23, 2015. Accessed at www.idigitaltimes.com/apple-allow-chinese-government-product-security-inspections-what-does-it-mean-410024 on October 24, 2015.

453. Nicole Perlroth and David E. Sanger, "Obama Won't Seek Access to Encrypted User Data," The New York Times, October 17, 2015. Accessed at www.nytimes.com/2015/10/11/us/politics/obama-wont-seek-access-to-encrypted-user-data.html?_r=0 on October 17, 2015.

454. Susan Landau, Surveillance or Security? The Risks Posed by New Wiretapping Technologies (Cambridge, MA: MIT Press 2013), p. 3.

455. Peter Swire and Kenesa Ahmad, "Encryption and Globalization," The Columbia Science & Technology Law Review, Vol. XIII, Spring 2012, p. 481.

456. Matt Olsen, Bruce Schneier, and Jonathan Zittrain, "Don't Panic: Making Progress on the 'Going Dark' Debate." Berkman Center for Internet and Society at Harvard University, p. 13. See also David E. Sanger, "New Technologies Give

Government Ample Means to Track Suspects, Study Finds." The New York Times, January 31, 2016. Accessed at www.nytimes.com/2016/02/01/us/politics/new-technologies-give-government-ample-means-to-track-suspects-study-finds.html on January 30, 2016.

457. Tim Cook, "A Message to Our Customers," February 16, 2016. Accessed at www.apple.com/customer-letter.

458. Pamela Engel, "Months after the San Bernardino attacks, the FBI still can't get into one of the shooter's phones," Business Insider, February 9, 2016. Accessed at www.businessinsider.com/fbi-san-bernardino-shooter-phone-2016-2 on June 9, 2016.

459. "Reform Government Surveillance." Accessed at www.reformgovernmentsurveillance.com/index.html on June 9, 2016.

INDEX

Republican Party, 134, 138, 167, 170, 217; Republican National Convention, 73

Richelieu, Cardinal, 2

Riley v. California, 214–215, 221

Risen, James, 31–32; *State of War: The Secret History of the CIA and the Bush Administration*, 31

Riverdale (NY), 147

Roberts, John G. Jr., 46–47

Robespierre, 203

Rockefeller, Jay, 169

Rodriguez, Jose A., 158–159

Roosevelt, Franklin D., 1, 14, 231

Rumsfeld, Donald, 83, 183

Russia, 21, 27, 53, 57, 67, 77, 94, 105, 107, 109, 111, 112–113, 120; Chernobyl Nuclear Power Plant, 115

S

Sadr City, Iraq, 8

Samarra, Iraq: Imam Ahmad ibn Hanbal Mosque, 26

San Bernardino (CA), 18, 28, 132–135, 151, 200, 225, 239, 249

Sandy Hook Elementary School, 128–129

San Francisco (CA), 143

Saudi Arabia, 133

Savannah (GA), 112

SBC, 50

Schultz, George, 95

Schumer, Charles E., 149

Sears Tower, 145–146, 230

Secure Democracy Clearly, 239

security and intelligence community: accountability, 1, 3, 221; budgets and funding, 19, 38, 39, 41, 52, 61, *63*, *65*, 93–94, 96, 231, 239; civil liberties, 1, 3, 4, 10, 13, 15–16, 29, 30, 33, 35, 42, 63, 73, 75–76, 146–147, 194, 195, 211, 215–221, 224–225, 227, 229, 232, 237–238, 240, 251; coercion, 85, 173, 192, 193, 194; control, 204–206, 246–247; counterterrorism, 2, 3, 5, 6–10, 17, 18, 19, 20, 21–28, 30, 34, 40, 41, 44, 48, 59–60, 66–67, 68–72, 73–74, 76–78, 80, 82, 91–93, 96–98, 101, 120, 124, 126, 135–136, 139–149, 154–156, 194–195, 197, 198, 199, 200, 210, 211, 219–221, 223, 227, 231, 232, 239, 251; data mining, 4, 12–13, 16–17, 32, 49, 50, 51, 52, 74, 193, 201, 204–205, 207, 208, 211, 215–216, 227, 233, 236, 242–245, 247–248, 250; digital sector, 12–13, 18, 32, 42, 43, 191, 207–214, 250–251; failures, 18, 28; fear, 93–95, 154, 156, 181, 194, 195, 206–207, 216, 229–231; foreign policy, 2, 25, 231, 251; informants, 6, 33, 147–149, 153; liberal democracy, 10, 11–12, 14, 16, 17–18, 19, 20, 22, 33, 36, 38, 42, 45, 47, 56–57, 76, 92–93, 121, 136, 151, 159, 167, 191, 192, 193–194, 198,

Soviet Union. *See* Russia

Spain, 8, 132, 200, 212, 233; Madrid Privacy Declaration, 233

Spokane (WA), 127

Stanford University, 67

State of War: The Secret History of the CIA and the Bush Administration (Risen), 31

Stevens, John Paul, 184

Stewart, Potter, 82

Stewart Air National Guard Base, 147–149

Stone, Oliver, 21

Stuxnet, 108

Sun Microsystems, 200–201

Sweden, 118; Stockholm International Peace Research Institute, 118

Swedish Television News, 48, 221

Syria, 18, 23, 24, 25, 27, 66, 77, 79, 80, 85, 87, 88, 91, 98, 103, 120, 135, 140, 143, 144, 145, 155

T

Taliban, 129, 188

Taney, Roger B., 179

Tanzania, 96

telecommunications industry, 209–210

Teller, Edward, 106

Tenet, George J., 159, 161, 164, 168, 170, 173, *175*

Terminiello, Arthur, 224–225

Terminiello v. City of Chicago, 224–225

terrorism, 5, 6–10, 11, 17–28, 29, 33, 34, 40, 41, 44, 48, 59–60, 66, 68–72, 73–74, 76–78, 79–91, *86, 87, 89,* 96–98, 181–183, 188, 189, 192, 194–195, 197–200, 202–204, 209, 210, 211, 216, 219–221, 223, 225, 227, 229–232, 233–239, 241, 246, 249, 252–253; catastrophic, 101–116, 120–121, 123, 124, 126, 152; conspiracies, 139–149; eco-terror, 137–138, 150; episodic, 101, 123–139, *125,* 152, 153; hate crimes, 136–137, 149, 150; mass shootings, 90–91; nuclear, 104–116; religious, 138–139; self-radicalization, 27–28, 79, 81

Texas, 77, 129, 138

Texas A & M University, 66

Thiers, Adolphe, 202

Third Force Act, 136

Thompson, Bennie, 39, 40

Tokyo, Japan, 9

Tor, 53

torture, 7, 10, 27, 29, 34, 42, 73, 103, 141, 157–177, 181, 185, 188, 194, 196, 197, 198, 223, 226, 227, 233; enhanced interrogation, 157–159, 171, 173–174, *175–176,* 177, 181, 192; *habeas corpus,* 160–161, 171, 172–173, 177–189, 192, 240

Torture: The Guantanamo Guidebook, 174

War Crimes Act of 1996, 172

Washington, DC, 9, 19, 31, 73, 76, 95, 101, 102, 123, 130–131, 178, 185, 231

Washington, George, 1

Washington Post, 15, 59–60, 129, 168

Wassenaar Arrangement, 117

weapons of mass destruction, 83–84, 91, 99, 103, 116, 117–118, 119, 123–124, 149, 155. *See also* nuclear arsenal

Weather Underground, 155

West Coast Airliner Plot, 141–143

WikiLeaks, 55

Wilson, Darren, 75

Wolfowitz, Paul, 183, 186

Woolsey, R. James, 26

World Trade Center, 8, 11, 23, 181. *See also* 9/11

World War I, 116, 120, 194

World War II, 1, 9, 14, 23, 43, 60, 73, 93, 120, 179–180, 214

Wyden, Ron, 169

Y

Yahoo, 52, 54, 250

Yemen, 18, 25, 103, 127–128, 140

Yoo, John, 159, 162, 178

Young, William G., 127

Z

Zangger Committee, 117

Zevallos, Hector, 139

Zubaydah, Abu, 157

Zuckerberg, Mark, 207

EAGLE VALLEY LIBRARY DISTRICT
P.O. BOX 240 600 BROADWAY
EAGLE, CO 81631 / 328-8800